JÜRGEN
KLOPP

JÜRGEN KLOPP

THE BIOGRAPHY

ELMAR NEVELING

EBURY
PRESS

1 3 5 7 9 10 8 6 4 2

Ebury Press, an imprint of Ebury Publishing,
20 Vauxhall Bridge Road,
London SW1V 2SA

Ebury Press is part of the Penguin Random House group of companies
whose addresses can be found at global.penguinrandomhouse.com

Penguin
Random House
UK

First published by Ebury Press in 2016
This revised edition published by Ebury Press in 2020
Originally published in Germany by Copress an imprint of Stiebner
Velag GmbH

www.penguin.co.uk

A CIP catalogue record for this book is available from the British Library

ISBN 978529109252

Printed and bound in Great Britain by Clays Ltd, Elcograf S.p.A.

CONTENTS

1

DORTMUND EUPHORIA: KLOPP TRIUMPHANT

Dortmund, 15 May 2011. A city in the mood for celebration. The main B1 road, usually jammed with cars, is closed to traffic and lined with crowds instead. In total an estimated 400,000 fans have turned out to watch the open-topped bus parade through the city to mark Borussia Dortmund's seventh German championship.

It is a parade that begins at Borsigplatz in the north of the city where, at the Zum Wildschütz tavern in 1909, the club was founded. A song has been written to commemorate these roots, and the tune captures the mood of the parade. *'Rubbeldikatz, rubbeldikatz, rubbeldikatz am Borsigplatz!'* The words might be unusual – 'rub the cat in Borsigplatz'[1] – but the tune, written by club legend Alfred 'Aki' Schmidt and the band Casino Express, is infectious. It feels like it's got the entire city on its feet. Even when it starts to rain, nothing can dampen the mood.

On the team bus, joining in the mass singing, is Dortmund's charismatic manager, Jürgen Klopp. Having slept only a couple of hours, Klopp hides his tired eyes behind mirrored aviators. His croaky voice betrays the hearty celebrations of the previous night, but his enthusiasm is undimmed. Klopp, who during his playing career only ever experienced the *Bundesliga* as a spectator, is manager of the German champions.

Standing next to Klopp, microphone in hand, is Dortmund's stadium announcer Norbert Dickel, the 'Hero of Berlin' from their

1989 DFB Cup triumph (the German equivalent of the FA Cup). Does Klopp have a quick greeting to the fans, already waiting for their hero in front of the Westfalenhallen, where the parade will culminate? 'This is just the warm up,' Klopp promises. 'We'll be right there, then we're going to have some fun. But first, we have to practise penalties!' As he does so, he holds aloft a handwritten sign that was handed to him, recommending exactly that. During a season of remarkable success, there had been one strange statistical anomaly: Dortmund had been awarded five penalties and missed every one of them.

Such was the volume of fans lining the streets, it took hours for the team bus to arrive in front of the Westfalenhallen. One by one, the players took to the improvised stage and received the tumultuous applause of the supporters. As Klopp took to the stage, a song specially dedicated to him by the singer Baron von Borsig blasted over the tannoy: *Kloppo, du Popstar.* Klopp's vocal cords were strained by the effort of talking over the noise: 'You'll have to be a bit quieter,' he told the cheering fans, 'my voice isn't so good right now. There's a good reason for that. Unbelievable, unbelievable day, an unbelievable fortnight [since Dortmund were declared champions].' Then he joined in the fans' chant: 'There's one and only champion of Germany, BVB, BVB!' (BVB is short for the full name of the club: Ballspielverein Borussia 09 e.V. Dortmund.) When Bayern Munich won the title in 2010, Louis van Gaal called himself a *Feierbiest* – a 'party monster'. In Jürgen Klopp, he had a worthy successor.

* * *

The contrast with the club's position a few years earlier could not have been starker. In 2002, Dortmund was a city still used to success: Champions League and Intercontinental Cup victories in 1997, *Bundesliga* champions in 1995 and 1996, UEFA Cup finals in 1993 and 2002. It seemed inevitable that the trophy cabinet in the Westfalenstadion would grow ever fuller. But then the club had flung money at sporting success and things had got out of hand. BVB had teetered on the brink of bankruptcy – not just in intensive care, but 'being readied for the autopsy', to quote one report. A complete meltdown was averted at the last minute, but the sporting development of the team was crippled as a result. The club had been saved because the creditors agreed to a rescue package, but the budget cuts left the team a shadow of its former self in the following seasons.

The sporting architect of the success story was Jürgen Klopp. Within three years, he had transformed an average, mid-table team into national champions. A charismatic and meticulous coach, he was described by Dortmund's sporting director as 'my best transfer'. The comparison with the previous Dortmund title-winning team was stark: while the champions of 2002 were a side filled with experience and international stars such as Tomáš Rosický, Jan Koller and Amoroso, Klopp's BVB was youthful and dynamic, boasting home-grown stars like Mario Götze and Kevin Grosskreutz. When he arrived in Dortmund, Klopp had promised 'full throttle football' – and he had kept his word.

The last time Dortmund had been champions in 2002, there had also been joyous celebrations in the city. But the 2011 vintage was something different. These were scenes that weren't planned, weren't expected and that no one had even dared hope for. There was an emotional bond between the players and the fans that hadn't been there before: an enormous wave of enthusiasm that reached far beyond the Ruhr metropolis itself. Klopp's Dortmund was a young team that had given everything in every game – a commitment to the cause that a whole nation could identify with. It would probably be fair to say that in 2011, the city of Dortmund cheered for its heroes more enthusiastically than ever before.

The triumph of Klopp and his team gave the city a reinvigorated sense of pride and self-respect. Dortmunders define themselves through the success of their football club in a way that only the other inhabitants of the industrial – or post-industrial – Ruhr understand. This is a city that has struggled with high levels of unemployment – 13 per cent at the time of the 2011 *Bundesliga* success – and which makes sporting success for the city all the more meaningful.

Klopp was well aware of the responsibility that put on his shoulders. Asked about his motivation early in his time as manager, he said, 'What we can do is give people a distraction, make people happy. [...] I can't do anything to improve the political circumstances, I can't change anything about the social reality – but we can give these people a moment of happiness.' This attitude is why so many of the fans loved Klopp. And why, with Borussia Dortmund, Jürgen Klopp found his second sporting love after Mainz 05.

Some of the Dortmund fans took their love of their manager further than others. In Spring 2011, die-hard BVB fan Martin Hüschen had a portrait of a shouting Klopp tattooed onto his back. Such was his faith in Klopp's managerial ability, he then added a second tattoo of the *Bundesliga* trophy, even before the title had been confirmed. The finished artwork covered the entire upper half of his back.

As Hüschen put it, Klopp was a 'great guy' who 'fits right in with the Dortmund way'. When asked about his thoughts on the tattoo, Klopp's response was that 'He's old enough. He knows what he's doing.'

The 2011 league title was just the beginning for Klopp's Dortmund side. Not only did the club defend the title in 2012, they won the double for the first time in the club's history with a rollicking 5–2 win over Bayern Munich in the DFB Cup final.

Dortmund had been reinvented as a major player both in Germany and on the European stage – the club's trademark black and yellow kit synonymous with attractive football on the pitch and a well-run club off it. Such was his influence in the club's success that when Jürgen Klopp announced his plans to leave the club at the end of the 2014–15 season, his name was inevitability linked with every high-profile managerial job going.

* * *

In October 2015, months of speculation about his career plans ended when Jürgen Klopp was announced as the new manager of Liverpool Football Club. As he adjusts to the challenges of life in the Premier League, it's time to get to know him a little better – both as a football person and also as a man. What qualities made him such a beloved, cult figure, not just for Borussia Dortmund supporters, but across Germany? How could the 'People's Manager' explain the intricacies of the game to millions of Germans in a language that non-experts could understand? What were reasons behind his era of success at first Mainz and then especially Dortmund – and now, for Liverpool fans, hopefully at Anfield as well? What drives him and how did he become a league-winning manager?

This book will attempt to answer these questions and many more. It paints a revealing portrait of Klopp's personality, the story of his career, his working methods and his tactical philosophy. This biography follows Klopp's progress first as a player, and then as a manager: it is not a history of his private life, but a study of his sporting and human character. As well as those with knowledge of the game, it draws on insights from experts who offer their own perspective from outside the world of football.

Klopp himself did not contribute to this book. Yet many companions from his early years get a chance to speak here, offering an objective view of his character and approach to life. They show that the superficial 'Jürgen Gob' cliché has little basis in reality, and that Klopp is much more than just a man-manager in a tracksuit.

This book takes us through the various stages of Klopp's footballing life, and reveals just how much he loves the game. It chronicles how he started as a youth player in Glatten, then became a second division pro; it explores his switch to management and a decade-and-a-half managerial career (so far), during which Klopp has created a persona all his own.

Jürgen Klopp is one of the leading football managers in the world – and also one with much more still to give. As he said himself, winning the *Bundesliga* title in 2011 was like 'winning a stage in the Tour de France'. There will be many more challenges before he finally reaches the Champs-Élysées, but his is a managerial career whose upward curve feels inevitable. This book will explore the rise and rise of this remarkable manager – a life that began in an idyllically situated spa town in the Black Forest …

2

YOUNG KLOPP

The sun shines through the open door of the Linde (The Lime Tree). It lights up the salt and pepper shakers on the tables, beaming the patterns onto the flagstones. Diners use them to flavour their roasts and their Wiener schnitzels with chips and salad. The portions are generous, they need to 'squeeze it down' as they say around here. Outside the bar are a couple of plastic tables. A handful of men from Glatten, Neuneck and Böffingen sit around them, smoking their way silently into the evening. The two 'lime trees' in front of the Linde are not limes at all, but oaks. But no one seems to have noticed.

Welcome to Glatten, a small, idyllically situated spa village in the heart of Germany's Black Forest. The village gets its name – and its existence – from the River Glatt that runs through it. 'Glatt' is derived from the old High German word '*glat*' (or '*glad*'), meaning 'clear, shining, pure'. The River Glatt is formed from the rivers Ettenbach, Stockerbach and Kübelbach in nearby Aach, a suburb of Dornstetten. It flows first south, then east, finally joining the River Neckar twenty-two miles downstream at Neckarhausen. Watermills and sawmills were built along its course, along with tanneries and breweries. Forestry and timber rafting depended on it: without the river, there would have been no way to transport the timber. The parish's coat of arms, appropriately enough, is a four-spoked waterwheel with a dozen blades on a field of red and silver.

11

Everything is uphill around here. At 530 metres above sea level, Glatten is low down for a village in the northern Black Forest. So the children who go to high school in Dornstetten or even Freudenstadt need a bike at least, or better a moped, or they have to take the bus. If they want to go to the cinema, the closest is in Freudenstadt. Or if they want to go for a night out, there's the Barbarina in Freudenstadt, or the Scotch Club or the youth club in Dornstetten, or the Ranch in Neuneck. All but one of the local men around the Linde tables are quick to swear on their mothers never having been in the Ranch. The description of what happens down on the Ranch is restricted to a rapturous expression, an 'ooh, aah', a raising and lowering of hands, accompanied by more oohs and aahs.

Since the parishes of Böffingen and Neuneck were incorporated into Glatten in the 1970s, the village has had around 2,300 inhabitants. An Alemannic grave field has been found here. In 1817, forty-nine impoverished *Glattemer* – as the locals call themselves – were sent to America at the cost of the parish; one child died on the way to New Orleans. Since then times have changed: by 1904 the village already had electric street lighting. Glatten certainly isn't poor anymore, and is a desirable and enticing place to live.

The centre of the village is Latschariplatz – from the Alemannic dialect traditionally spoken in the Black Forest region. There's a fountain here, above the Bürgenbach beck, where the local teenagers meet up, chew gum, spit on the ground, smoke, and flick their fag ends into the beck where the trout swim. There are disposable knives and forks floating in the beck as well, quite possibly from Glatten's kebab shop, and if the teenagers are feeling particularly full of bravado, their beer bottles too. The fountain is a meeting point: this is also where the squad of the sports club Sportverein

Glatten Kreisliga gather before away matches. The youth teams too. It seems like the fountain is *the* place to be in Glatten.

Also in the centre of Glatten is the Hotel Schwanen ('The Swan'). And opposite this once stood the Reich brewery. This belonged to the family of Jürgen Klopp's mother, Liesbeth, the reason why this future football manager had a Black Forest beginning to his life.

* * *

Jürgen Klopp was born in Stuttgart in June 1967 and grew up in Glatten. His mother Liesbeth had her roots in the village, while Klopp's father, Norbert, originally a furrier by trade, moved to Glatten from Dornhan. Norbert then started work for Fischer-Dübel in Tumlingen (Artur Fischer, born in Tumlingen in 1919, invented the plastic wall plug in 1958). Those who knew Norbert Klopp say that he was an elegant man: capable, a good salesman, confident, a man who treated children with respect – and whose influence and encouraging of his son's footballing career was absolute.

The house where Klopp grew up is right next to the smart new town hall and the primary school – Klopp only had to cross the street to get to class. Today, a black and yellow flag hangs from a window: the flag has nothing to do with his mother or sister, who still live here, but with a tenant. The tenant must be the only Borussia Dortmund fan in the village. Traditionally, *Glattemer* are either Bayern Munich or Schalke supporters. It's like some ancient feud with the next parish: no one remembers who started the argument, back in the grey and misty past, but that doesn't mean there will be peace any time soon.

The young Klopp, by contrast, supported the team of his birthplace: VfB Stuttgart. He had a small attic room under the roof of his parents' house: it was full of Stuttgart pennants and the bed was placed where the roof pitched down, ready to bang your head. Those are the memories of Jens Haas, who lived next-door to the Klopps and played alongside Jürgen for SV Glatten up to Under-17 level. He remembers listening to the *Bundesliga* on the radio with an eleven-year-old Jürgen. Even then, he was analysing the Stuttgart manager's decisions: 'He's got to take Klotz off now.' That was the era of German greats such as Hansi Müller, the Förster brothers, Karl Allgöwer, Walter Kelsch and Helmut Roleder in goal. It was probably Jürgen Sundermann who took centre-forward Bernd Klotz off, or earned himself a hail of criticism if he hadn't heeded Klopp's advice. It might even have been Lothar Buchmann.

Such is the beauty of Glatten that many residents spend their lives here and many of those have fond memories of the young Jürgen. At the bakery, Bäckerei Trik, Gerhard Trik has pitched in for twenty-five years. It is a family business: Gerhard's brother, who's in his sixties now, and who greets his sibling with a curt, friendly grunt, is in charge. It is the last independent bakery that still bakes its own bread – each of the other bakeries in the village is part of a chain.

Gerhard Trik, who became the groundsman of local club SV Glatten and runs the clubhouse, remembers one occasion with Jürgen all too well. It was a Saturday sometime in 1974. The coaches from SV Glatten came round to the bakehouse at eight in the morning to see 'back-up' baker Gerhard Trik, because they knew he would have time at that hour, and wanted him to step in to drive them to Kirn. Their ordinary driver couldn't make it. The Under-19s were playing there. Trik let them talk him into it, and got behind the wheel. That's how it is in this village: people help each other out.

Along for the ride were Norbert Klopp and his eight-year-old boy, Jürgen. Klopp senior was known locally as a good tennis player and not bad at football either. He played with Turn- und Sportfreunden

Dornharn in the amateur league second division and had a trial with 1. FC Kaiserslautern. He played midfield for SV Glatten when they were short of players. He was ambitious when it came to his boy too. Especially when it came to his boy.

Having arrived in Kirn, the Under-19s game got underway. Klopp senior was watching the youth team play. Klopp junior tapped a ball across to Trik. Trik, not lazy, passed it back, and they continued knocking the ball back and forth. Then Trik slipped. The grass was wet, he says, and down he went, his ankle in a bad way. 'Get help,' said Trik, who was down on the ground and couldn't stand. Jürgen ran for help in a flash. After a medic arrived with a stretcher, Trik was taken to hospital. He walks with a limp now, has arthritis in his ankle, and that's why his hip hurts. Overcompensation. An early memory of Jürgen he'll never forget.

Other *Glattener* have fonder memories. Astrid Wissinger was a classmate of Jürgen's and has a school photo, framed, from the mid-seventies, when they were ten or eleven years old. She can't put a name to the teacher, though remembers that she always read *Jim Knopf und die Wilde 13*, a Michael Ende story, to them. She looks very young. It's a very seventies photo: they're all wearing nice jumpers and look like very well-behaved children. They're all holding very still. You can spot Klopp – everyone called him 'Klopple' ('little Klopp') back then – in an instant.

There were forty-five pupils in the first primary-school class. 'It only worked because we all loved going to school, and the pressure wasn't so bad then as it is today,' says Astrid, and she ought to know: she has a child going to school. That said, there were teachers in Glatten primary school who would strike the children. 'With the side of the hand,' Astrid says as she demonstrates and the side of her hand cracks in the air.

There are twenty-three children in the picture. More girls than boys. 'She's still here, her too,' says Astrid, going through one by one. In total, twelve of the twenty-three still live in Glatten or nearby. Some of those who stayed never go further than Dornstetten or Freudenhaus. Astrid is one of those who does: there's a company called Wissinger, on the edge of the village just before the turnoff to Lombach, who make decals for cars, for motor racing too, and plastic wraps that protect vehicles from stone chips. One of their customers is Maserati.

Astrid recalls visiting Jürgen's mother Liesbeth and his sister Stefanie: 'We hadn't seen each other for twenty years, then we were sat in the kitchen half the night chatting away. It was all very nice and friendly.' Mrs Klopp told her the story of how Klopp senior had cleared out the living room to make a goal on the wall for three-year-old Jürgen to shoot at. 'Aim at the goal, boy, not at the glasses,' he had warned him.

After Borussia Dortmund won the *Bundesliga* title in 2011, there was a big victory party at Glatten's Riedwiesen sports centre. Such were the demands of those wanting to speak to him, Klopp needed three-quarters of an hour to eat a *bratwurst*, and he apologised for not having enough time for his school friends. 'This here, this is home, and that's cool,' Klopp told the crowd. Every now and then he slipped into Swabian dialect and the applause got even louder. It was still early when he had to start fending off tipsy guests in the beer tent who didn't want to go home, but he did it 'with style', says Astrid with a nod. Klopp's very clear when it's too much for him, when it's too cramped, when he needs time to himself. When he feels he needs to, he leaves. He's a man completely in control.

* * *

The sports centre where the *Bundesliga* celebrations took place is the home of the local football team, SV Glatten. It opened in 1983, the last time SV Glatten played in the *Bezirksliga* – level eight of the German football pyramid. The nearest they came to returning was in that 2010–11 season, but in the end they could only manage third. They had another crack the following season, with player-managers Croatian Tomislav Gelo, thirty-five, and Bosnian Senad Sencho Kacar, thirty-nine. Both coaches had other jobs, receiving a little money on top for coaching. The rest of the team was 'local' as Gerhard Trik put it. It wasn't to be enough, and they finished a disappointing seventh.

The pitch itself is a verdant green. 'Like Wembley,' says Trik, 'but only if yew squint.' In truth, it is a swamp in winter, hard as stone in summer. 'What we have here,' Trik continues, 'is a pitch you need to put a tent over.' Today, the pitch is soft as butter, the Under-17s trained here yesterday, and have kicked whole clods out of the turf. Not intentionally, just in the normal course of training. 'The day will come,' Trik says, 'when we won't be able to play anymore, the risk of injury will be too big.'

'Riedwiesen needs to be properly fixed up – urgently,' says Trik. But the council doesn't want to pay and the club doesn't have the money. It would cost €130,000 to restore. Württemberg's sports foundation would put in 30 per cent, the council would have to take on some of the expense, but the club would still be stuck with making up the difference.

All the while, the ground gets its fair share of use. Training takes place here seven days a week. An average crowd of 100 to 150 come to the games to support the local teams. The *Glattemer* stand on the steep bank that rises up to Neunecker Strasse, the away fans stand opposite. Fortuna Köln and 1860 Munich have played practice matches here. A crowd of 800 came to see a friendly between Mainz 05 and SV Linx – when Klopp was still playing for the former. During the 2011 celebrations, Klopp was asked if Dortmund were ever coming to Glatten. 'That might take a while,' was his answer: with not enough decent opponents in the area, practicality came before sentimentality.

None of the locals, Trik included, are sure whether Klopple ever played on the 'new' pitch (that's already thirty years old and counting), but the general feeling is that he probably didn't. Either way, in the clubhouse there are a couple of trophies in the cabinet, which Klopple helped win. Where Klopp definitely used to play was at the Waldplatz, the club's original pitch. All the teams, including the three women's teams, which train twice a week, rotate between the 'new' pitch and the 'old' one. The Waldplatz is especially popular in summer, it's nice and shady here, and you don't get that across the way.

The gate – neatly painted in the yellow and black of SV Glatten by Trik – is supposed to stop 'young people, middle-aged people, old people coming here in the night and getting up to nonsense'. The pitch, snug and secluded, is a place that begs you to get up to mischief. It's exactly what you imagine a Black Forest pitch to look like: lush green, surrounded by trees, with the stump of a fir tree on the touchline. Not long ago they set up a net to catch the balls flying towards the Lauter, the beck that rushes past five yards from the edge of the pitch. 'We were always losing balls in the Lauter,' Trik explains. Originally, there was a pole specially to fish them out. It wasn't too bad at low water, but when the beck was at its normal level, the ball had 'gone to the devil'. The way Trik pronounces 'devil' conjures images of Satan in football hell, having a kickabout with the damned – using balls from Glatten.

In front of the touchline stump the otherwise smooth, mani-cured turf is a little higgledy-piggledy and crumbly. There are little brown mounds of soil – moles have been digging their tunnels and pushing the spoil onto the pitch. The moles, of all things, manage to stir Gerhard Trik's blood – a man otherwise generously endowed with patience and poise. 'I'm fighting the moles with all available means,' he growls, counting them: poison and traps. He's put paid to one or two moles, but these molehills are fresh. 'They weren't there yesterday,' he says.

He'll have to get the traps out again. 'I don't like doing that while training's on.' He marks the place he's set a trap with a stick, but the kids pull them out and then the traps are lost because he has no way of finding them again. For Trik, there's no way of knowing how many of the enemy he has to face. 'Could be there's only the one, but blast, he's digging the whole pitch up,' Trik curses. Not that he's completely unsympathetic to his foe: 'In the fields, that's all right by me, but they ain't got no business on a football pitch.'

Like Gerhard Trik, Jan Haas both remembers Klopp growing up and is still involved with SV Glatten today. An engineer by trade, he trains the Under-9 team. There was no Under-9 team back when Jürgen and Jens started playing. The youngest side was when Ulrich Rath founded an Under-11 team in 1972, in order to have somewhere for his sons Ingo and Hartmut to play. Today, SV Glatten joins forces with other local clubs to put out youth teams in the higher age groups, as they wouldn't be able to get a team together on their own.

Children don't gather for kickabouts in the way they used to when Klopp and Haas were young. The kids have simply got too much to do in school these days, and no free time after school either. Stress, plain and simple. Haas recalls that, back in the early 1970s, 'either we were kicking the ball about, or training'. Football, every day. Homework? 'If at all possible, none at all,' he laughs. And if it absolutely had to be done, then it was done quickly and then out to play football. After playing, Klopp and his mates went down into the cellar of the Schweizers – another local family – and treated themselves to fizzy pop. During the title celebrations in Glatten, Klopp thanked the Schweizers once again for their hospitality. Who knows what might have been if it weren't for that fizzy pop?

The local boys all met at the fountain on their bikes, ball on the pannier: leather balls were no problem then, not like in Gerhard Trik's time, a generation before (leather balls and bicycles were still a rarity in those days). The rules of a kickabout works the same the world over: the players are picked in turn, and the best players are picked first. As Haas ruefully recalls, Klopp was a first pick and he wasn't. It was soon clear to the other boys that Klopple had talent. It was obvious to everyone by the time he was playing for the Under-13s.

When you play with someone who's 'got it', you start to realise how much more average you are yourself. The decisive thing Haas remembers about Klopp was that 'he never made it obvious. Sure he might have let out a few choice words during a game, but everyone did that at that age; he never got personal.' To this day, Klopp isn't the type to look for confrontation: he gets on with everyone and never makes anyone feel that they don't belong. He can see things through, but he does it in his own style, clear and polite. So while he criticised the Stuttgart manager when watching on television, he would never make the same comments directly to the SV Glatten manager. Besides, there was another managerial influence who had a strong bearing on his son. 'His dad was usually with him, any problems, any questions, he talked [them] out with him,' says

Haas. Even when Klopp junior was playing for Mainz in the second division, Norbert would drive down there and shout instructions onto the pitch. 'A powerful voice,' Haas noted.

To nobody's surprise, Klopp was team captain by the time the pair had graduated to the Under-15s. Klopp 'radiated composure', according to Haas. He was a 'central figure' who you could rely on 'in any situation on the pitch'. He was always open to receive the ball; you 'couldn't say a word against him, not as a footballer, not in how he carried himself'. When a lesser player like Haas started getting the feeling that things were going wrong, he would look over to Klopp, who would convey the opposite feeling. Was there anything Klopp wasn't good at? 'Losing,' answers Haas in a flash. Sparks would fly when that happened – a response none too different from that of Klopp the famous manager, well-known for giving his emotions full rein.

Haas remembers his teenage friendship with Klopp with affection. Both had mopeds: Klopp's was orange, a Vespa. 'Mine was faster,' says Haas. 'That peed him off, but he was sporting about it.' There was good-natured competition between them on the road; the mopeds were all souped up to give them an edge. Not that riding bikes came without its dangers: Astrid Wissinger remembers someone around their age who lost an arm in an accident and 'He was ruddy lucky it was no worse than that.'

Even though Klopp was team captain, even though he scored a hatful of goals for the Under-15s, even though he was selected for the local and regional elevens, Haas never imagined his friend would actually make it as a pro. Not even when he switched to the Under-19s at TuS Ergenzingen, a club in a small town fifteen miles to the east with a good reputation. It was a time when Klopp wasn't just changing clubs, but schools as well: he was one of three

Glattemer who made it to the grammar school in Dornstetten. For the first year or two, the ties to his school friends in Glatten stayed firm. Then, Haas noticed a 'parting of the ways'. It wouldn't be the final one. It had nothing to do with how they treated each other – it was a case of different paths rather than a change in the feelings they had for each other.

Today Haas finds himself watching his son, and how he reacts to Klopp on the TV, when he appears in adverts. 'He reacts just like he would to anyone else in an ad,' says Haas. For his son, this is Klopp: the impossibly distant figure on the Dortmund bench and on TV. For Haas senior, it's different. He knows two Klopps: 'When he does an advert on TV, he's a TV character. When he comes here to join in the festivities, he's my old school chum and teammate, and he asks me how I'm doing and I ask him.'

* * *

As soon as you enter Walter Baur's home, you know that a real football fanatic lives in this house. Brazilian and German flags fly from the balcony: the Brazilian for the academy player who also lives here. There are footballs in the garden, and lights on in the office where the nameplate on the door reads Baur. Inside, there's a tactics board on the floor, shelves filled with books, all of them about football: World Cup '74, modern defending, modern fitness training. There are jerseys on the wall, trophies on the desk. Hanging on the back of the door is a photo of the 1986 TuS Ergenzingen Under-19 team. It's not just any photo. Kneeling in the front row, in the bottom-right corner, with his blue shorts, yellow jersey, moustache and captain's armband, is the seventeen-year-old Jürgen Klopp.

Klopp's transition from captain of SV Glatten's Under-15s to under-19 captain of TuS Ergenzingen was not as smooth as it might first appear. During the first year at the club, he spent most of the time in his tracksuit, warming the bench. Walter Baur, the coach, remembered Jürgen as no footballing prodigy. 'He couldn't do three keepy-uppies in a row,' he recalls with a chuckle. Pulling out a file, he flicks through it until he finds the player notes on Klopp for a particular match, TuS Ergenzingen against SSV Reutlingen. *Completely useless, didn't win a single tackle.*

In fact, it was more luck than judgement that brought Klopp to Ergenzingen. There was a Jürgen playing for SV Glatten who had piqued the interest of Hermann Baur, another youth coach at the club. But it was striker Jürgen Haug who'd made Baur sit up and take notice: the other Jürgen wasn't worthy of a single line. In the end, transport seemed to play a factor in the transfer. Joining TuS meant travelling twenty-five miles to training three times a week, there and back. It was Klopp's father Norbert who was willing to make the journey. Even today, Klopp still has the feeling that his dad's car was the most important factor in his transfer to TuS.

Making the journey was just the beginning of the travails for Jürgen. Once there, there was a lot of time for a detailed personal critique. Klopp senior was Jürgen's biggest critic, a perfectionist who expected 100 per cent from his son. It drove him to achieve more. 'Jürgen was very grateful for his father driving him to training, and he wanted to repay him. He was incredibly ambitious,' Baur recalled. But Klopp was always eager to learn. He was the one who paid close attention to both his father and Baur, while his teammates would chat among themselves during team talks in the dressing room. Klopp remembers some of Baur's sayings to this day.

After the team talk, Klopp would go out and try to juggle the ball. 'After half a year, we had players at the Christmas party, they were like seals. They sat down with the ball on their heads and stood up with it balanced there.' Klopp would never be a 'seal', but he didn't stop learning. By his second year in the Under-19s he was captain – and not just on the pitch. He organised the Christmas do and the team parties. He was a hit with the local girls too. The lanky lad – 'Schlacks', as Baur called him – had a lot of female admirers. Jürgen met his girlfriend at a party in Ergenzingen.

Klopp's determination to win was clear. At one traditional Whitsun Under-19 tournament, Klopp and the boys fought their way to the final, to meet the Czechoslovakian participants Vitkovice Ostrau for the trophy. The score stood at 0–0 after normal time – it would go down to a penalty shootout. Baur wanted to let the 'poor Czech boys' win. Klopp's response was simple. 'Are you crazy? They're all going in the back of the net.' Sure enough, at the trophy presentation, it was Klopp who lifted the cup to the heavens.

That was Klopp's last act as a youth player. His first as a senior was soon to follow. When he found out that local rivals VfL Nagold were hunting his signature, the eighteen-year-old went straight to the TuS board and demanded that his Under-19 coach Baur take over the first team. He did, so Klopp stayed.

In July 1986, *Bundesliga* team Eintracht Frankfurt came to the Breitwiese in Ergenzingen to play a friendly. In the team was Thomas Berthold, the Germany defender fresh from the World Cup in Mexico. Before and after the game, Berthold was hustled by autograph hunters. During the game, however, he was hustled by right-midfielder Klopp. 'Jürgen played out of his skin and got away from Berthold time after time,' said Baur. On top of this, he got the consolation goal that made the score 9–1.

Frankfurt manager Dietrich Wiese was astonished. 'Who's this lad?' he asked his friend Baur. Later on he would frequently ask how the 'lad' was progressing. And progressing Klopp was, outgrowing the relationship and influence of Walter Baur. That winter he switched to lower league team 1. FC Pforzheim and from there he transferred to Eintracht Frankfurt Amateurs in the summer of 1987. The Ergenzingen club are said to have received the fantastic sum of 12,000 Deutschmarks from Pforzheim.

Though his career had moved on, Klopp and Baur kept in regular contact. When Klopp started his career as a manager in 2001, it was Baur whom he rang. It was 11.50 on Carnival Monday, the Monday before lent, when he called. 'Walter, guess who the new Mainz manager is?' Klopp asked. Baur got it wrong once, twice before Klopp revealed the truth. 'For the last ten minutes – me!' In 2008, when Klopp exchanged Mainz for Borussia Dortmund, Baur was coaching the Under-19s at VfL Nagold. Baur, who had scouted Mainz's opponents for Klopp, kept a lookout for good young players in southern Germany for the new BVB manager too. His finds included Lars and Sven Bender (1860 Munich) and Mats Hummels (Bayern Munich).

After the *Bundesliga* title was won, Baur wanted to send his congratulations. Yet before he called his former player, he contacted Klopp's assistant Željko Buvač, 'because no one thinks about him in all the euphoria'. A lot of people in Ergenzingen would like to see Klopp at their Whitsun tournament, and come back to do this or that. Baur is supposed to be the one to set that up. But he is protective of his former player, weighing up what is fair to ask of *Der Jürgen* and what is not.

'That wherever you were, you made it a little better. That you gave all you could. That you loved, were loved, and didn't take yourself too seriously.' This was Klopp's answer in 2008 when *Stern* magazine asked him what counted in life. Baur, certainly, is someone who never took himself too seriously. He didn't accept the invitation to BVB's championship party. He was fighting a relegation battle in the *Oberliga* with his youth team, and had to go to the match against VfR Aalen. When the Under-19s were relegated, Baur wanted to retire from coaching. But he kept going. That is Baur through and through, giving all he can. Klopp gives all he can too – that's something he took with him from his time with Baur.

3

THE JOURNEY TO MANAGER

Jürgen Klopp's playing career following his move from Walter Baur's tutelage at TuS Ergenzingen was marked by a continual switching of lower-league clubs over the next few seasons. Having joined 1. FC Pforzheim in 1987, he switched a few months later to Eintracht Frankfurt, where he combined playing for the Amateurs with studying sports science and coaching the Under-13 side. In 1988, he continued his journeyman-player route by signing for Viktoria Sindlingen. The following year he moved on again, this time to Rot-Weiss Frankfurt, and by 1990 he had switched once more, this time to FSV Mainz 05. Only at this latter club did Klopp finally cement his position. Indeed, he would go on to play for Mainz for the whole of the next decade, as well as beginning his managerial career there.

The English football league structure has long been based on four national divisions. In 1990, they were still running under the 'old money' names of the First, Second, Third and Fourth Division. This was all about to change, of course, with the formation of the English Premier League in 1992 and the remaining Football League divisions eventually becoming the Football League Championship, Football League One and Football League Two. Unlike the English system, where there are a further two divisions before football becomes regional, with the National League North and South, the German football pyramid splits into regional divisions further up.

Since 2008, the German system has consisted of the two *Bundesliga* divisions, *Bundesliga* and *2.Bundesliga*, with a third national league, *3.Liga* beneath this. Feeding into this are then five *Regionalliga* divisions, with various local *Oberliga* competitions underneath.

Back in 1990, when Jürgen Klopp was a Rot-Weiss Frankfurt player, there was no third tier *3.Liga*. Instead, with Frankfurt having won the Hesse Regional League, they were entered into a six-game mini-league, Play-Off Group South, from which the winners and runners-up of both groups (north and south) achieved promotion to *2.Bundesliga*. As it turned out, Rot-Weiss Frankfurt didn't make it to *2.Bundesliga* on this occasion, but Klopp did. Rot-Weiss Frankfurt managed only a single point in six games – the group winners Mainz 05, beating them twice. Mainz's manager, Robert Jung, was impressed with the playing style of the then winger and signed him. 'I picked up on him because he was great in the air, and that's exactly what our squad was missing,' he later explained.

Although FSV Mainz 05 – Fussball und Sportverein Mainz 05 e. V. to give them their full name – have been a fixture in the *Bundesliga* in recent years, the club has for much of its history been more regularly found in Germany's second tier and lower divisions. Originally formed in 1905 as 1. Mainzer Fussballclub Hassia 1905, the club combined with FC Hermannia 07 to become 1. Mainzer Fussballverein Hassia 05, before joining forces in 1919 with Sportverein 1908 Mainz, forming 1. Mainzer Fussball und Sportverein 05, the basis of the modern club. The team plied their trade in various South West and Hesse Leagues (Hesse being the region in Germany) for several decades. When the *Bundesliga* was formed in 1963, Mainz's position was predominantly as a mid-table second division side. Financial difficulties led to them dropping out of the *2.Bundesliga* in the late 1970s, but a decade later they returned briefly to the *2.Bundesliga* in 1988–89, before being promoted back into the division in 1990.

Klopp was brought to Mainz from Rot-Weiss Frankfurt as a striker. As a young player, his pace had been instrumental to his switch from amateur to professional football. Certainly, he was quick to make an impression with the Mainz fans. Right at the start of his Mainz career, the club faced Erfurt in the Steigerwaldstadion in August 1991. Klopp ran for everything, and everything ran for him. Klopp became was the first *Mainzer* to score four goals in a single game in the second division.

Klopp would play for Mainz for the best part of eleven years, making 325 appearances for the club and scoring fifty-two goals in the process. He switched position in the team on a number of occasions during this time. Like so many attacking players, the longer Klopp's career went on, the further back on the pitch he moved. Following on from his attacking role, manager Josip Kuze then moved him to the right of midfield. Subsequent manager Wolfgang Frank shifted Kloppo to the right side of defence for good.

No other Mainz 05 player has as many second-division appearances for the club as Klopp. In many ways, he was the perfect fit for this level of football, where effort, know-how and footballing acumen can be as important as raw ability. Looking back on his playing days, Klopp has wondered if he might have done better playing in England: 'I might have had a better career there. Pump it into the mixer and then get your head on it,' he pondered in 2002.

Wolfgang Frank felt that Klopp's limited technical ability was one of the reasons behind his emotional outbursts: 'Sometimes he lost control out on the pitch because he had so many good ideas in his head, but not the footballing talent to act on them. That wound him up so much sometimes that I'd have to take him to one side,' he recalled in 2011.

As his playing career started to wind down, even the pacy Klopp couldn't avoid using some tricks of the trade. He became an old pro who could dish it out when necessary, but also had to take it on occasion, as illustrated by an altercation with the St Pauli midfielder, Bernd Hollerbach. The pair had a coming together during a match at the Millerntor stadium in Hamburg, as Klopp recalled in a 2002 interview: 'We'd broken clean away when Hollerbach caught me on the thigh on the halfway line and gave me a dead leg like you wouldn't believe. That was an injustice that no one saw, the whole stadium was jeering at me for simulation. Only two men knew the truth – me and Hollerbach. As a result, the next time I met Hollerbach on the pitch I made sure to show him what's what.' According to Klopp's Mainz teammate, midfielder Christian Hock, that was the footballing realities of the lower leagues in those days. 'OK, you had a lot of space on the pitch, but you always had a man marker chasing you down ready to hack your ankles.'

Klopp's competitiveness was clear on the training pitch as well. There was little team unity to witness when Klopp and Hock met in training. The contrast between the nippy left midfielder Hock at five foot eight and the lumbering right-back Klopp at six foot three made for an interesting contest: one owed his success to agility and a powerful left foot, the other to his strength in the air and dogged perseverance rather than any great technical ability. 'There were many occasions when we'd be having a go at each other the whole length of the pitch,' says Hock. 'Kloppo could be very impulsive.'

The impulsive behaviour could land Klopp in trouble. In summer 2005, Klopp agreed to be attached to a lie detector by the editors of *RUND* football magazine and was asked what his biggest meltdown was. 'Shortly before I was made manager, I headbutted a very good friend of mine, Sandro Schwarz. He'd put me on the floor twice in training. I got up, all I could see was his face in front of me, and then he was down on the ground. I wanted to die, I just wanted to die, I couldn't bear the thought of what I'd done.'

* * *

For the first few seasons following Mainz's return to *2.Bundesliga*, the club's main goal was simply to survive. This was a time when the threat of relegation was a constant premise. Somehow, each season, Mainz survived by the skin of their teeth, ready to do battle to stay in the division the following season. It was a sequence that couldn't go on. After a terrible start to the 1995–96 season, with the opening seven games resulting in one point, no goals scored and thirteen conceded, the Mainz manager Horst Franz was shown the door.[2]

Enter Wolfgang Frank. Frank was born in 1951 and during his playing career, he was a centre-forward for teams including Stuttgart and Borussia Dortmund. He was a particularly good header of the ball despite standing at only five foot eight. Before taking charge of Mainz he had managed in Switzerland and at Rot-Weiss Essen, then in the second division. Despite being a *2.Bundesliga* team, Frank took them to the final of the 1994 *DFB-Pokal* – the German Cup – where they lost 3–1 to Werder Bremen at the Olympic Stadium in Berlin.

Wolfgang Frank lived and breathed football like few others and his influence on the Mainz players was clear both immediately in the club's performances and in the number who later followed him into coaching. Many of those who sat through the long team meetings went on to become managers themselves after their playing careers ended. 'That's definitely no coincidence,' says Christian Hock. 'We spent so much time working on tactics that it was just a short step from there to coaching a team.' Alongside him and Klopp, Torsten Lieberknecht went on to manage Eintracht Braunschweig, Jürgen Kramny managed Stuttgart Amateurs and Sven Demandt managed SV Wehen Wiesbaden in the third division. Peter Neustädter, who managed TuS Koblenz, and Peter Stöver, who coached at Kaiserslautern, were also graduates of Wolfgang Frank's Mainz managerial academy.

Frank – sometimes nicknamed 'The football professor' – arrived to take over a Mainz side seemingly doomed to relegation from the second division. Their form had been woeful and performance-wise they were the worst team in the league. The fact that the team were so terrible was, in a curious way, a bonus for Frank. Being so bad is never good, but being so bad also allows you – even forces you – to try something new.

Germany in the mid-1990s was the land of the *libero*. The sweeper position had its origins in Italian and Swiss football in the 1950s. It allowed for an extra body in defence – a 'free man', hence the name – and over the years Dutch and German football made the position more forward looking, encouraging a skilful, ball-playing footballer to bring the ball out of defence. Classic exponents of the role were the likes of Velibor Vasović at Ajax and Franz Beckenbauer at Bayern Munich. By the start of the 1990s, even the England side were experimenting with the system: Mark Wright played the part in Bobby Robson's side that reached the semi-finals of the 1990 World Cup.

Such was the influence of the *libero* system that other tactical set-ups were all but unheard of. Germany possessed two of the finest proponents of this position in Lothar Matthäus, the 'eternal Loddar', and Borussia Dortmund's Matthias Sammer: every other team attempted to emulate them. Indeed, when Jupp Heynckes had attempted something different at Eintracht Frankfurt, playing with a flat back four the previous season, he gave up in the face of stubborn resistance from his own players, the media and the fans. There was a manager in the amateur leagues in Württemberg, Helmut Gross, who passed on his ideas for a zonal marking system to up-and-coming coaches, but hardly anyone in the professional game had dared to try out the tactic.

Wolfgang Frank, however, was more receptive to trying something new and in particular to the idea of playing without a sweeper. The new Mainz boss had enjoyed a more positive experience in Switzerland with FC Aarau, FC Wettigen and Winterthur – where a wider variety of tactics were used than in Germany at the time.

Mainz were in such a desperate situation that trying something new seemed worth a shot. 'If you're bottom, you need to do something different,' says Christian Heidel, sporting director of Mainz at the time. During the winter break, Frank told him: 'We're going to play 4–4–2 without a sweeper.' Heidel thought to himself: 'Oh God, oh God, no sweeper, that too now … Well, we're already up shit creek without a paddle anyway.'

From the very first sessions with his players, Wolfgang Frank had demonstrated to the team what the solution to their problems might look like. He drew on videos of legendary AC Milan and Italy manager Arrigo Sacchi's training drills, and showed the team recordings of a Swiss youth team playing in this different style. 'The video was always on,' remembers Christian Hock. 'Frank marked out where everyone had to move in the new system with sticks, and they worked with ropes as well. Tied together standing ten metres apart, four players could cover fifty metres – almost the entire breadth of a pitch in the professional game, which is usually somewhere around seventy-five yards.'

The players were receptive to Frank's ideas and, in training, they started practising zonal instead of man marking. The squad seemed to be coping with it, so Frank decided to take the gloves off. They played for the first time using the new tactics in a friendly against FC Saarbrücken: zonal marking, with the defence set up as a flat back four in a 4–4–2 formation. The *Mainzer*, who had been practising moving as a unit for weeks, were 4–0 up after half an hour. When the referee blew the final whistle with the score at 5–0, Hock says that, 'We all saw it: we've got something here. We might just have the players to play a back four.'

Frank had won over his team to his new tactics. From now on, his players would press, disrupting their opponents high up the pitch, close down opposition defenders, and win the ball much closer to the opposition goal. For most of the Mainz squad, it was a new way of playing. In contrast to the traditional man-to-man marking system that directly targeted opposition players, the zonal marking and pressing system works by targeting space. The aim is to close down opponents in possession through clever positioning and break up their build-up play. To do this, the players have to move towards the ball as a unit: that requires being tactically disciplined and, to sustain this strategy for a full ninety minutes, extremely fit.

The theory is that possession will be regained by the pressing and proximity of players forcing the opponent with the ball into a mistake. It's a tactic whose success is not always understood in football reporting. So for example, when Klopp's Dortmund beat Bayern Munich for their first away victory against them for two decades, the focus on the media was the moment when Bayern midfielder Bastian Schweinsteiger lost the ball to Kevin Grosskreutz, who played in Lucas Barrios to score. The German media put this down to a mistake on Schweinsteiger's behalf. The harrying, the pressing, the kilometres the players put behind them that led to the turnover of possession and *forced* the mistake on Schweinsteiger went largely unnoticed. Yet these turnovers define modern football. Wolfgang Frank knew this; Klopp was to learn it at first hand from him.

Not that Klopp was Frank's right-hand man at this juncture. Over the winter break, Frank and Mainz worked on zonal marking, moving as a unit and pressing. Frank also seized the opportunity to give the team a new leader, taking the captain's armband from Klopp and making Lars Schmidt captain instead. He was now stationed in central defence and seemed to grow as a player with the new responsibility. The squad – and Klopp – took the decision with equanimity. Armband or not, said Hock, '"Kloppo" was still one of the players we looked to for leadership, and he got the gaffer's message across.' That's what nearly everyone in Mainz called him: Kloppo.

Mainz entered the second half of the season propping up the table with scarcely a point to their name, but at least they had a plan now – most of them for the first time in their career. Under Frank, everyone had a job to do when they didn't have the ball. 'Everyone knew what his role was,' says Hock. 'If you made a mistake, you could be sure that someone would be in their preordained position covering, and you didn't actually have anything to worry about. That was the most important thing.' Admittedly, to make sure this cover was complete, they had to start running a lot harder than before. But they were professionals, and smart enough to see the new turn of events as an opportunity rather than an imposition. After all, they were in a unique position – the only way from the bottom of the table, as Hock put it, was up.

And up the team went. They tore up the second half of the season, not because the players were suddenly better, or at least not just because they had improved, but because the manager had a vision, and no one else in the league had an answer to it. Nowadays, a back four is common practice in German football, but this was the formation's beginning, a bumpy road bypassing the footballing mainline. The football establishment watched and waited, and later copied (Bernd Krauss and Ralf Rangnick went on to successfully employ the system with Borussia Mönchengladbach and SSV Ulm respectively)

Mainz were the standout team in the second half of the season, and ended up finishing eleventh. In just a few months, Wolfgang Frank had transformed the club. Whereas previously the only way for Mainz to leave the division was through relegation, now Frank talked openly of promotion to the first division and challenged chairman Harald Strutz to expand the Bruchweg stadium, even though Mainz had rarely come close to selling out the 13,000 capacity. His ambitious attitude didn't stop there – he wanted to improve his players as well. Team meetings focused increasingly on mental training. Some tried to use this to their advantage, although there were those who felt they were being treated like children. 'With the benefit of hindsight, trying to force changes didn't work. You can't make someone who doesn't want to work on their psychology. In reality it becomes counterproductive,' says Hock.

The increasing number of mental strength exercises took nothing away from the positive impression the Mainz players had from their intensive training sessions. Even so, Frank made it more and more difficult for them to switch off after they'd put in the hard miles. During the following season's winter break, a ten-day training camp in Cyprus was scheduled for January 1997. Frank was so enthusiastic about the excellent conditions for training – in comparison with icy pitches in Mainz – that he extended the trip to three-and-a-half weeks. 'He was stubborn and couldn't find the balance to say to us: Take it easy now and then. We were basically under high pressure for an entire three weeks. That took a toll,' said Hock.

It was the players who reacted first. Mentally burned out, the *Mainzer* lost twice in succession on their return from Cyprus. But then, to everyone's surprise, the results took their toll on the manager, too. Frank resigned. His players, Klopp foremost among them, attempted to change his mind. But responsibility was his watchword, and he stuck to his decision. No one was able to persuade him to stay. As quickly as he had blown in and turned the team around, Frank was gone.

* * *

In the Bruchweg stadium is the office of club's sporting director, Christian Heidel.[3] There are reminders of Klopp everywhere. Not just in the pictures on the wall, but primarily in Heidel's enthusiasm, the sheer joy he shows when he talks about his friend, with whom he spoke on the phone 'not two days ago'. Heidel talks fast, the words spill out of him like water, so much does he have to say. The happiness his memories evoke has much to do with the working environment he enjoyed with Klopp.

Heidel laughs a lot, smiles and grins when he thinks back to Klopp's time at the club. He has at least as much fun looking back on it now as he did experiencing it then: how Mainz 05 were transformed from a permanently relegation-threatened second division team to solid *Bundesliga* regulars, a process started under Wolfgang Frank.

But when Frank resigned, it left Heidel with a problem, one that would recur repeatedly over the following seasons every time a manager departed. Heidel needed a manager who would follow Frank's tactics – a flat back four, 4–4–2 formation, a pressing game. He didn't want to give that up, and nor did the players. The problem was that there were no coaches versed in this system. 'Germany didn't have a problem with young players coming through then, like everyone claimed, but a coaching problem,' says Heidel. It was a both a national problem and one for Heidel personally.

Mainz needed the right manager for a team that was mourning Frank and wanted to retain his system. The club also needed a big name for the outside world as a statement of the club's intent. This was to rebut the ambitious Frank's bitter complaint that 'Mainz don't *want* to get promoted.' Frank's replacement was the forty-five-year-old Reinhard Saftig. Saftig was a former Bayern Munich caretaker manager, and would go on to manage clubs including Borussia Dortmund, Bayer Leverkusen and Galatasaray.

Heidel was to discover, however, that securing the manager's signature was the start rather than then end of his difficulties. His pitch to prospective managers – and Mainz was a much less attractive proposition then than it is now so they weren't exactly queuing round the block – was loud and clear in what he wanted from them: pressing, pressing, pressing. The managers-to-be would cheerfully agree – then once in charge would do the exact opposite. Not because they wanted to, but because they had to: they weren't capable of coaching a different system, but wouldn't admit it because they wanted the job. 'Today,' said Heidel, 'Mainz is a club with an identity, a philosophy. We tell the manager how we're going to play, his job is to implement it.' Within the boundaries of that concept, the manager can do what he wants, but until the Rivers Rhine and Main run uphill, Mainz will never see another sweeper. That, following Frank's departure, was the theory anyway.

The fact that Reinhard Saftig and his successor Didi Constantini both dropped the flat back four after a brief transitional period didn't sit well with the squad. Core players were convinced that they would have done better by keeping Frank's system – including Klopp and Hock: 'We had and still have similar ideas regarding that.'

At a team meeting before a match against Rot-Weiss Essen, Saftig explained his revised tactics: three men at the back, goodbye to Frank's system, hello to the standard *Bundesliga* tactical set up. After the meeting, Klopp knocked on Heidel's office door, a little worked up. At this point, things got a little conspiratorial: 'Should we play like we always do, or how Saftig wants it?' Klopp asked the sporting director. Knowing the consequences full well, Heidel didn't hesitate: 'Play like you always do.' That is to say, with four at the back, just as Saftig had agreed before signing. The 'shadow cabinet' as Heidel called it, was formed. But it was no long-term solution, as the sporting director was fully aware.

'This is the table,' Heidel says, smacking it so hard that the coffee cups lift off: the table where he and Klopp sat and talked over the tactics Mainz needed to be using, despite the manager. 'This is how we're going to do it, just like this,' Klopp responded. Yet eventually Saftig managed to get his way against the player rebellion initiated by Klopp – and made a couple of mistakes that the players weren't able to correct. Under his leadership Mainz finished fourth, just missing out on promotion with the top three being promoted. VfL Wolfsburg – before they were rebranded with the VW logo – went up. It was the first of Mainz's ominous series of fourth-place finishes.

The following season, Saftig got the sack, to be replaced by the Austrian Didi Constantini. Like Saftig, Constantini came with strong managerial credentials: he had managed the Austria national team alongside his mentor Ernst Happel. Like Saftig, Constantini didn't want to play the Frank system and brought back the *libero*. Like under Saftig, the players weren't happy.

In the DFB Cup, Mainz were drawn against the third division side, SSV Ulm 1846. Not only did they suffer a humiliating 4–1 defeat against a lower league side, but to rub salt into the wound, Ulm's manager Ralf Rangnick had his team playing in the Frank way. Heidel remembers thinking to himself, 'Ulm are playing the way we'd like to play.' He watched ruefully as a bow-legged Serb, Dragan Trkulja, laid on two assists and scored one himself. He pressed, that Trkulja.

As for Klopp, he wasn't even in the starting eleven for the cup defeat. He had a difficult relationship with Constantini, which resulted in him being left out. It's always a risky strategy as a manager when you leave out influential players and results don't go your way – doubly so when playing with a tactical system against the wishes of your sporting director. With too many games ending in draws, Mainz's chances of promotion under Constantini fizzled out. After a 3–1 home defeat to SG Wattenscheid that left them just a point above the Stuttgarter Kickers in fifteenth place, Constantini stepped down, unable to escape the shadow of his predecessor. 'There's only one man who can help you in this damned difficult situation,' he said to Heidel, 'and that's Wolfgang Frank.'

* * *

Constantini, it turned out, was both right and wrong. By this point, Wolfgang Frank was in charge at Austria Vienna. Heidel made the call and to the delight of both the fans and the players, Frank came back. Such was the delight of the supporters that 1,200 fans travelled to the match against Stuttgarter Kickers, Frank's first of his second spell. 'Messiah, Messiah,' they chanted from the stands. Many of the players felt the same way: there was an atmosphere more reminiscent of Mainz Cathedral than a football stadium. Playing without a sweeper, Mainz won 2–1. With Frank back in charge and his pressing tactics deployed on the pitch, Mainz finished tenth in the 1997–98 season, and seventh the following year.

But then, in April 2000, following a 1–0 home defeat at the hands of Cologne, Frank openly conducted talks regarding a switch to MSV Duisburg despite still being under contract until 2001. The club had no choice: he had to go. For two years, he and Heidel didn't speak a word to each other. Frank's assistant Dirk Karkuth took temporary charge and the relegation-threatened team managed to stay in the division.

Once again, the club faced the difficult situation of a manager wanting to play a different way to that desired by Klopp and the other senior players. 'Our team was superbly educated tactically by Frank. The managers we had after him weren't on that level,' says Heidel. 'The players were better tacticians than their managers.' There were added problems now with new recruits on the pitch as well, because the veterans were accustomed to the old system that the newcomers never learned – the new managers were incapable of teaching them.

A familiar pattern re-emerged with the new manager, the Belgian René Vandereycken. Once again Vandereycken was no slouch as a coach – he would go on to become Belgium national coach between 2006 and 2009 – but his desire to play with a sweeper brought him into conflict with the senior players. Vandereycken confronted the old pros, and once more Klopp found himself out of the team. Once again, too, results did not go the new manager's way. On 11 November 2000, after a 2–0 home defeat to Hannover 96, Mainz found themselves with just twelve points from twelve games. The Belgian was history.

Vandereycken was succeeded by Eckhard Krautzun, who rather than confronting the senior players attempted to get them on side. Before his interview for the job, he had the foresight to give Klopp a ring – just to see how he was getting on, he assured him, making no mention that he was eyeing up the manager's job. Klopp told him what was working in the team, what wasn't working and why, and what needed to be done to fix it. During the interview with the Mainz board, Krautzun shone thanks to his inside knowledge. He told them how the back four needed to work, without mentioning that Klopp had just told him everything over the phone. As Heidel said later, 'We had no idea about this conversation between Krautzun and Klopp.'

The worldly coach was less successful in his dealings with the media, however. He got off to a rather unfortunate start when he declared at his first press conference that he was happy to be working 'in the Pfalz and by the Bruchsee' – somewhere many miles upriver from the actual location of his new Rheinhessen employers. It didn't go down well. In the meantime, the club was flirting with relegation again. Under Krautzun, who was nearly sixty and whose vocabulary was coloured by the experiences of the war generation, they won a point against St Pauli, then three against Nürnberg, followed by seven games that produced just two points. 'The tide of battle was against us,' Krautzun growled. By late January 2001, a goalless draw with Stuttgarter Kickers left Mainz in sixteenth place – one place lower than when Vandereycken was shown the door.

By the time the season paused for its winter break, Heidel had decided that 'we need to do something'. He started looking for a new manager. On the Monday before the start of Lent – known in

Germany as *Rosenmontag* or 'Carnival Monday' – he found himself sitting at home leafing backwards and forwards through *Kicker* yearbooks (a leading German football magazine). 'There wasn't one CV I liked the look of,' says Heidel. He had no idea as to whom the new manager should be.

The team were at a training camp with Krautzun at Bad Kreuz-nach, escaping the all-consuming *Määnzer Fassenacht* carnival. The club board were taking part in the procession in the city centre. Heidel was sitting on his sofa, thinking hard: 'Where do we go from here?' At some point, he hit upon the answer. Heidel said to himself: 'They can sort out their own mess. The team can shoulder some responsibility. The players, they can do it themselves, we've four or five leaders in that group, we can manage ourselves.' The team's problems, Heidel concluded, had nothing to do with defiance, nor was it because the team was 'unmanageable'. The players had an understanding of football matched by very few managers in Germany at that time, and Krautzun wasn't one of them. It was time for the players to step up.

Mainz's next fixture was on Ash Wednesday against promotion hopefuls Duisburg: the following Saturday they faced bottom club Chemnitz. 'The first thought on my mind was to survive these next two games,' said Heidel. He rang team captain Dimo Wache at the training camp and told him his thinking. Then he called Klopp, who also at the training camp, despite being injured and unable to play. 'I knew that he wanted to go into management one day,' Heidel says. Even so, he was nervous of suggesting his plan to Klopp: that he should take over as player-manager with immediate effect. Heidel was worried that he'd say, 'You must be joking.' But when Heidel offered him the post, Klopp didn't hesitate: 'I'll do it.' There was just one proviso: he didn't want to be a player-manager, just a manager, nothing else. Klopp hadn't taken long to weigh his options up: a playing career in the second division that was winding down, or a new career that he backed himself to succeed at. Heidel was surprised at Klopp's response – and pleased. 'Good for him,' he thought, and agreed. As he put the phone down, Jürgen Klopp's playing career was over.

4

MAINZ MANAGER

Klopp's appointment as the new manager of Mainz did not go down well with everybody. By the time Heidel got in his car and drove to Bad Kreuznach, all the key players knew what was going down. The only person who didn't know what was happening was Eckhard Krautzun. 'Give me one more game,' he pleaded when Heidel broke the news. Heidel's response was a firm 'No'. Krautzun asked him what he was planning to do. Heidel told him that, 'We're taking Klopp.' Krautzun's thoughts on Klopp's appointment were clear cut. 'No,' he replied. 'Think of the club. You have a responsibility to the club.' But Heidel wouldn't be budged.

Krautzun's dismissal of Klopp's appointment was echoed by the response of the press. The club called a press conference where Heidel would present the new manager. The *Mainzer* journalists had caught wind that something was up – firings weren't exactly a rarity at the club – and when they saw who was with Heidel, wisecracked, 'What's Klopp doing here, has he got lost?' When Heidel told them he was going to be the new manager, the laughter really started. The scepticism carried on in the subsequent newspaper reports. Mainz were portrayed as a joke club that has lost touch with reality and given up on staying in the second division. Kloppo, meanwhile, was depicted as a player who had developed megalomania. 'They did a number on us,' Heidel reflects.

But within the team itself, Klopp's appointment had the opposite reaction. When Klopp held his first team meeting, Heidel listened in and was hugely impressed. 'If they'd have given me boots, I was ready to run out onto the pitch, and I'd have fought like a lion,' he said. Mainz might have been relegation certainties, but Klopp was totally convinced that they would beat promotion-chasing Duisburg. 'The players were champing at the bit to get out there and give Duisburg a good going over,' Heidel recalled. He remembers thinking to himself: 'OK, he knows his football' – he knew that from the 'shadow cabinet' days – 'and he can talk too.' That ability to motivate people is a real asset in a manager.

Only 3,500 fans turned up to see the match against Duisburg. Like the media's reaction to Klopp's appointment, this was scepticism on display. But against the odds, Mainz won 1–0 thanks to a Christof Babatz goal. 'Good,' Heidel thought. 'Kloppo can take charge against Chemnitz as well.' Once again Babatz put them 1–0 up, the final score being 3–1 to Mainz. After a terrible run of results, here were two priceless victories in just four days.

As well as the team impressing on the pitch, Klopp was impressing off it. His press conferences were a revelation, his post-match interviews just as good. 'He can do that too,' Heidel thought. 'Good, he's got till the end of the season.' They shook hands on it. Back on the training ground, Klopp put Frank's principles into practice. The team worked on movement again, they pressed and played attacking football with 4–4–2 and zonal marking. The result? Mainz stayed up, Klopp stayed as manager, and a formal contract was signed.

A decade later, at the International Sporting Conference in Bochum in July 2011, journalist Max Jung asked Klopp about the beginnings of his managerial career:[4] 'I still remember that Monday, the day before, the day after,' Klopp told the audience. 'I could tell you everything that happened on those days, all of it. That was a critical point in my life. You mustn't forget, at that point I was an aging second division player with Mainz […] It was a pretty enjoyable transition, from leggy pro to freshly baked manager. Straight away I had the feeling that life was on the up. And then I was allowed to take over the team. I don't have many talents, but I seem to have something of a talent for that. And at that time, working together with the team, it was enough to drag us out of what looked like an impossible situation and stay in the division.'

Klopp admitted to the conference that, 'I didn't really think about it at the time, but today I realise: if I had gone down with Mainz at the age of thirty-three, two or three matches before the end of the season, then my managerial career would have been in trouble. Big trouble. I'd have had this on my CV: First managerial position, went straight down. No one would have come knocking […] and given someone with that record a second chance. So I had to hope for a lot of luck and put a lot of faith in the players to get the job done.'

As soon as Klopp took the job, he realised that 'management was something I wanted to do for the rest of my life. But you can't rely on that. You can't say: "Guys, look, I might not be such a good footballer, but I've halfway understood how the game works, so put me in charge of your team." It doesn't work like that. With my record as a player, you'd normally have to start off in the fourth of fifth division […] I had the great good fortune as a mediocre player to get my start in the second division.'

As starts to managerial careers go, six wins out of seven is hard to beat. 'We had to,' Klopp remembered. 'We needed every single point. It was pretty dramatic, although it didn't feel that way to me at the time. We were relatively relaxed, because we were already as good as done for. All we could do was try to pull off a miracle, and it turns out that's exactly what we did. In terms of character, that team was exceptional, everything we worked on together they took on board. We had a fantastic time as a result of that.'

As an example of the buoyant atmosphere in the camp, Klopp cited the time they were returning from a victory at Ulm: 'We said to the coach driver, "Pull over on the right," and we stopped at a petrol station. We all got out with our sunglasses on and grabbed a beer. Anyone who saw the Mainz 05 team bus would have said to themselves, "Who are all those donkeys spilling out of that coach?" It wouldn't be possible today. But with that team, who were all about the same age as me, it wasn't the wrong approach. That was more than ten years ago, it was a different time.'

By making Klopp the permanent manager, Heidel had finally found what he has been looking for. With Klopp, there was a bridge, a context, a connection: everything fitted together. Frank had a successor. Yet Klopp's style, while following Frank's principles, had its own identity to it as well. While under Frank, the Mainz system meant rigidly following a plan, and woe betide anyone who departed from it in the slightest. Klopp, by contrast, promoted individual initiative to complement the tactical plan. A major factor in this was that he had more technically gifted players under his command than Frank did. Klopp got the best out of his squad and developed a tactical style that was part Frank, part himself.

* * *

What was it about Jürgen Klopp that allowed him to manage the transition from player to coach so effortlessly? It was because he was 'authentic' as a manager, as Heidel put it, calling it his 'greatest strength'. He inspired trust, that rare commodity, and people trusted him implicitly: 'You had the feeling that when he said something, you could rely on it.' When Klopp gave an opinion, he really meant it, there was no dissembling. There are managers who try to act the tough guy when they're not. That's not Klopp's style.

Klopp is a 'what you see' kind of guy, the sort of person who as manager will have a go at a referee, hurdle advertising hoardings, get sent to the stands, jump up and down, pull terrifying war faces, shout, roar, bare his teeth, run on the pitch – whatever he does it is always 100 per cent Klopp. 'He never worries about how it might look,' said Heidel. 'Tuchel [Klopp's successor at both Mainz and Dortmund] is exactly the same.' It says a lot about a coach when the players he trained aren't put off from the job, but want to go on and manage themselves. Just as Frank's teams boasted a number of future coaches, so a whole cohort of Klopp's players ended up in management: Otto Addo, Sandro Schwarz, Christian Hock, Jürgen Kramny, Sven Demandt, Petr Ruman, Tamás Bódog, Marco Rose, Sven Christ, Peter Neustädter, Ermin Melunović, Marco Walker.

Looking back, Klopp was well aware that there was a huge amount of good fortune involved him getting the Mainz 05 job. He wasn't complacent about what it meant to be a *Bundesliga* manager: 'It's something I feel every day,' he reflected a few years later. But he's also well aware that the clubs also have a hard job finding the right manager, and he's not afraid to say so if asked – or even if he's not asked:

'I've got to know a lot of people in this profession by now. Either I got my badges with them, or I got to know them over the course of time. If I'm speaking to a chairman on the phone, then I'll say to him: "Look, I know someone you might be interested in." I think that the decision makers need as much help as possible, particularly when it comes to choosing a manager. Either because they don't have enough information, or they don't have the time to think things through and come to the right decision. Or they aren't brave enough. They were brave at Mainz, they were brave at Dortmund, and I benefited from that. And that doesn't mean I have to be the only lucky one.'

It quickly became clear that Klopp was a draw in getting players to join Mainz. Heidel explains that he had never previously brought managers along when he was signing new players: he was afraid that they'd be put off. It was different with Klopp – he was his strongest argument: 'We almost never lost a player when he was there.' Dennis Weiland was one such recruit, joining in summer 2001 from VfL Osnabrück. The previous season, Mainz had played at Osnabrück on 22 October 2001, when both teams were battling relegation. Mainz midfielder Jürgen Kramny had to be substituted after fifteen minutes with a muscle tear; Klopp came on and played against Weiland, who assisted Daniel Thioune's goal that gave Osnabrück a 2–1 win. 'That earned you a place at Mainz,' said Klopp to Weiland, once he had become his midfield 'tin opener' for his ability to unlock strong defences with his passes and often score the first goal of the game.

When Mainz showed their interest, Weiland asked Christof Babatz, a friend and former roommate at Germania Grasdorf, what was what at Mainz. Babatz was happy there. 'You knew that they played with a back four, they had good strikers in Michael Turk and Blaise Nkufo, and they were looking for a left-footer,' said Weiland. A player like him, in fact. In Osnabrück they warned him against joining: 'Why go there? You'll play in front of 3,000 fans and next season you're down too.' Weiland, though, was no fool. He checked out the Mainz squad and saw that they had the quality for the second division. 'We had the potential to play 4–3–3,' said Weiland. That would suit him.

Gradually, Klopp incorporated the new recruits into his way of playing. They had to learn the system. 'The system had priority,' said Weiland. The core message was to anticipate, to sense what the opponent was going to do next, to keep mentally alert. It was anything but the blunt object of man-to-man marking. You had to be prepared to press, too.

Weiland recalled one incident when he had played the ball in for his brother Niclas, who had also joined Mainz as a striker, into space behind the defender. But Niclas didn't make the run, a classic misunderstanding. Dennis was furious and had a few choice words for his brother: 'Hey mate, you know I'm going to do that!' Klopp's response to be was angered by the fact that Dennis had lost his cool rather than simply playing on. 'And once he loses his temper, well …' says Weiland. It gets lost and it stays lost. 'Then you have to bust a gut for him to get another chance.'

Weiland believes that Klopp had a massive role to play in the team staying together after Mainz twice missed out narrowly on promotion. He didn't criticise the players; the players didn't criticise each other. 'Anywhere else, you'd be chased out of town if that happens. In Mainz, they had our backs,' says Weiland. 'Not everyone gets to experience that.' Even after the second missed promotion, there were no thoughts of a curse, no psychological barriers, no worries of a lack of killer instinct. 'We wouldn't let anyone get into our heads like that.' Weiland describes Klopp as 'an emotional man who lives his emotions, and he did that when we didn't go up too, but then he got a grip and got back to business. He made it clear to us that this wasn't the end of the road, that we'd get another chance.'

Weiland's trust in Klopp as his manager is clear: 'I always had faith that the boss was good for the team, was doing the right thing, even when I wasn't playing,' said Weiland. There were decisions, particularly towards the end of his time at Mainz in 2006, that he couldn't understand, when he was hoping to get back in the team after coming back from injury, but it didn't happen. 'Even then, you think there's reasoning behind it.'

Laughing, Weiland recalled the club's European adventure after Mainz mananged to qualify for the UEFA Cup via Fair Play. It pitched them against Mika Ashtarak in Armenia, Iceland's Keflavik IF and Sevilla. Klopp showed them a video of Keflavik and had to remind the players to take it seriously, himself having to keep a smile off his face as they watched the Icelanders pump corners and free kicks high in the air in the hope that the wind would catch them and carry them towards goal – or even straight in, which it did.

Weiland's contract expired in 2006 without being extended. He doesn't make a big deal of it. He doesn't need to; he's not bitter. 'It hurt, a bit,' because Weiland sensed that he was losing something that he wouldn't be able to replace: the feeling that everything was in its right place, both in footballing and human terms. Antônio 'Toni' da Silva arrived at Mainz, a decent player. Weiland suffered an ankle injury and never regained his place. His brother was also set to leave, and soon Babatz was gone as well. When Dennis went to Eintracht Braunschweig, the difference was huge.

The way Weiland describes it, Klopp embodies a unique combination of affability, humour and very serious, very meticulous preparation. Practise, practise, practise, until you can do it in your sleep. Keep an eye on the fine details. And pinch shampoo from your players. 'Where's your shampoo then, mate?' Klopp would ask. 'You know where,' says Weiland. That was Klopp's reign in Mainz all over. When Klopp moved to Dortmund, Weiland could see the way Mainz had played reflected in the way Dortmund were now playing, but with new additions. It was a style bearing Klopp's hallmark, but always developing.

* * *

For all the success of Klopp's system at Mainz, his belief in his tactics – and the belief of others in him – was tested by the team narrowly and repeatedly missing out on promotion to the *Bundesliga*. On 5 May 2002, Mainz played Union Berlin in the Alte Försterei. It was the final game of the season; Mainz need just a single point to go up. They'd already had two chances to take this vital point, in Duisburg and at home against SpVgg Greuther Fürth. 'Fürth!' said Klopp, 'Fürth!' It was the 'Fürth curse' – a Mainz bogey team. In both games the scoreline was in Mainz's favour before they let it slip. And they weren't to fare any better in Berlin.

Mainz lost 3–1. VfL Bochum went up in their place with a win over Alemannia Aachen. Klopp broke down in tears before an interview with the German national broadcaster ZDF TV. At the official press conference he said: 'I don't want to dwell on it anymore. We had it in our hands and we failed. Our fans had a dream, and we didn't make it reality. We'll have another crack at it.' Later on, Klopp admitted, 'I cried in Berlin like never before in my life. But when you get knocked down, you can get up. As far as I'm concerned, we start again, tomorrow. We've come a long way and we can go even further.'

The following May, Mainz found themselves in a similar situation. On 25 May, the final game of the season saw Klopp's team up against Braunschweig. The previous season they had needed a point, this time they needed a goal. The final league table couldn't have been any closer. Mainz swept Eintracht Braunschweig aside 4–1.

It felt like enough: no one thought anything of the consolation goal, or the numerous chances Mainz also spurned. But then in injury time, Mainz's promotion rivals Eintracht Frankfurt scored to make it 6–3 against Reutlingen. That left both Eintracht and Mainz on sixty-two points. But with that injury time goal, Eintracht had a superior goal difference of one, and went up. The scorer of their promotion-winning goal was Alexander Schur, a friend of Klopp's whom he had played with at Rot-Weiss Frankfurt under Dragoslav Stepanović.

It was a day of contrasting emotions for Klopp. The Mainz match finished first: the squad were all on the pitch, arms around each other's shoulders. Then the news broke of Schur's late goal. Andriy Voronin consoled his manager, his manager consoled him. Klopp ran into the dressing room, where Christof Babatz was in tears. Klopp, still only thirty-six, held it together until at the entrance to the dressing room his son asked him if he had to go to school the next day. 'Then I cried like a baby,' Klopp said.

In the press conference afterwards, Klopp declared: 'I don't believe in a football god, only in God. I believe that everything that happens in life has meaning. Someday, I'll find out what today really meant.' On the way back, the players celebrated defiantly with beer and singing: 'Second division, never again.' The next day, in front of the theatre in Mainz, thousands of people came out to support their team. Klopp tells the crowd, 'Yesterday I asked myself what it all means, and then I realised: someone has decided that it's necessary to show people that you really can get knocked down once, twice, three, even four times, and still get up again, and they thought, there's no better city for it than this.'

The following season, incredibly, Mainz found themselves play-ing the last game of the season with promotion once again in the balance. This time round, the table offered more permutations than in the previous seasons. Alemannia Aachen were third on fifty-three points, but with a worse goal difference than Mainz, and had to face Karlsruher SC (KSC), who were fighting to stay in the division. Mainz 05 were fourth on fifty-one points and faced Eintracht Trier. Also on fifty-one points, but with an inferior goal difference, were Energie Cottbus, who just a couple of weeks before had looked like certainties to go up. Some pundits also gave Rot-Weiss Oberhausen, on fifty points, a chance.

Christian Heidel's daughter was attending her First Communion that day: the sporting director couldn't get out of going to church in strongly Catholic Mainz. At the end of the service the Albanskirche priest and organist struck up: 'Stand up if you're a *Mainzer*.' All stood and sang along. The priest grinned. Heidel believed they could do it: 'With help from above, what can go wrong?'

The afternoon starts well. Thurk puts Mainz a goal up after twenty-three minutes. But then Oberhausen and Cottbus take the lead in their games too. Then, in the forty-third minute the crowd watching the big screen that's been set up behind the stadium jumps for joy: KSC have taken the lead against Alemannia Aachen thanks to striker Conor Casey, who will later go on to play for Mainz. In the sixty-third minute. Mainz are awarded a free-kick. Babatz can pick out his man, crosses it in. Manuel Friedrich gets a head on it, then manages to strike the ball home: 2–0. The fans are still celebrating when Babatz plays in the lively Thurk, who lifts the ball over Trier keeper Axel Keller. Game over.

It's down to the other results now. Karlsruhe are still playing. To make matters worse, the team are down to ten men, with their player Marco Engelhardt having been shown a red card. But somehow,

Alemannia Aachen can't find a way through. Karlsruhe cling on, and hold on to their place in the division. Mainz, at the third attempt, are in the *Bundesliga*. Klopp says, 'That's no normal promotion.'

* * *

Mainz spent three seasons in the *Bundesliga* under Klopp: they finished eleventh in 2004–05 and again in 2005–06. But success brought its own problems. When the club found themselves in the UEFA Cup, it was an extra challenge that was a curse as well as a blessing. On top of this, the players had reached a level that was attracting the attention of other clubs. Central defender Mathias Abel went to Schalke 04, midfielder Toni da Silva to Stuttgart. Three strikers also left: Benjamin Auer to VfL Bochum, Michael Thurk to Eintracht Frankfurt, Mohamed Zidan to Werder Bremen. The players who came in couldn't fill the gaps.

In the first *Bundesliga* season Mainz suffered seven defeats on the trot and went nine games without a win. Klopp said, 'As a manager, you're on your own, you can't ask another manager: What do you do after five, six, seven losses on the go? No one can give you an answer to that, because any other manager would have been sacked before that point.' In the first half of the 2006–07 season, Mainz collected just eleven points. Klopp couldn't sleep, spent his nights brooding. He asked himself, 'What can I do?' He increased the pressure on the team, banned *schunkeln* (the beery reverse-Poznanesque swaying celebration) in the stadium, and challenged the fans to cheer every tackle won. Klopp tried everything, but it was only when he reverted to 4–4–2 that the team returned to form – with a little help from the psychologist Hans-Dieter Hermann and new signings in the winter break. There were some good moments, but in the end it wasn't enough. Mainz lost to Bayern, and after having come eleventh the two previous seasons, they were sent back down to the second *Bundesliga* division.

Back in *2.Bundesliga,* the expectation was that Klopp would take Mainz straight back up. But the 2007–08 season in the second division wasn't normal. The level was unusually high thanks to the inclusion of Borussia Mönchengladbach, 1. FC Köln, SC Freiburg and 1. FC Kaiserslautern. And Mainz 05 too, of course. Klopp came to an agreement with Heidel: he would only stay if Mainz went up. Heidel had a handsome offer ready in his desk drawer for when promotion came.

Once more, Mainz's season went down to the wire. On the final day of the season, Mainz were up against St Pauli: a win would only be enough if third-placed Hoffenheim failed to win at home against SpVgg Greuther Fürth. 'Fürth!' said Klopp, 'Fürth!' It was the Fürth curse again: if they were involved, things were going to be tricky. Mainz did their job by blowing Hamburg away 5–1. But Hoffenheim wiped the floor with Fürth, 5–0, and went up.

Klopp was in tears again. Missing out on promotion meant his goodbye from the club he'd been at since 1990. Petr Ruman embraced his manager. Klopp took a bow in front of the south stand, started a lap of honour. He could only complete two-thirds. Then he escaped his emotions and the fans in the dressing room.

Around 20,000 people flocked to Gutenbergplatz in Mainz on 23 May 2008 to give Kloppo a proper send off. 'All that I am, all that I'm capable of, you all made that possible,' an emotional Klopp told the crown, having difficulty getting the words out, while the Mainz fans chanted 'Jürgen, Jürgen.' He continued: 'Christian Heidel and Harald Strutz gave me the opportunity to do my dream job. I was given support like you wouldn't believe. I had a chairman in Harald Strutz who was my friend before I even knew it […] I'm sure you can all imagine that I'll never forget you.'

5

A MANAGER'S SECOND LOVE

Christian Heidel had been in touch with Borussia Dortmund chairman Hans-Joachim Watzke regarding his manager two years before Klopp went to Dortmund. 'I told him: He's the best manager in Germany,' said Heidel – even if that was bad for Mainz 05. Inevitably, Klopp's time as manager of Mainz had attracted the interest of various *Bundesliga* clubs: Bayer Leverkusen, Hamburg, Bayern Munich and Borussia Dortmund were among those sniffing around.

Not everyone understood the appeal and approach of Klopp's management style. Hamburg were interested in Klopp and sent a scout, who noted Klopp arriving late for training and smoking. He didn't know that it was a tradition at Mainz for Klopp to be the last one onto the training pitch. As for the smoking, Klopp simply shrugged his shoulders. Far from being laid back, a decent scout would have seen that when he was training with the team earlier, Klopp put his heart and soul into it. 'He always managed to put one in the back of the net, striker that he was,' said Weiland. He put his all into the sessions, and he put plenty of willpower in there. Willpower was something that Klopp had a lot of, and something he valued greatly in others. 'If someone didn't show it, determination, you could see Kloppo's blood start to boil,' said Weiland. A decent scout would have taken note of the happy working environment in Mainz, the enthusiasm and will to get stuck in, how the manager enjoyed training, the fun the players had during training, and the precision, the meticulous detail. In the end Hamburg strung him along for so long that Klopp decided to call the whole thing off.

Another team in need of a new manager was Bayern Munich, whose manager Ottmar Hitzfeld had announced he was stepping down at the end of the 2007–08 season. But here, there were doubts as to whether Klopp could handle big-name players. After all, there weren't any of those in Mainz. Klopp was seen purely as a motivator who could whip his team up, a bit of a wild man – a bit too wild, perhaps. At Bayern they were unsure whether someone like Klopp – never still on the touchline, unshaven, wearing jeans with holes in – was really a Champions League manager. That got on Klopp's nerves. The Bavarians said to him: 'We're going to decide between you and an internationally recognised manager.' Klopp told them thanks but no thanks; Bayen went for Jürgen Klinsmann instead.

This left just two potential suitors: Bayer Leverkusen and Borussia Dortmund. Bayer made it clear to him that rather than being in charge, Klopp would be number two to Mirko Slomka. Bayer eventually settled on Bruno Labbadia. So after leaving Mainz, having failed to get promotion, Klopp was left with one option: the club to whom Heidel had been singing his praises several years before.

* * *

Borussia Dortmund parted ways with manager Thomas Doll in summer 2008. He had relied on a squad of mostly aging players. That was expensive in terms of the wages and the Borussians were in financial difficulties. They were looking for a manager with a new philosophy: one based around young, hungry (and cheap) players who could offer the fans in Signal Iduna Park more exciting football. Klopp seemed to be the perfect fit for their new direction.

He had forged a team that played attractive and tactically mature football without any big stars.

On the same wavelength from the start, it didn't take much for the Dortmunders to convince Klopp to step on board. Relations were excellent from the beginning, with BVB officials Michael Zorc and Hans-Joachim Watzke giving him the feeling that they didn't want anyone but him. 'To be honest, we [Klopp and his assistant] knew straight away we would do it. We were just playing hard to get after that,' revealed Klopp years later.

When he arrived at the club, Klopp announced with a cheerful, knowing smile that 'Borussia Dortmund wasn't the worst offer you could get.' From the very beginning, Klopp's consummate media skills radiated positivity with lines like these – a positivity that had been in short supply in Dortmund in the previous few seasons. Klopp's charm offensive continued with his admiration for the club's ground: the Westfalenstadion: 'The first few times you come to our stadium and you see 80,000 fans there, you think: Wow! And it never becomes routine. You get the same rush every time you come here. It sends a shiver down your spine, every single time.'

For all the positivity, Klopp knew that he was a young, relatively inexperienced manager (he was forty-one years old when he took over) being put in charge of a heavyweight club in serious need of an overhaul. The once proud club – who had won the Champions League just a decade before – had now descended into mediocrity. They had finished the 2007–08 season a dispiriting thirteenth in the table. The only highlight of a disappointing season was that they had qualified for the UEFA Cup by reaching the DFB Cup final, where they lost 2–1 to Bayern Munich after extra-time. This defeat had been a much better showing than most had hoped for: just a few days earlier they had been crushed by the same opponents 5–0 in Munich, revealing how hopelessly outclassed they were. Finding themselves four goals down before half time, the Dortmund fans responded with gallows humour – celebrating imaginary goals until they were 'leading' 5–4.

The travails of Dortmund's 2007–08 season were succinctly summed up by Philipp Köster, editor-in-chief of *Kicker*, who wrote the following report in April 2008: 'In the time it took for the ball to be won by the Dortmund defence and moved upfield to the strikers, some of the fans in the south stand managed to go and buy a beer. Twice. Dortmund can carry on like this. Or someone can ask themselves how they can get this team playing. That would be a real breath of fresh air.'

This is what Klopp had to deal with when he arrived. He was there to rebuild; to give the team an attractive and successful sporting identity. Expectations were high for what he might achieve, but they were also grounded in realism. The 'black and yellows' were hungry for their team to play attractive football, but most of all they wanted to see some passion and commitment. Titles might be beyond their reach, but having a team that made it easy for you to identify with them – that was what they wanted in Dortmund. Klopp understood this: his first promise to the fans was to deliver 'full throttle football'. His challenge now was to coach the players to achieve this.

* * *

Dortmund's financial state had changed the face of the team, seeing the departure of the big names of the club's turn of the millennium generation. The Stefan Reuters, the Jürgen Kohlers, the Jan Kollers – all were now Dortmund history. Instead, the new star of Borussia Dortmund was the manager. Larger than life, Klopp towered above the city from billboards along Bundesstrasse 1, the motorway that runs through the heart of the city and past Signal Iduna Park: 'Don't lose your place!' That was the message for season ticket holders who could barely remember what good football – clever combinations, mazy dribbles, pace and aggression – looked like. Weekend after weekend, they had subsisted on gruel. Most only turned up to the home games, and that was more out of habit than anything else. It was a Dortmund thing – the current crop of players might not have had much to offer, but the fans still loved the club.

Previous managers had come to Dortmund with intentions similar to Klopp's, but had been unable to bridge the gap between ideas and implementation. Klopp's pre-predecessor Jürgen Röber had also spoken stirringly of passion and putting yourself on the line for the club at his introductory press conference. He was gone within three months. Dortmund was euphoric during the 2007–08 pre-season when they hammered AS Roma 4–0 in a friendly. The truth was the Italians had only just returned from their summer holidays and still had one foot on the beach. Reality soon reared its head as a 3–1 away defeat to MSV Duisburg signalled the start of a painful season that by its end also saw Röber's successor Thomas Doll out of a job.

'None of my teams has ever played "lawn chess",' said Klopp on being unveiled as the new manager in May 2008. He wanted to imbue his team with a new philosophy. Their playing style should have an identity, be 'recognisable'. And he was brave enough to deal with the old guard straight away, packing the man-marking school embodied in Christian Wörns and Robert Kovač off into retirement.

Instead, he set his stall by two nineteen-year-olds: Mats Hummels and Neven Subotić – Klopp brought the latter with him from Mainz, where he had established himself in the first eleven the previous season. It was the youngest central-defensive partnership in *Bundesliga* history, and lovingly described by the press as the *Kinderriegel* (a pun on a Kinder chocolate bar and 'defence kids'). There was no traditional playmaker in the BVB set-up. Instead, the midfield consisted of a central 'double-pivot', Tinga and Sebastian Kehl, with Jakub 'Kuba' Błaszczykowski (already lauded as the 'Polish Luís Figo' when he signed in 2007) on the right and Tamás Hajnal on the left flank tasked with compressing the space. But there was still much to be done, and Klopp knew it.

In the east of Dortmund is the surburb of Brackel: the name is drawled out: 'Braakel' rather than 'Brakkel'. It is here that Dortmund have their training complex and where in the summer of 2008, Klopp got to work. Right from the start, he was completely in his element at the BVB training complex. An all-action figure, he worked on everything from improving Nelson 'Couldn't hit a barn door' Valdez's shooting accuracy, to bringing out the 'wild boar' within from Giovanni 'Stroller' Federico. The true hardcore fans who turned up at Brackel to watch every day – the *Trainingskiebitze* as they are known – immediately saw for themselves that Klopp was much, much more than a TV personality: he was a professor of football working tirelessly to make his ideas a reality on the pitch. One of the dedicated fans who watched the training sessions spoke on behalf of many supporters when he said: 'Actually, I was planning to give my grandson my seat next season; he might have had the patience for the rubbish we've had to put up with the past few years.' Now, he wanted to go himself and hold onto his regular seat. 'Because of Kloppo,' he said.

As with his Mainz players before them, Klopp's players were drilled hard on playing without the ball, defending as a unit. There was to be no skiving: the midfielders and forwards had defensive responsibilities now. In the previous season, Dortmund had shipped sixty-two goals, more than any other team in the league. That wasn't going to happen again under Klopp, and everyone had their part to play in ensuring that.

Klopp repeatedly interrupted the training drills, making them do them over until they got it right, until they could do it without thinking. The 'flat bank of four' in midfield still wasn't working properly. Ingraining training ground routines was vital. Klopp knew that, out on the pitch, if you have to stop to think, you lose: 'If I break through along the byline and someone's completely free in the area, ideally I'd be spotting him. That means I should already know exactly where to look for the midfielder bursting into the box,' said Klopp.

In the curtain raiser to the 2008–09 season, Borussia Dortmund played Bayern Munich in the T-Home Supercup: the German equivalent of the Charity Shield that season. Klopp's team reversed the score of the DFB Cup final at the end of the previous season, beating Bayern 2–1. The result was almost too good: Dortmunders began to dream that 'this year might be our year'. The user 'Ikpeba' spoke for many fans when he posted on the popular German football website *transfermarkt.de*, 'Kloppo, make football fun again!' Many fans expected nothing less than that. Klopp, however, was more circumspect. He knew that in order satisfy the Ikpebas, the whole Dortmund system would need overhauling. That was a big job: to the point that rather than buying a home in Dortmund, he rented at first – you never know. Instead of inflating the fans' optimism, he sought to lower expectations to a sensible level. It was only after a hard-fought win over third division Rot-Weiss Essen in the cup that he said: 'Today, the team has shown a glimpse of the new look we've all been talking about these past weeks.'

* * *

Despite their thirteenth place finish in 2007–08 – their worst for exactly twenty years – Dortmund continued to boast remarkable attendances: an average of 72,510 watched their home games that season. Yet the point had been reached where the legendarily atmospheric stadium was approaching library status. The sporting spectacle that had been the norm when the stadium still went under its traditional name (the Westfalenstadion) was just as much a thing of the past.

The expensively bought titles under chairman Gerd Niebaum and manager Michael Meier had raised fan's expectations. Extensions had almost doubled the capacity of the stadium, but the number of 'true' fans who came to support their team rather than those who might uncharitably be described as glory hunters hadn't kept pace. Home advantage had been reversed: at times, it seemed as if the players lived in fear of the restless – and gigantic – South Stand (Gelbe Wand). When a pass was intercepted, the sound of 25,000 people falling silent could be very loud indeed. The atmosphere at away games was, in contrast, completely different. These were the BVB supporters who would sacrifice their weekends to travel to all corners of Germany: the fans who stayed loyal to their club through the mid-eighties when there were scant prospects of any future success. Who could cheer on their team even in the midst of a five-goal thrashing in Munich. The sort who responded to such situations with humour, rather than turning on the players.

Klopp was tasked with awakening the old South Stand spirit, winning back the fans' unconditional love for Borussia Dortmund. Sure, when one victory follows another like in the 2011 championship-winning season, that's no hard task. But there was more to it than that, as this reaction to the Champions League tie against Arsenal in September 2011, a 1–1 draw, shows. Before the match 'Wenger has described the Westfalenstadion as the temple of German football and it was hard to disagree. The huge Gelbe Wand, [is] like Villa Park's Holte End, only bigger. As kick-off approached it also became a wall of sound,' wrote Glenn Moore in the *Independent*. It took a powerful Ivan Perišić shot in the 89th minute to earn the late but deserved equaliser that Dortmund had been chasing since they fell behind against the run of play at the end of the first half. The last time they had been in action, they had suffered a sobering 2–1 home defeat at the hands of newly promoted Hertha Berlin. Now, against Arsenal, the 'Yellow Wall' exploded into life and fired the players on tirelessly, driving them on to the equaliser with sheer willpower – an encouragment that rippled out from there to more shy and retiring wallflowers in the rest of the stadium.

Just as Klopp had asked, thousands of fans renewed their season tickets and retained their *Stammplätze* (regular seat). After record sales the previous year, when 50,549 season tickets had been sold, despite the club's poor finish to the previous season, the club still managed 49,500 for Klopp's first season. Thanks to some excellent performances, the 50,000 mark was broken again the next season, and after the championship season 53,000 season tickets were sold, a new *Bundesliga* record. The new manager had convinced more than just his players.

Klopp's hard work soon bore fruit on the pitch as well: the 2008–09 season got off to a perfect start with a 3–2 win away to Bayer Leverkusen. However, it came at a heavy price: left back and Dortmund legend Dedê, one of the first names on the teamsheet since 1998, suffered a cruciate ligament injury and faced months on the sidelines. The following week saw Klopp's home debut. The 1–1 draw with reigning champions Bayern Munich was at least a moral victory. Beating Energie Cottbus one-nil away gave the team a further boost going into the *Reverderby* – the *'Ruhr clasico'* – against arch-rivals Schalke 04.

The match was not just Klopp's first Ruhr derby, but a milestone in his debut season with Borussia Dortmund. All newcomers to Dortmund or Schalke have it drummed into them right from the start: there are thirty-four games in the *Bundesliga*, but two matches are about more than the three points. The derbies determine bragging rights in the Ruhr and the workplace atmosphere for fans in black and yellow or blue and white. And it was to be one of these very matches, with their long tradition of intensity and passion, that was to be one of the defining ties of Klopp's early reign.

The game started badly for the home team. With two-thirds of the game gone, Borussia Dortmund were three goals down in front of their own fans. For all the optimism of the opening three matches, this was like a cold, wet flannel in the face. It could have been worse: Schalke forward Kevin Kurányi had a golden opportunity to make it 4–0 and put the game beyond Dortmund's reach – but he wasted it. Soon afterwards, Dortmund defender Neven Subotić showed him how it was done, making it 3–1 in the sixty-seventh minute. It was a goal that breathed new life not just into his team, but also the 25,000 fans in the South Stand. Driving their team on with ever greater intensity, they got their reward just three minutes later when Alexander Frei, who had been brought on at half-time, put a dream strike in the top corner to cut the deficit to just a single goal (albeit from an offside position that escaped the linesman's notice).

Schalke were now on the back foot and started to lose their nerve. With a little less than a quarter-hour to go, they found themselves down to nine men with first Christian Pander and then Fabian

Ernst being sent off. At first though, it seemed as if the equaliser was destined not to come, despite relentless Dortmund pressure. Until, that is, the ball was fired against Schalke defender Mladen Krstajić's arm inside the box. A somewhat questionable penalty was awarded. Whether it was justified or not made no difference to Frei: he made no mistake with the spot kick and Dortmund had done the seemingly impossible in the penultimate minute of normal time. Signal Iduna Park went wild. It was a remarkable comeback: both for Dortmund and for Frei himself, being the Swiss striker's first game back after being out injured for months. In the end, the only thing that saved the shellshocked visitors was the referee's whistle – with no injury time being played, they were spared a likely fourth goal and a humiliating defeat.

Like Klopp, Schalke had a new manager, Fred Rutten, experiencing the intensity of the match for the first time. Klopp marvelled after the game, 'That was a crash course for both of us in just what can happen in a derby.' A derby for which Klopp and his coaching staff had spared no effort to motivate their team. Before the game, they had shown the players a video of highlights of past derby wins – and told them this was their chance to go out and make history. Even if events probably hadn't quite gone to Klopp's original game plan, there was no doubting that his players had been paying attention. And there was the feelgood factor from fighting back from a seemingly impossible position.

If he didn't realise it after this first match, then Klopp would have recognised the enormous significance of winning the Ruhr derby when BVB put in a majestic performance in the lion's den of Schalke's Veltins-Arena to triumph 3–1 two years later, again on the fourth matchday of the season. As the team bus returned to Dortmund, the conquering heroes were mobbed by hundreds of ecstatic fans, who hoisted Shinji Kagawa – who had scored a brace – onto their shoulders. 'That was pure ecstasy. Goosebumps, incredible, I've never experienced anything like it. No one could deny just how much a derby win means after seeing that,' Klopp said in astonishment at the time.

Back in 2008, the late comeback against Schalke meant that BVB remained undefeated four games into the season, level on points with their Gelsenkirchen neighbours. The tender shoot of hope that Klopp had been nurturing since his arrival could now grow and flourish. Even a clear 4–1 defeat at Hoffenheim a week later did nothing to deflate the mood of the campaign.

That was sustained despite other first season setbacks. Klopp's first appearance with Dortmund on the European stage was to prove slightly less successful than the September 2008 derby win. They came up against Udinese in the first round of the UEFA Cup and suffered a sobering 2–0 home defeat after leaving themselves rather naively open to the counter. The return leg was to be an inspiring contrast: they fought back with a 2–0 win of their own before the match went to extra-time and then penalties. However, losing the shootout meant missing out on the group phase. The Italians reached the quarter-finals where they were themselves knocked out by Werder Bremen.

Borussia Dortmund had a rocky start to the new year to cope with as well: the first seven games of the second half of the season brought only one win. That didn't stop the club leadership showing their confidence in Klopp with an early contract extension taking him up to 2012, and there was an instant reward: they won the very next game, 1–0 against Werder Bremen. The final ten matches of the season included eight wins that lifted *die Schwarzgelben* to sixth place.

For *Kicker* reporter and Dortmund expert Thomas Hennecke, Jürgen Klopp proved his steadiness under fire during the 2009 winless streak by staying true to his philosophy. 'Around that time there were headlines like "Has Kloppo lost his mojo?" He didn't let it affect him in the slightest. That's when I learned that he doesn't work week-to-week, or see things in black and white. He sees the shades of grey, and – keeping on the colour theme – he keeps following the golden path that he's set for himself with unshakeable consistency. No matter what anyone writes or says, or what tactical changes they demand.'

For Hennecke, this strength of character is key to Klopp's success: 'Even at sporting low points he doesn't deviate from his chosen course by a millimetre. That's because he has total conviction in what he's doing. And how things played out in the months that followed proved him to be 100 per cent in the right. For me, that's a really crucial part of his make up, that he isn't reactive and ready to change course. Whatever direction the wind is blowing from, he never loses his bearings. He's steady at the helm, and it pays off.'

The standard was set. At the end of Klopp's first season in charge, the club had ended up just two points short of Europa League qualification. If anything, the final position was something of a disappointment: Hamburg had moved past them into fifth place at the last possible moment with an injury-time goal that should not have stood. The goal that made it 3–2 against Eintracht Frankfurt came from an offside position. Nevertheless, Dortmund had taken enormous strides forward in comparison to their thirteenth place the previous season. It was the start of the beginning.

6

CHAMPIONS

Klopp had already started making big changes to the squad during his first season. The 2009 January transfer window saw Antonio Rukavina, Diego Klimowicz, Giovanni Federico, Delron Buckley, Marc-André Kruska and Robert Kovač leave the club after being reduced to bit-part players. Even before the season started, veteran defender and long-time captain Christian Wörns, who had spent nine years at the Westfalenstadion, had not been offered a new contract and decided to retire.

After three years in Dortmund, the hero of Klopp's first derby, Alexander Frei, also left the club in 2009, returning to his home country by signing for FC Basel. One of the reasons Dortmund let him go was their new philosophy under Klopp. The classic fixed formation and fixed player roles were now passé. As Thomas Hennecke of *Kicker* magazine explained, 'With Klopp, the boundaries between the different parts of the team blur. Defenders start phases of play and push up the field. The forwards are responsible for the first defensive phase. So Klopp's players need to be as flexible as the system. He let strikers like Mladen Petrić and Alexander Frei go because they didn't put in the hard running he demanded. I was not the only one to have doubts about them leaving in 2008 (Petrić) and 2009 (Frei), but ultimately Klopp's decisions made sense. And he found the perfect successor in Lucas Barrios. He was a poacher who was also capable of holding up the ball and bringing others into play, and followed his boss' tactical instructions to the letter.'

Barrios wasn't the only success story among the new recruits. BVB proved to have an excellent eye for talent in this period, with almost all the new additions coming good. As well as Neven Subotić, another ex-*Mainzer* had joined the squad along with Klopp in the summer: striker Mohamed Zidan, in a swap deal for Mladen Petrić. The forward had shown his best form to date at Mainz under Klopp. Nuri Şahin, who had made his BVB debut at sixteen, returned from a loan spell at Feyenoord and soon developed into a crucial cog in the Dortmund midfield.

Other transfers who proved to be successes included Brazilian central defender Felipe Santana, Hungarian midfielder Tamás Hajnal, and German international Patrick Owomoyela. Another new addition was South Korean full-back Young-Pyo Lee, who was brought in to deputise for the injured Dedê. During the first phase of Klopp's time at Dortmund they all became stalwarts of the overhauled squad. Kevin-Prince Boateng was also brought in on loan from Tottenham Hotspur that winter break, and showed hints of the talent that would blossom at AC Milan. The shock therapy had worked. Klopp's new team was taking promising shape.

The 2009–10 season was to prove another year of stabilisation for Borussia Dortmund, who showed their consistency by reaching fifth place. Yet at the beginning of the season, things had been looking far from rosy. Unlike Klopp's first season in charge, it proved to be a bumpy start and they had to come to terms with some painful setbacks: losing 4–1 at Hamburg in their second game was the first indication that team wasn't managing to properly implement Klopp's cherished 'playing without the ball' system. If you include the five goals conceded to Real Madrid in a friendly, Klopp's troops had let in nine goals in the space of five days. Suddenly, it seemed the Dortmund defence was all over the place and it wasn't to end there. Dortmund's fifth league game of the season brought Bayern Munich to Signal Iduna Park, and the Borussians were trampled 5–1.

To make matters worse, Dortmund also lost their next home fixture, this time just 1–0 – but against, of all teams, Schalke. After seven league games, Dortmund had a solitary victory to their credit, leaving them in fifteenth position, just one point above the relegation zone. Just a fifth of the new season had been played, but the situation already seemed grim. Adding to the pain, all of this was happening while Dortmund were celebrating their centenary season – that had been the reason for the friendly against Real Madrid, which had seen them outclassed and mercilessly humiliated.

Yet just as they had done at the turn of the year in Klopp's first season, Dortmund now kicked into top gear and started overtaking the pack – without the inspiration of a Klopp contract extension this time. The *Jungs* – Klopp's 'lads', as he liked to call them – marched on up the table all the way to the winter break, losing not a single game as they rose to fifth place. They were able to defend that position until the end of the season, earning direct qualification to the Europa League.

There were some chastening defeats in the second half of that season: it hurt to lose 2–1 to Schalke 04 in Gelsenkirchen, meaning their Ruhr rivals had done the double over Klopp's team. And then there was a mixed return to Bruchweg for Klopp and a one-nil defeat to newly promoted Mainz. Nevertheless, fifth place and European qualification in 2010 met with enthusiastic celebrations from the Dortmund fans. Little did they know the incredible grounds for celebration their team would provide the following season.

* * *

Klopp's third season in charge of Dortmund would not only mark the completion of a decade of his time in management, but would prove to be the highlight of his career so far. It wasn't just the fact that they won the *Bundesliga* title – it was the way they did it that impressed most of all. In Klopp's own words: 'This kindergarten is tearing through the league like there's no tomorrow. It's truly extraordinary.'

It certainly was. When Dortmund beat Nürnberg by two goals to nil at home, Klopp's team had put the title to bed a full two weeks before the end of the season. After the final game of the season, the squad kicked off the celebrations in an Italian restaurant before heading to a club and partying away until dawn approached. 'And the squad partied just like they'd played: passionately,' Klopp later revealed. Throughout, they stayed true to the gaffer's motto: 'Work hard, play hard.'

At the beginning of the season, however, such scenes would have been unfathomable. Once again, Dortmund got off to anything but an auspicious start, losing 2–0 at home to Bayer Leverkusen to kick off the season. What no one would have suspected at the time was that this would be their final defeat until the very last game of the *Hinrunde* – the first half of the season – which they lost 1–0 away to Eintracht Frankfurt. Sandwiched between the two defeats was a thick filling of success, including one draw and fourteen wins. It was the second best *Hinrunde* in *Bundesliga* history.

Dortmund experienced many highs during the 2010–11 season, but for Klopp one moment in particular from the first half of the season remained fresh in the memory, in a manner which perhaps only managers who sweat over the set up of their team can understand. This image of perfection came during their sixth game, in the build up to Shinji Kagawa's goal for 2–1 against St Pauli (the final score was 3–1). Klopp was in raptures as he told the story: 'It's not possible to have your players better positioned in the penalty area than what happened in that moment. During a well-organised attack we always want at least three, but preferably four players in the opponent's box, and at least two more on the edge of the area. Götze took the ball to the right of the goal, squared it from the goalline towards the penalty spot where Grosskreutz was standing. He could have taken a shot, but he didn't, he dummied, but he knew without looking that Kagawa would be completely free behind him, because that's exactly what's in our game plan. So Kevin let it run for Shinji, who passed the ball into the corner of the net. If the shot had hit the post, then Bender was there waiting for the tap in, also according to plan. The image of perfection. I watched it back, and I was made up.'

The image of perfection. Klopp puts a lot of effort into analysing games, treating himself to up to thirty DVDs per week so he can show the team the good – and bad – phases of play, divided between defence, midfield and attack to focus on each player's needs. He's a manager who hands his players a training schedule before they leave on holiday and has them text him how well they're keeping up with it. He's a perfectionist: and when it all goes to plan like this, the results feel extremely rewarding.

The question on everyone's lips during the winter break was whether or not Klopp's young side would have the maturity to keep up this level of performance through to the end of the season. Would the pressure cause them to start questioning themselves and rob them of their footballing innocence? It's lonely at the top, as the saying goes, and throwing away a ten-point lead is not unprecedented. If, if, if. But it didn't take long for the front-runners to prove the doubters wrong: their first act of the second half of the season was to comfortably exact their revenge on Bayer Leverkusen, defeating one of the most persistent members of the chasing pack by three goals to one.

Another crucial milestone on the road to the title was to be reached in February 2011 in Munich. Bayern Munich entered the match having just given themselves a welcome confidence boost by beating defending champions Inter Milan 1–0 in Italy in the Champions League. Now they were ready to seize their last chance to turn the domestic title race in their favour. Bayern chairman Uli Hoeness optimistically declared to *Bild* newspaper that the match would be an 'unambiguous victory by a margin of two clear goals'. His prediction turned out to be correct – except that the 3–1 winning scoreline ended up in the guests' favour.

Jürgen Klopp got his tactics spot on for the match, setting up his team to neutralise the frightening attacking threat emanating from superstar Bayern wingers Franck Ribéry and Arjen Robben. Dortmund's left flank was defended by Marcel Schmelzer and Kevin Grosskreutz doubling up on Robben; on the right, Ribéry had no joy against Łukasz Piszczek, with Mario Götze also dropping back to lend support. If gaps opened up in midfield, the double-pivot of Nuri Şahin and Sven Bender was quick to close them down. By defending from the front and closing down relentlessly, Dortmund didn't allow Bayern to get their game going. They also decisively limited the impact Bastian Schweinsteiger, the vital cog in the Bayern midfield, could have on play.

All of this was achieved with Borussia Dortmund fielding the youngest team in their *Bundesliga* history, with an average age of just 22.3. The records kept tumbling: the victory at Bayern was the first time Dortmund had beaten the Bavarians on their home turf since 1991. Following the match, players and club officials started talking openly of potential title ambitions. Previously it had seemed as if anyone who uttered the taboo 'M-word' – *Meister* (Champions) – would face a club fine, such were the lengths they went to avoid using it. Now, with a massive twelve-point advantage on second-placed Bayer Leverkusen – and an even bigger sixteen-point lead over the defending champions from Munich – naming any other target would have defied common sense. And so it proved. Klopp's side defended first place through to the end of the season to clinch the title. With an average age of 24.2 over the whole season, the Dortmund 'Kindergarten' became the youngest team in its history to lift the *Bundesliga* trophy.

The relief at never having lost sight of the finish line, and finally crossing it, was palpable. For although second place would still have been considered a fantastic result the previous season, that year, after Borussia Dortmund had swept all before them, only first would do. Motorists driving through Dortmund on the B1 motorway enter a tunnel a mile from Signal Iduna Park. Fixed above the entrance are the words 'We are good football' in giant steel letters. By winning the title, Klopp's young side had made those words a reality.

* * *

That title-winning season, Borussia Dortmund played in some breathtaking games that captured the imagination not just of their own fans, but football supporters more generally. Their champagne football earned the admiration of many, with an appeal that extended far beyond Dortmund's city limits. But how exactly did the Dortmund system work? What was the tactical basis for the grandiose performances of Klopp's team?

During the 2010–11 season, Dortmund played in a 4–2–3–1 system with Nuri Şahin and Sven Bender acting as the double-pivot in defensive midfield. While the tough-tackling Bender concentrated almost exclusively on his role as a stopper, shielding the defence, Şahin's role was to organise and set the tempo, transitioning the play from defence effortlessly into attack. This is why Bender is placed slightly further back in the diagram (see p. 91). Şahin often dropped deep as well in order to keep play ahead of him and to pick up the ball directly from the defensive players before initiating a new attacking phase. As a result, Şahin frequently had more touches than any other Dortmund player.

The creative impulse in attack was provided by the 'magic feet' of two men in particular: Mario Götze and Shinji Kagawa, who were not just dangerous goal threats themselves, but also gave target man Lucas Barrios the platform from which to shine. Kevin Grosskreutz made a huge contribution to the attacking three-man midfield with his commitment and willingness to run to the byline. The midfield would dominate the ball and pull the opposition defence apart with a quick, short passing game, waiting until they created a gap. Switching the ball between flanks put further strain on the opponent.

When the opposition had the ball, Grosskreutz and Götze would push high up the pitch. By closing down the flanks, they aimed to force the opposition to attempt to start their attack phase by passing into the packed midfield, where Sven Bender and company were stationed, ready to win back the ball. All the outfield players operated as one, pushing high up the pitch into the opposition half to win early possession – an effective but energy-sapping tactic. This proactive and relentless *Gegenpressing* when the team didn't have the ball was one of the key factors in their amazing winning run.

Leading the line, Barrios interpreted his role not as that of a traditional centre-forward, waiting for the ball to be played in to him, but more about laying the ball off to the advancing midfielders to bring them into the attack. Once Barrios reached the penalty area, they would then play the ball back to him, where he could take advantage of his eye for goal. The Argentine-born Paraguay international was equally deadly in the air or on the ground: as long as the midfielders could get the ball to him, it was a recipe for goals. As their sole nominal striker on the pitch, Barrios had to rely on regular support from the midfield if he was to avoid becoming isolated – and they provided it.

Borussia's full-backs Marcel Schmelzer and Łukasz Piszczek frequently pushed high up the pitch when the game situation demanded it, creating a dominance in midfield and adding their own goal threat down the wings. As they moved into an offensive position, Grosskreutz or Götze would move into the centre to create space for them. When the opposition was in possession, Schmelzer and Piszczek would fall in line with the central-defenders, Hummels and Subotić. Both extremely comfortable on the ball, the two central defenders would win the ball then initiate attacks themselves: Hummels in particular made a speciality of sending long balls to the forwards, quickly bypassing the midfield and taking advantage of the disorganisation of the opposition in the moment they lost possession. Because the central-defensive duo held their positions, they have no movement arrows on the diagram. Hummels and Subotić moved upfield only for set-plays, corners and free-kicks, to take advantage of their strength in the air. They were then covered at the back by the full-backs and the defensive midfielders. Behind the defence, keeper Roman Weidenfeller was also capable of coming off his line and tidying up.

Essentially, Klopp's team acted as a compact and cohesive unit that united all players in both attacking and defensive phases. There was no strict division of roles. Parallel movement towards the ball restricted the amount of space between defence, midfield and attack, and balanced out to cover over as much of the pitch as possible. Thanks to a tactical maturity beyond their years, Dortmund conceded a mere twenty-two times in thirty-four games and kept fourteen clean sheets – with a little help from Weidenfeller's excellent reflexes.

To give his players a chance to rest, Klopp did occasionally vary his starting eleven, but injuries to key players such as Kagawa and Şahin made it impossible to implement a full rotation policy. Kagawa suffered a broken metatarsal while on international duty with Japan in the Asian Cup and missed almost the entire second half of the season; Şahin also missed the run-in thanks to a knee injury.

As a result, the changes were usually forced rather than voluntary. To compensate for the loss of Kagawa, who had been playing on another level during the first half of the season, Götze moved inside and Kuba took his place on the right. Alternatively, Robert Lewandowski would drop into the number-ten role and Götze would stay in the inside-right position – as he did for the 3–1 win in Munich. 'Supersub' Lewandowski would step in for Barrios, scoring four goals in the league after coming off the bench.

Antônio da Silva was the first choice to replace either Bender or Şahin in defensive midfield. Captain Sebastian Kehl, who was equally at home in that position, missed the majority of the season due to injury. Felipe Santana proved himself a worthy deputy for Hummels and Subotić in central defence. Back-up keeper Mitchell Langerak, meanwhile, played only once – of all games in the rip-roaring defeat of Bayern Munich, where he kept goal flawlessly.

Such was the success of the system that in the following 2011–12 season, the story of Borussia Dortmund's playing philosophy was mostly one of continuity, with just two changes to the basic starting eleven: Nuri Şahin moved to Real Madrid and his place next to

Dortmund's Tactical Set Up in the 2010–11 Season

Bender in the midfield trenches was taken either by the now-fit Kehl or new addition İlkay Gündoğan. Lewandowski replaced Barrios as the focal point of attack.

* * *

Dortmund becoming league champions so quickly under Klopp's tenure had been beyond anyone's expectations. After the club's near bankruptcy the Borussia Dortmund fan community hadn't dared dream of another title. The years that followed, characterised by a downhill trend of sporting mediocrity, seemed to confirm this. Sixth place in 2004 was followed by seventh in 2005 and 2006, ninth in 2007 and then a miserable thirteenth in 2008 – before Klopp came in and managed to reverse the club's fortunes.

The last BVB manager to guide the club to the title had been Matthias Sammer in 2002. Yet there was little in common between his title-winning team and that of 2011. The spine of the turn-of-the-millennium team consisted of experienced and often expensive stars: the likes of Jens Lehmann, Jürgen Kohler, Stefan Reuter, Christian Wörns, Dedê, Miroslav Stević, Jan Koller, Marcio Amoroso, Ewerthon and Tomáš Rosický. Home-grown players like Lars Ricken and Christoph Metzelder were thin on the ground, in stark contrast to the 2011 generation.

The financial situation meant that BVB made the best of a bad job by giving youth a chance, betting on young, untested but hungry players. The side no longer consisted of grizzled, seen-it-all veterans, but 'wild ones', like the Dortmund born and bred Kevin Grosskreutz, who embodied the 'We're all Dortmund lads' feeling like no other. At his side were equally ambitious young professionals such as Marcel Schmelzer, Mats Hummels, Mario Götze, Nuri Şahin and Sven Bender. Young, freewheeling and fearless, these football cavaliers made it easy for the fans to feel they were all in it together.

BVB fans found themselves revelling in the warm glow of a football side that was rooted in their city and their region, where 'fans and club as one' was more than empty rhetoric – it was a living, breathing reality. It was one of the main reasons the 2011 side achieved so much admiration, from across the footballing world. It was a team whose achievements were pithily summed up by goalkeeper Roman Weidenfeller for an Middle-Eastern station on live TV: 'I think we have a *grandiose saison gespielt*.' The Queen's English it wasn't, but the memorable, spontaneous 'Denglisch' outburst (an amalgamation of *Deutsch* and English) got to the heart of the matter: 'I think we played a fantastic season.' Weidenfeller's quip was to become the motto of the subsequent title celebrations.

The Dortmund party lasted a full two weeks, starting with the victory over Nürnberg. 'We were lucky enough to confirm the title before the end of the season so we could start celebrating straight away, in beautiful weather, completely spontaneously, completely from the heart. It was incredible fun,' Klopp later said, looking back fondly. He made clear just how much the intensity with which the fans celebrated the title moved him in an interview in May 2011: 'This weekend, in the stadium, at the parties in the evening, on Sunday during the victory parade, many times I've thought to myself: I'll never experience anything this beautiful again! That was it, the pinnacle! And then you turned the corner, and you were overwhelmed again. People have understood for the first time how big this club really is. Borussia Dortmund, that's an unbelievably powerful energy.

'Almost all of us had tears in our eyes at one point or other, some of them were really bawling with happiness. That's an experience you want to repeat. What you realise on a day like this is that in Dortmund, football is a lot more than a pleasant distraction, it's the main attraction. For the men and women of this city, and this is something I truly came to understand on Sunday, if I hadn't understood it before, they're just as much there for BVB in the bad times as they are in times like these. And this solidarity ensures that the bad times never last long.'

As the twenty-third manager to win the *Bundesliga* since the league's foundation in the early 1960s, Klopp didn't feel so much personal pride at what he'd achieved, but rather a deep joy that they had made a dream come true for the people of the region. Since the club had last won the title in 2002, the hope of many fans was simply for the club to survive. Now not only was the future secured, but they were champions as well. Winning the title was a thank you for the immense goodwill that the club had always had banked with its loyal fans – even when the banks threatened to close the club's gates for good.

Klopp – and, by extension, his team as well – was rewarded for these achievements in July 2011, when he was voted Manager of the Year by German sports journalists, succeeding former Bayern Munich manager Louis van Gaal. The result was never in doubt. Claiming 743 of the 972 votes cast, Klopp polled an remarkable 76 per cent of the poll, way ahead of Mirko Slomka (Hannover 96) and Lucien Favre (Borussia Mönchengladbach), who claimed the next two places with 52 and 38 votes respectively. When Dortmund defended their title the following season, Klopp also kept a tight grip on the Manager of the Year award: 496 votes were cast in his favour, putting him firmly ahead of Favre (138) and SC Freiburg manager Christian Streich (101) in second and third place.

For all the accolades, it didn't take long before Klopp was looking back on his first championship with sober pragmatism and thinking ahead to the next battle: 'By the time I went on holiday, it was already history. It's hard to explain. I'm making it sound like it was a formality, but it's not that at all. It's a wonderful feeling, but you don't get carried away.' Even immediately after the title was secured, Klopp stressed that his initial reaction was relief rather than a wave of euphoria (a wave which broke all the more powerfully during the club's title celebrations).

It was an attitude that Matthias Sammer, who led Dortmund to the title in 2002, could well understand. He approached Klopp at the 2011 International Coaching Conference in Bochum and told his successor: 'Jürgen, when you became champions of Germany, you said: "This isn't how I expected it to feel." But I'll tell you something: it's part of you now. In that moment, you felt pure relief – and that's what the true greats feel.'

7

JÜRGEN KLOPP'S PLAYING PHILOSOPHY

When asked which of his coaches had influenced him most during his playing career, Klopp was quick to answer: 'Wolfgang Frank! Frank made us see the game in a whole new light. It was no ordinary day when he became part of our football life. It was no longer about how good you were as an individual, but how good we could become as a team. It was the most influential period in my playing career.'

Before his death from a brain tumour in 2013, Wolfgang Frank had words of praise for his 'model pupil' too. Looking back in 2011, he responded to the suggestion that he had taught his squad at Mainz that having the best plan rather than the best players was the key to success: 'That's exactly what Jürgen has done, flawlessly. Many players in the *Bundesliga* are on a similar level, so in the end it's self-confidence, belief and motivation that decide who wins.'

Known for his reserved manner, Frank compared his and Klopp's way of dealing with things: 'For years, my biggest problem was dealing with defeats. When my team lost I could almost have died and I felt like I was the only one responsible. Fear of failure held me back for a long time. Jürgen can move on much faster. Maybe his emotional reactions on the touchline help him come to terms with disappointments more easily.'

For all the revolutionary introduction of the flat back four, what particularly seems to have impressed Klopp about Frank, as a manager, was his team-building ability: 'He was fantastically good at it.' As a member of the 'Frank School', one of the first areas to be tackled in training for Klopp was working as a defensive unit. Or as Klopp himself put it in his own inimical style: 'What do we do when the other lot have got the ball? We never used to care about that here in Germany.' Training had traditionally focused on practising offensive phases such as getting crosses into the box or getting in behind the defence. For Frank and Klopp, though, a stable defensive unit was of critical importance.

There was a significant advantage in concentrating on defence first and building a team up from the back. Compared with attacking, defending is much less dependent on the technical ability of the players. 'When we show our team spirit out on the pitch, if everyone does their job, then we can really cause the opposition problems,' explained Klopp. 'And that's the whole point of what we're doing: we're not trying to show off how fantastically progressive we are tactically, we're making our opponents weaker.'

Of course, if your team is studded with stars, your chances of winning will be that much greater. But stars aren't everything: 'The big difference though is that the best team doesn't always win. You don't need to be a gifted footballer to set up defensively against an opponent.' Quality counts, but form and tactics count more. As Klopp put it, a well-organised defence can cause any opponent 'maximum problems', making it one of the 'critical steps in building a team' and a priority when developing your team's play. Setting up a team to react to opposition possession made sense for Klopp because 'It's something that you can absolutely train for and has very little to do with the talent at your players' disposal – it's got much more to do with character and being prepared to learn and work hard.'

Even as a novice, Klopp made tactical preparation central to training – a reality far removed from his image as a pure motivator and man-manager. As soon as he took charge of relegation-threatened Mainz in 2001, Klopp started work on the defence. 'I had them training without the ball and nothing else at first. As regards confidence, they were pleased with themselves if they managed to find their way to the stadium without getting lost. If I'd started discussing passing accuracy and things like that with them, I'd have got an earful.'

When starting as Mainz manager, Klopp had himself been just one of the team only days before and was all too well aware of the low morale in the camp. 'The last game I played in was at Greuther Fürth; we lost 3–1. I was pulled in the second half, not because I was tired, but because I was terrible, plain and simple – and so was team morale.' The side lacked all conviction. They needed to get things together fast if they were to have any chance of staying in the division.

But under Klopp, confidence (and success) was quickly restored – very quickly: 'We were 70 per cent better at playing without the ball within a week,' said Klopp, clearly pleased with the achievement. Results soon confirmed his assessment: Mainz won six of his first seven matches in charge. Staying up was no longer wishful thinking.

That Mainz were grinding out ugly wins was neither here nor there. It certainly didn't bother Klopp: 'I can remember our first three goals, they were set up, and this is frowned upon these days, with long balls upfield. Christoph Babatz headed them on for one of the midfielders to take a shot from distance. I was very happy that we didn't try to play our way up the pitch, that wouldn't have worked, it would have been asking too much. We knew what to do without the ball, but with it, we needed a little help from above.'

Points on the board were the only thing that mattered. For Klopp, pragmatism counted, not aesthetics: 'You need to do the right thing at the right time, that's what it's all about – and that's what that was.'

* * *

The tactics employed by Klopp at the start of his time at Mainz were a short-term measure: putting almost everything into defence with only the odd moment of attacking football to look forward to is not a recipe for ongoing success. Where Klopp is really in his element as a coach is when he has a chance to build a team step-by-step – from a stable base up through progressively more advanced levels of development, until finally the players match his understanding of attacking football.

It was the process that Klopp took Borussia Dortmund through in the three years of his reign leading up to winning the *Bundesliga* title in 2011: 'If a club's appointed me their new manager that means something's not working there, otherwise they wouldn't need to make a change. You can improve things by working defensively as a group. That will make any team stronger by an order of magnitude instantly.'

At Dortmund, as with Mainz, Klopp began by administering his 'first aid' kit for clubs in crisis. A glance at the stats shows just how badly the Dortmund defence was in need of stabilisation when he took over in 2008. Under Klopp's predecessor Thomas Doll the club had conceded sixty-two times in the league in the 2007–08 season. In Klopp's first season in charge, they conceded just thirty-seven: the following season, forty-two goals were conceded and in the first championship-winning season it was a mere twenty-two. That was a reduction in goals conceded, then, of almost two-thirds in three years. Only one team had been more miserly in defence in *Bundesliga* history: in the 2007–08 season, Bayern Munich conceded just twenty-one times, one goal fewer than Dortmund in 2010–11.

In order to patch up the leaks in the Dortmund defence, Klopp implemented a 4–4–2 formation, with a flat back four and eschewing a midfield diamond for two central holding players, with a left and right midfielder supporting on the flanks.

Klopp and his assistants had good reason to choose this set up: 'We introduced a 4–4–2 because we're convinced that this is the most effective system to play without the ball. It's the easiest system to implement because the running lines are the simplest.' Almost always when Klopp is explaining important tactical decisions, he refers to 'we'. He sees himself as a team player, as part of a coaching trio consisting of him, Željko Buvač and Peter Krawietz, who we will learn more about later.

Klopp's method for beefing up the defence involved order and discipline – but nothing agricultural. Referring to two of the old guard of BVB defenders in the 2011–12 *Bundesliga* Special Edition of *Kicker*, Klopp said: 'Jürgen Kohler and Christian Wörns were fantastic defenders. The systematic weaknesses of their teams often left them in one-on-one situations. They had to jump in because they were the last line of defence. Our philosophy is this: if you make a tackle, you know you can make it cleanly because there is always someone covering. There should be absolutely no need for last-ditch tackles anymore.'

Klopp's justification for the 4–4–2 with flat banks of four is that it is much easier to hold the right position than with a midfield diamond. Additionally, the two banks of four are 'lines' that function in the same way, and that makes getting the system right in training easier. Using a midfield diamond, in contrast, means that losing possession demands a different reaction from the midfielders, due to their positioning.

As his Dortmund side continued to develop, Klopp began to move away from the flat bank of four in midfield: 'Eventually we moved closer to having a midfield diamond, because this corresponded to the strengths of our players.' The attitude of the coaching team also began to change: 'In the beginning we weren't focused on what was good for the players, but exclusively on the best way to teach them our system.' This is an interesting insight, especially given that the conventional wisdom is to adapt your system to the players and not the other way round. Klopp, however, sees playing without the ball as being so critical to the team's success that this must be the first step to drill into the team. Only when this has been internalised can the system progress and be adapted to accommodate the individual strengths of the players.

The next stage in the development of a Klopp team is in honing the attack, which begins directly from defence. After winning possession, Dortmund defenders would look to play an attacking ball, ideally releasing a quick ball fowards to start a counter attack. Lateral right to left passing, nudging it on to a midfielder, was no longer de rigeur. One keystone of this new system was Mats Hummels, who signed in February 2009 after previously playing on loan from Bayern Munich. He was the embodiment of a modern central defender: a robust and disciplined tackler, good in the air, with excellent positioning and, critically, consummate ability on the ball. Hummels was capable of playing pinpoint balls upfield that enabled lightning attacking transitions. Neven Subotić had similar capabilities and together the pair made for a formidable defensive partnership.

In the 2010–11 season, retaining possession came to be an increasingly important focus of the training sessions – along with playing long balls, or as the German media described it, *vertikalspiel* ('playing vertically'). Klopp said, 'We've started putting a much, much greater focus on vertical passes now – if not as dogmatically as some people imply.' Looking back, Klopp was convinced that the gradual development of tactics and organic growth were key to Dortmund's eventual success. It was a case of choosing the right moment 'to start on a new stage of development, which steps can we take with the team and when'.

As simple as it sounded in theory, the title – along with exciting football – took time to arrive. Even the best manager is dependent on the possibilities his players offer him. This applies above all to attack, where good technical ability makes quick, direct and accurate passing possible. By 2010–11, Dortmund had a rich pool of talent up front. With Nuri Şahin, Shinji Kagawa, Mario Götze, Mats Hummels and Lucas Barrios, they had some of the most willing as well as most gifted players in the league, whether the players had come through the youth ranks as Götze and Şahin had, or been brought it in like Kagawa and Barrios.

'I've got a team with fantastic technical ability. With players like these you have a chance to keep possession and stay in control at the extreme tempo the *Bundesliga* is played at,' Klopp said, praising one of his team's key strengths. The reverse of this situation is one of his pet hates – when a team is asked to play a system they don't have the ability to cope with. 'There's nothing worse that giving a team instructions and on the weekend they all go flying out the window. You stand there and realise it was all a complete waste of time.'

Klopp saw Dortmund's famous 3–1 win against Bayern Munich in February 2011 – a 'big three points' on the way to the title

– as an example of his plans being put into practice. His team didn't have huge amounts of possession, but when they did have the ball they were extremely focused and proactive in moving it forwards into threatening positions: 'What's important is having dangerous possession. Let's imagine that I said before the Bayern game, "When we've got the ball we'll really make them run."' Yet, queried Klopp, what if it's Bayern that dominates possession? His instructions would have been completely hollow: 'Then the players will be saying to themselves: "What was the gaffer on about?" So it's crucial to ask myself *what* I coach in the run up to a game and *when*. It's not what you do in training, but how you coach.'

This assessment of the Dortmund–Bayern Munich clash was something Klopp had alluded to before: 'If we hadn't double- and triple-marked Robben and Ribéry in our win in Munich, I don't know what would have happened. Bayern couldn't live with us that day, but we by no means dominated them. We won with goals on the break instead. If you really keep things like this in mind you realise: we shouldn't lose our cool because we ran ourselves ragged.'

The success of Klopp's tactics raised the question of why other *Bundesliga* teams weren't copying Dortmund's system – especially those who had money to burn on the right players for it. Mats Hummels had a ready answer during the first half of that title-winning season: 'Obviously we're tactically very disciplined, trying to get the ball forward quickly from a structured base. But that's just what most teams are trying to do. What we've got at the moment is genuine passion. We're properly up for it.'

So did the 2010–11 and 2011–12 vintage Dortmund sides simply have more willpower than the competition? It wouldn't be the least of the Klopp's achievements to have instilled this ambition, this unshakeable will to win in the first place. Certainly, as long as the team kept up the playing style from the championship-winning seasons, the Dortmund first eleven was an almost ideal embodiment of the Klopp ethos: 'The squad as it is now really suits me, we've got a real good spirit here. It wouldn't be easy for me if I had to work with a team where I had to tell them [slows his voice]: "Okay, pay attention, we're switching from left to right and then from right to left. And if a gap happens to open up anywhere, please play the ball into it."'

JÜRGEN KLOPP'S FOOTBALL PHILOSOPHY

- To differentiate between possession and opposition possession: first set up to be secure when not in possession, only then go on the offensive.
- To have passion and fighting spirit: get stuck into every game.
- Run hard and far to always have a free man ready to receive the ball in attack.
- To focus on group rather than individual tactics: the team needs to defend with discipline and as a unit, with a high press in order to put early pressure on the opposition.
- To dominate play and possession instead of relying on counter-attacks.
- To ensure fast transitions in both directions: balance between defence and attack.
- To play with 'vertical penetration': no sterile, square passing but attacking, proactive play towards the opposition goal.
- To employ quick and direct 'one touch' combinations without holding onto the ball any longer than necessary, unsettling opposition defences and provoking errors.

- To control the movement of groups of players towards the ball in order to occupy the relevant zone of play and prevent the opposition from playing their game.
- To quickly win the ball through pressing and *gegenpressing* (pressing directly after losing possession in order to regain it).
- To replace injured or suspended players directly, rather than changing the system or playing players out of position.

Derived from these principles, Klopp's tactics make the following demands of his players:

- To think fast and act fast – slower players tend to play backwards because they are afraid of one-on-one situations.
- To have incredible stamina, both physical and mental – full concentration and action is needed for the entire ninety minutes.
- To be technically proficient – and be able to receive and accurately pass the ball at pace.
- To have tactical discipline while maintaining attacking intent predicated on flexibility. Players are not obliged to stay in their positions at all costs, as long as they have cover to fill the gap (this is only possible with mutual trust).
- For full-backs and wing-backs to have equally significant attacking as well as defensive roles. Since they have to cover the full length of the pitch and put in repeated intensive sprints, they have to be incredibly fit. Unlike central defenders, they have little chance of taking a break from play.

8

DOING THE DOUBLE

The start of the 2011–12 season seemed to confirm what the sceptics had been saying all along: Borussia Dortmund's title had been a fluke and thoughts of defending it were mere pipe dreams. Certainly, the club officials, always cautious, had refused to set the title as their target for the season. Understatement had served them well in the past and they saw no need to change that now. The official aim was to qualify for the Champions League.

During the 2011 summer break, Klopp was already anticipating the difficulties that might lie ahead: 'We're going to have a lot of problems this season, that's normal. The next time we lose a game we're going to see what the reaction is.' Crucial for Klopp was to avoid constant comparisons to the extraordinary title season and above all to take the pressure off his players: 'We mustn't compare. We can't play Hamburg this season and think to ourselves: "Last year we wiped the floor with them." We have to continue taking each game as it comes and focus completely on the task at hand. If we do that, then we have a relatively good chance of having another decent season.'

Dortmund were to encounter difficulties sooner than Klopp would have hoped. Expectations continued to soar after a brilliant 3–1 win at home over Hamburg, but were immediately dampened a week later with a – by now almost traditional – 1–0 away defeat at the hands of Hoffenheim. Following further defeats, at home against promoted Hertha Berlin and away to Hannover 96 (both 2–1), BVB were left in a lowly eleventh position after six games and three defeats. They had already lost more games than they had in the entire *Hinrunde* the previous season. With a mere seven points from six games, they had endured the worst start of any champions defending their title in almost three decades.

At the press conference after the Hertha Berlin game, Klopp was calmness personified: 'Sometimes you have to take the rough with the smooth. OK. It's going to feel that much better the next time we win.' The defeat in Hannover, however, was rather more painful. After leading 1–0, BVB let the ball into their own net twice in the last five minutes to gift the game to their opponents. Having felt that victory was safe, BVB had given up the initiative and let Hannover back in. 'We let the match slip out of our grasp. It was an active process that led to passivity,' Klopp rather paradoxically put it afterwards. What really frustrated Klopp was that of the six goals Dortmund had conceded in these opening games, four had been from set-plays: 'That's unacceptable. So the players don't get the impression that the defeat in Hannover was down to bad luck,' he was going to 'make things very clear' to them. There had been a lack of desire.

It was obvious by now that the mantle of champions was weighing heavily on Dortmund's young shoulders. Every game they played was now like a cup final for their opponents – having won the league the year before, they were a scalp to be taken. Klopp was to speak later of a 'rucksack' that his team had been carrying and had needed to accustom themselves to: Dortmund were being 'seen differently' by their opponents now. They were no longer the underdogs, even if the club still preferred to present itself that way, but the defending champions.

Chairman Hans-Joachim Watzke said again and again that they were 'no normal defending champions', not least as an attempt to relieve some of the pressure on the players, but no one else seemed to be buying his line. On top of this, Dortmund seemed to be suffering from the way that great success can dull the edge of concentration and determination, at least temporarily. Combine that with opponents who were giving 110 per cent every week, and you start having problems. At the start of the 2011–12 season, Borussia Dortmund didn't seem to have the answer.

In Neven Subotić's opinion, one of the changes since becoming champions was that from the start of the 2011–12 season their competitors had adopted increasingly defensive tactics when playing Dortmund: 'Nearly everyone we played against started playing much deeper. It's hard to think of a team that was prepared to trade blows with us. Nearly all the play was constricted in midfield, everything was a battle. Even so, we had a lot of chances, but we didn't take enough of them.' The Serbian international added that Klopp had been unmoved: 'I've known him for five years, he's the same as always.'

In order to create chances against teams who were set out to stifle their natural gameplan, Klopp demanded that the team play laterally, moving the ball patiently from one side of the pitch to another until an opportunity presented itself. Keeping patient was to be one of the main challenges for the Black and Yellows that season.

* * *

Borussia Dortmund had another difficulty to overcome at the start of their title defence. Just as in the previous season, they were running themselves into the ground to create a multitude of chances, but when it came to pulling the trigger, they lacked a killer instinct. As ever, the players were working as hard for each other as Klopp could wish for, moving up and down the pitch as a unit. But in contrast to 2010–11, when they had also wasted a litany of chances but usually managed to win nevertheless, the team was no longer being rewarded for all its hard work with victories.

The absence of striker Lucas Barrios was keenly felt. He had been Dortmund's top scorer by far the previous season with sixteen league goals. But the Paraguay international had suffered a muscle tear during the *Copa América* that summer, which kept him out for several weeks. With Barrios gone, the Dortmund attack lacked bite. Though Klopp wasn't a fan of these kinds of comparisons, a glance at the statistics was enlightening: during their first six league matches, BVB managed to put away only 20.6 per cent of the thirty-four chances they created, making them the most profligate team in the *Bundesliga*. After the frist eight games of the 2010–11 season they had been twenty goals to the good; in the new season they managed only thirteen in the same number of games. It wasn't just for his goals that Barrios's absence was being keenly felt: he was also missed for his ability to hold up the ball and bring the attacking midfielders into play.

The club had decided not to reinforce this position during the summer transfer window. That they believed they didn't need another finisher was beginning to look like an error of judgement. Of course, if Barrios had stayed fit, any new transfer would merely have been forced to warm the bench, which would have brought problems of its own. And as it turned out, the decision not to buy another striker was eventually proved to have been the right one.

The eighth game of the season was to see one of the existing squad members emerging as the answer to the club's goalscoring problems. Robert Lewandowski had previously been standing in

Barrios's shadow: now it seemed his time had come, hitting a hat-trick in a 4–0 demolition of promoted Augsburg. Increasingly, he was growing into the all-round modern attacker that Klopp had previously made of Barrios.

Lewandowski had been in the starting eleven from the season's beginning thanks to Barrios's injury, but without ever being particularly convincing. His goals against Augsburg started a fire that kept burning brightly – his impressive consistency meant that he made the centre-forward position his own. With twenty-two goals and ten assists, the Poland international played the season of his life (so far). It was a bitter pill to swallow for Barrios, who had previously been an equally reliable goal machine: even when he returned to fitness, there was no way back for him. He eventually decided to leave the club in spring 2012 for Guangzhou Evergrande in China.

Yet even if Lewandowski hadn't 'exploded', it wasn't Klopp's style to pin the team's bad patch on individual or absent players. Instead, he felt the team was suffering from a more fundamental problem – they needed to get back to basics: 'We're allowed to hoof the ball into row Z too if we have to. If we're looking wobbly in defence, then we need to break up the game by putting the ball out of play. If an attack looks like breaking down, then we need to take a shot at goal. These are all things we're struggling to do at the moment.' Nevertheless, in those first few weeks of the season it was clear that Dortmund were going to have to make some kind of adjustment to their game to compensate for the loss of their midfield generals.

With former linchpin Nuri Şahin now plying his trade at the Bernabéu for Read Madrid, Klopp needed to find a way to restructure the team's approach. Şahin had been a midfield mastermind who rarely misplaced a pass. He had regularly dropped back into defence to collect the ball; from that position he had the game ahead of him and could weigh up the situation without the threat of being closed down. Although Dortmund now had İlkay Gündoğan, who had been bought from Nürnberg, as well as Sebastian Kehl and Antônio da Silva, who could play next to 'water carrier' Sven Bender, the team still sorely missed the metronome who had set the tempo for their midfield.

The result of the lack of ideas in midfield led to an increase in the number of safety-first balls being played backward rather than forward. Dortmund's build-up play seemed to be beginning much deeper than before, often directly from defence. A look at the statistics confirmed this impression: media reports had the central defensive partnership of Hummels and Subotić on around sixty touches each per game in the 2010–11 season; in the first seven games of the following season they averaged around ninety each. As well as his tactical importance for the team, Şahin had also contributed six goals and nine assists to Dortmund's title win and had been a quality option on dead balls. It came as no surprise, then, that Dortmund struggled to adjust to life without the Turkey international. (Şahin, meanwhile, had difficulties of his own adjusting to life in Madrid. Injury kept him from playing in the first weeks of the season, and he barely figured in José Mourinho's first eleven when he did return from injury. With Sami Khedira and Xabi Alonso blocking his way into the Real midfield, he was finally loaned out to Liverpool for the 2012–13 season.)

One of the strengths of the 2010–11 Dortmund side was that it was a team with incredible focus. The players had impressed with their ability to maintain concentration for the full ninety minutes. Faster than the wobbly start to the season might have suggested, the team managed to regain this focus, whose edge had been temporarily dulled during the summer break. Self-confidence returned, and their role as defending champions was embraced. Just as Lewandowski had found his form, sidelining Barrios, so Kehl and Gündoğan found their feet and were increasingly adequate replacements for Şahin.

That early loss in Hannover was to be the last league defeat of the season. With the exception of five draws, Dortmund were to go on to win every one of their remaining games. The fuse for this turnaround was lit in the seventh game of the league campaign: a lucky last-minute Łukasz Piszczek goal gave Dortmund a 2–1 victory and all three points from the match against Klopp's former side, Mainz 05.

The game had played out almost identically to the previous week's clash with Hannover – except the positions were reversed. Ivan Perišić managed to cancel out Mainz's opener with an hour gone, but it seemed as if it wasn't to be BVB's day as they failed to take any of the numerous chances that would have given them the win: Mainz keeper Heinz Müller seemed unbeatable, pulling off a series of fine saves. The game was wide open by the final minutes, with play flowing from one end of the pitch to the other and with both sides having good chances to steal the win. This time, though, it was Dortmund who were destined to come away with the spoils. In the ninetieth minute, the ball fell to Piszczek twenty-five yards out after Müller had punched clear from a free-kick. His volley bobbled through a host of players before finally scuffing into the net. It was one of those goals. But it still counted. 'The fact that the ball went through about fifteen players before rolling directly in the corner of the goal was ruddy lucky, there's no denying that,' admitted Klopp at the post-match press conference, although he emphasised that 'over ninety minutes, we were still worthy winners'.

The momentum behind Dortmund was picking up speed again. The next home game – the 4–0 demolition of Augsburg – was, as mentioned above, Lewandowski's day. The quality of the 2011–12 BVB vintage was confirmed thirteen games in when Dortmund found themselves up against Bayern Munich. Bayern had been leading the table comfortably with a five-point gap between them and Borussia Dortmund, whose return to form had propelled them up into second. It was an opportunity for Munich to put clear water between them and their closest rivals, but was one that they missed. In an unspectacular game defined by a tactical battle, a Mario Götze goal gave Dortmund a 1–0 win and three points in the Allianz Arena. The title race had been blown wide open.

The battle between Bayern and Borussia continued in the months that followed, with surprise contenders Borussia Mönchengladbach also managing to keep in touch with the title rivals. The defining fixture of the season arrived thirty games in as Klopp's side played host to their main rivals. Would Bayern be able to take revenge in Signal Iduna Park? The teams were well-matched, but once again BVB took the upper hand and ultimately the three points, putting them six points clear at the top of the table. The 1–0 scoreline was secured by a combination of Robert Lewandowski, who with his back to goal flicked in a Kevin Grosskreutz shot, and Roman Weidenfeller, who saved an Arjen Robben penalty in the final minutes. Dortmund rode their luck in the dying minutes, when a botched injury-time Subotić clearance hit the bar, before the ball was skied by Robben when it would have been easier to score. But Bayern failed to score and the spoils went to Dortmund.

Interviewed by Sky afterwards, Klopp was clearly still riding the emotion generated by the tumultuous final phase of the match: 'That was real edge-of-the-seat stuff right to the end. It was just unbelievable in those final minutes. Hats off to my team, you can't play much better than that.' Klopp couldn't make his feelings clearer: 'I don't want to exaggerate or sound melodramatic, but what we're doing here wasn't the work of one evening. We put our heart and soul into this, end of. We've all got a bit of a crush on this club. You can't always keep that locked inside.' As soon as the final whistle blew, Klopp had faced the Yellow Wall and beat his chest – the BVB badge – and made a heart with his hands. It was melodrama through and through, but it was genuine. That gesture, those words – they weren't put on, they came straight from the heart.

Just four days later, Klopp's team completed the perfect BVB week when they beat the eternal enemy Schalke 2–1 in Herne-West. The Dortmund fans were euphoric: BVB had done the double over both Bayern Munich and Schalke 04 and for *die Schwarzgelben*, it doesn't get any better than that. Yet even with just three games of the season to go and an eight-point lead, Klopp was clear that there were to be no premature celebrations. He preferred to speak of the 'hard work' that had got the win for a 'fortunate' Dortmund. These were memories of so narrowly missing out on promotion at Mainz talking: never celebrate before victory is certain.

Victory over Mönchengladbach meant that the title was sealed with two games still to go. Given that BVB managed to see out the rest of the season with a 100 per cent record (in contrast to the previous year which had seen them lose in Bremen after they had confirmed the title), they had become record breakers. In thirty-four games they had collected eighty-one points – the highest points total ever. Their run of twenty-eight games undefeated wasn't a record – yet. This stood at thirty-six games, set by Hamburg over the course of two seasons thirty years earlier. The challenge to better that lay ahead. Sporting director Michael Zorc was perfectly justified in speaking of a 'historic season'.

Not everyone was as fulsome in their praise for Dortmund's success. Their rivals for the title, Bayern Munich, were fuming. For the first time since 1996 (when Borussia Dortmund claimed back-to-back titles) they had gone two seasons without winning the league. Their response, delivered by chairman Uli Hoeness, was to point at Borussia Dortmund's lack of success in Europe, which, so they claimed, had given them the advantage of fresh legs in the *Bundesliga* while Bayern fought all the way to the Champions League final (the notorious *finale dahoam* – Bavarian for 'final at home' – in which they were beaten in their own stadium by a resilient Chelsea).

Hoeness was only prepared to accept Borussia Dortmund as equals to Bayern if they managed – without resorting to a spending spree – to compete on multiple fronts at once, as he emphasised during a discussion on Sky90 in April 2012: 'Dortmund have had a fantastic season, but for me you can only say they're the real deal when they have a fantastic season in the *Bundesliga and* are competitive in Europe. Two years ago they were knocked out of the Europa League without a whimper, and this year, in a very weak group, they didn't just come third, they came fourth. Only if they can bring the two together, when they show that they can compete in Europe, am I prepared to say they've really earned my respect.'

It was unlikely to be a coincidence that Uli Hoeness chose the moment when Bayern were being confronted by a competitor that was proving to be a sporting equal to make public what for eight years had been a closely guarded secret. In February 2012, the Bayern chairman revealed to a supporters' gathering up in Hamburg that, 'Back when the Dortmunders were at the end of their tether and couldn't even pay the players' wages, we gave them €2 million.'

Borussia chairman Watzke confirmed that the Bavarians had come to their rescue at a time when Dortmund were facing financial catastrophe. 'It's true. That was 2004. We paid back the last of three instalments by the middle of 2005.' Watzke, who was appointed chairman in 2005 – that is to say after the deal with Bayern had been made – found it hard to understand what his predecessors in charge of the club, Gerd Niebaum and Michael Meier, had been thinking. 'I would never have done anything of that nature. Taking money from a competitor is an impossibility. Clearly, it seems there was no other option.'

Not letting up, Hoeness went on to describe Borussia Dortmund as being in a 'protected oasis', which was contributing to Dortmund's success, something else he revealed during the TV interview: 'Gündoğan goes from Nürnberg to Dortmund, for nine months he barely plays. In Munich, people would have been writing it off as a failed transfer; in Dortmund, he's given the time he needs to develop. In Munich, he would have been long since written off. They're still living in this oasis.'

Certainly it could be said that Dortmund and Bayern had different approaches to their transfers. Bayern had a 'forever number one' self-image that put pressure on them and the players they bought. Dortmund didn't subscribe to this approach and indeed, the İlkay Gündoğan example demonstrated perfectly one of Klopp's decisive managerial gifts. He recognised when players needed protection, to be nurtured and allowed to develop step-by-step. When it appeared as if the pressure of following in Şahin's footsteps was cramping Gündoğan's game, Klopp took him out of the press firing line by 'resting' him every few games during the first half of the season. The talented midfielder benefited from the enforced break, blossoming into one of the team's key players during the second half of the season. Gündoğan's well-earned reward was to be called up to the Germany squad for Euro 2012 in Poland and Ukraine, although he didn't play.

* * *

While a number of Hoeness's criticisms seemed wide of the mark, there was at least one thing the Bayern chairman had got right – there really was a sizeable gap between Dortmund's league success and their European form. There was little hiding from the fact that Europe had been a continual disappointment for the club. As much as Klopp's tactics had resulted in *Bundesliga* success, their style of football had brought them rather less success on the European stage. Indeed, one could accuse them of having been naive at times: uncharacteristic individual errors in defence had led to senseless goals being conceded.

One 'golden' example was in the Champions League group game at the end of September 2011 away against Olympique Marseille. Dortmund had dominated play and had carved out some decent opportunities, yet the the French were the first on the scoresheet, aided by a slip from Neven Subotić. Dortmund pressed hard for the equaliser after the break, but when a second goal came, it was once again Olympique who scored. At fault this time was an unnecessary header back into midfield by Mats Hummels which turned into an inadvertent assist for the opposition. The dubious penalty that made the final score 3–0 was almost irrelevant by that point. Three-nil: it was a humbling scoreline that stood completely at odds with the run of play throughout the match. Dortmund had created opportunity after opportunity but when it came to taking their chances they had hesitated, overthought and the moment was gone.

It was no surprise, then, that the players were frustrated given the avoidable mistakes that had led to defeat. They had been the better team, only to deprive themselves of the fruits of their labour. Klopp himself seemed to undertake a complete rethink after that demoralising defeat. The fact that his team could lose a game in this manner annoyed and ate away at him. Yet the commonplace explanation that mistakes are punished more harshly at the European level was as valid on this occasion as ever. It was a maxim eloquently elucidated by the experienced French, who were more accustomed to the Champions League and seemingly more incentivised: several of their players were seizing their chance to make an impression on the big-money stage in front of millions of TV viewers.

No less frustrated than Klopp or the team was sporting director Michael Zorc, who was in Marseille for the match. He made the following analysis for TV during half-time: 'We've got more possession, cover more ground, but we're behind. The players look nervous and we've given the ball away cheaply. We have to change the way we're playing.' But *how* would they change the way they were playing? It was question that *die Schwarzgelben* could find no answer to during the remainder of the group phase, where they signed off by losing to Marseille again, this time 3–2 at home. The final group table didn't make for good reading: played six, lost four; final position fourth out of four. Dortmund hadn't even done enough to secure third place, which would have brought qualification to the Europa League. Their European adventure for the season was over, and it wasn't even Christmas.

One indication of the reason for the lack of competitiveness was revealed by a Dortmund official who in summer 2012 anonymously speculated that on their Champions League debut, the team had shown their opponents a little too much respect. It seemed that on entering Arsenal's Emirates Stadium, one or two of the Dortmund pros had let an overawed 'Wow!' escape from their lips – when of all teams it was Borussia Dortmund who were famed for their intimidating home atmosphere at Signal Iduna Park. Was the team simply still too 'green' in that first season of Champions League football? Were slips in concentration really punished more harshly at that level than in the *Bundesliga*? It's hard to explain how Klopp's players could perform heroics in cauldrons like the Allianz Arena or *auf Schalke*, yet when it came to London, Piraeus and Marseille, their hearts seemed to fail them slightly.

* * *

Although Dortmund were out of Europe, they eventually found cup success that season in another knockout competition. Up to this point, BVB had not exactly been a 'cup team' under Klopp. Their record in the DFB Cup included a last-sixteen exit at the hands of eventual winners Werder Bremen in the 2008–09 season, and in the following two seasons they were knocked out by lower league opposition: first VfL Osnabrück (again in the last sixteen) and then Kickers Offenbach (this time in the second round).

Dortmund had enjoyed success in the DFB Cup in the past. From their famous 4–1 victory over Werder Bremen in the 1989 final, they knew that the Olympiastadion in Berlin where the final is hosted is well worth the visit. Twenty-three years later, Dortmund would once again pick up the thread of this defining moment in their history, which had kick-started an epoch of success. The 2012 final was to be no less spectacular and the end result would be a Klopp triumph unique in the 103-year history of the club: the league and cup double.

The road to Berlin started at third division SV Sandhausen: a Kagawa brace and one from Lewandowski gave them a 3–0 away win. In the second round they met fellow 'black and yellows', Dynamo Dresden. Lewandowski scored again, as did Mario Götze to give them a deserved 2–0 win over the second division team. But a more difficult challege followed in the last sixteen, when BVB were drawn away to another *2.Bundesliga* team: Fortuna Düsseldorf, who were to gain promotion to the *Bundesliga* via a relegation play-off win over Hertha Berlin at the end of the season.

With key players already missing in defence, Dortmund found themselves a man short after half an hour when Patrick Owomoyela was sent off: the full-back had found himself switched to an unaccustomed central defensive berth and picked up a second yellow card and his marching orders. Yet Fortuna found no way to take advantage of their extra man, or their home advantage. After 120 goalless minutes, it all came down to penalties. Just moments beforehand, Klopp was sent to the stands as a reward for his protests – just as Düsseldorf coach Uwe Klein had been shortly before extra-time. All of Dortmund's penalty takers held their nerve – and keeper Roman Weidenfeller made himself a cup hero by saving the decisive penalty from Düsseldorf's Thomas Bröker.

After all that drama, BVB had a much easier time of it in the next round, the quarter-final against *Regionalliga* side Holstein Kiel. Kagawa and Lewandowski put them two up within eighteen minutes to make anything but a Dortmund win an implausible result. Lucas Barrios and Ivan Perišić then each bagged a goal for a clear 4–0 final score. The final hurdle before the final proved to be another tricky opponent from the second division: SpVgg Greuther Fürth, who would also succeed in achieving promotion to the *Bundesliga* in 2012. Gündoğan's 'lucky punch' making it

1–0 in the last minute of extra-time prevented another penalty shootout.

His late goal was particularly galling for Greuther Fürth manager Mike Büskens. In expectation of the 'inevitable' penalty shootout, he had brought on sub keeper Jasmin 'Penalty Killer' Fejzić in the 118th minute – but the penalty killer's luck was out when Gündoğan's shot came back off the post and bounced off his back into the net. This substitution and winning goal prompted Klopp to fire off a hand gesture towards the opposition dugout that could have been interpreted as mocking. He later admitted: 'I could have been a bit smarter.' Yet when the ball's in play, emotions can take the upper hand even in otherwise completely reasonable people like Klopp. Handbags after the final whistle between Kevin 'Mr Dortmund' Grosskreutz and Fürther's Büskens and Gerald Asamoah, who had both spent many years at Schalke 04, were an unnecessary epilogue to a tense match and stoked a battle of words that continued after the game.

Once the fallout from the match had subsided, anticipation for the final started to build. It was to be a repeat of the 2008 final against Bayern Munich. Four years before, the then seemingly unstoppable Bavarians had been taken to extra-time before they finally ran out 2–1 winners, just a matter of weeks before the Klopp era at BVB began. In the run up to the 2012 'clash of the titans', first versus second in the *Bundesliga*, the media hype was enormous. The betting was on a close match similar to the duals they had fought out in the league, which had both ended in BVB's favour by a goal to nil. In fact, the match turned out to be anything but.

In the first thirty minutes of the final Bayern held their own, even slightly outperforming BVB. Robben had been able to cancel out Kagawa's third minute opener from the penalty spot – despite his misses in the league, the Dutchman was back on spot-kick duties and this time he had made no mistake. Yet BVB too were to be awarded a penalty, just minutes before the break: Hummels hit it a bit too close to Neuer, who got a hand on it, but couldn't prevent it going in the corner to put Dortmund back in front: 2–1.

Now the Lewandowski show was about to begin. He added the third in first-half injury time, sending Bayern into the dressing room with their heads bowed: 3–1. When he scored again in the fifty-eighth minute, they were completely demoralised: 4–1. Like fellow Bayern dangerman Arjen Robben, Franck Ribéry had another poor game against BVB, but he did manage to pull one back from the edge of the box after making space with some skilfull footwork: 4–2. But Lewandowski restored Dortmund's three-goal cushion five minutes later – his cup final hat-trick the icing on the cake: 5–2, a remarkable final and a remarkable result, giving Dortmund their third DFB Cup victory, to go with their previous successes in 1965 and 1989.

It wasn't just the Dortmund fans who enjoyed the clash. Manchester United manager Sir Alex Ferguson had been watching from the stands – and a few weeks later, one of the heroes of the final, Shinji Kagawa, was on a plane to Old Trafford. Ferguson was also said to have been extremely interested in Lewandowski, but this time he wasn't able to put a deal together – Dortmund had declared him not for sale at any price. This was the downside to success. BVB's competitors were watching wide-eyed, waiting to pick apart the squad. It was only going to get more difficult keeping this dream team together.

A typically animated Klopp was impressed by the way his team held their nerve, as he revealed when speaking to Sky shortly after the final whistle blew: 'That was a cup final they way you expect it as a *Dortmunder*. There were plenty of tricky moments, but that ice-cold finishing – brilliant! Some of our goals were works of art. Bayern had a lot of phases where they made us work. But we came here to work. We did what we needed to do in the decisive moments. It's impossible to put into words how we all feel right now.'

Even if Bayern had appeared to be on a par with Dortmund for long stretches of the first half, they didn't take advantage when they had the chance, in complete contrast to the Westphalians, who ruthlessly took advantage whenever they created an opportunity. In any case, the scoreline made any discussion about who had more of the play or who looked the better team redundant.

Together with four consecutive *Bundesliga* wins against their southern rivals, the DFB Cup final made it five wins in a row for BVB against the once supremely dominant *Rekordmeister*. It was a run that was ended by the Supercup defeat in August 2012 – 2–1 in the Allianz Arena – but in any case, Klopp had given talk of a permanent changing of the guard in German football short shrift. He would always stress when anyone made that implication that: 'This isn't about world domination.' Even so, the cup-final victory over Bayern and the first double in the club's history was a moment for both Klopp and Dortmund to cherish.

9

INSPIRATION NOT IMITATION: KLOPP'S TRAINING METHODS

Though the greatest inspiration for Jürgen Klopp's managerial career has been Wolfgang Frank, he was not the only manager he had learned from. In his eleven years at Mainz as a player, he played under another nine coaches: Robert Jung, Josip Kuze, Hermann Hummels (the father of Mats Hummels), Horst Franz, Reinhard Saftig, Didi Constantini, Dirk Karkuth, René Vandereycken and Eckhard Krautzun.

Even as a player, Klopp had finely tuned antennae and a natural 'filter' that allowed him to 'pick out the right things. You could learn something from every manager. For me it was less about the training drills we did than what the manager was like as a personality. What's his philosophy and how does he get it across? Those were the things I always paid attention to.' Not that Klopp has any records of those training sessions, having made a conscious decision not to keep notes: 'I've always thought, I can remember the important stuff and forget the rest.'

Once a manager, Klopp has taken a similar approach to the latest advances in football management. Klopp is sometimes considered the embodiment of the modern manager, thanks to his understanding of the game and ability to see beyond the traditional, but he is no blind follower of the latest trends. As with observing his different managers at Mainz, he has the knack of taking on board what is useful and discarding the unhelpful.

In recent years, professional football has been subject to an ever greater influence from sports science. Managers have been turning to new methods that are often reliant on information technology. The field of statistical analysis in particular, whether the data is taken from training or from a match, has seen exponential growth thanks to technological developments. Today's managers have numbers at their fingertips their predecessors never had: How many kilometres has a player run? How many tackles completed? Who has had how many touches of the ball? There are any number of specialists in charge of different areas that a modern manager can call upon: conditioning trainers, goalkeeping coaches, video analysts, scouts and so forth.

Yet for all these possibilities, Klopp has always been circumspect in his use of new technology, particularly the role of statistics. Take his opinion on the work of sports scientist Dr Roland Loy, an authority on the use of statistics in football. He has written a number of books on the subject, as well as developing databases for the football show *ran* on German channel Sat1 and advising the sports department of the broadcaster ZDF. For his research, Loy has analysed more than 3,000 football matches in the last twenty years, in the process disproving many common assumptions. For example, he discovered that the hardest tackling team doesn't always win (only in 40 per cent of matches); and rather than the received wisdom that attacking down the wings is more likely to lead to a goal than going through the middle, his analysis showed that both routes are equally likely to lead to a goal. Klopp, however, has limited interest in Loy's work: 'I know Roland, we worked together in [TV presenter] Johannes Kerner's team at the World Cup in South Africa. I place 0.0 per cent faith in his statistics and he knows it too. I've said it to his face so I feel perfectly comfortable saying it in public.'

Klopp isn't dismissive of statistics per se, adding that, 'I'm a huge fan though of stats that look at the last game or maybe evaluate the entire season.' But certainly he puts a lot of faith in his observations, rather than numbers on a spreadsheet: 'I'm a big proponent of the idea that you have to see for yourself. Most of the time I'll know if our build-up play is too slow before anyone hands me any data. After all, I've got nothing else to do but train a team and deal with football day in day out. I don't need any hard numbers for that. I've been trained to spot these things myself.'

One area where Klopp puts more faith in scientific methods is on the question of stamina. Advances in sports science have made it possible to tailor training regimes to the fitness level of individual players. A player who's 'raring to go' can be handled differently from one recovering from injury, who's just returning to full training after a long period of convalescence. Klopp's maxim is that no player should have too much – or too little – asked of them in training. To make sure this happens, Klopp uses lactate tests: lactate is produced as a metabolic breakdown product during exercise, as soon as the muscles can no longer produce enough energy from aerobic oxygen; lactate concentrations therefore offer a guide to the stamina levels of the player. Lactic acid levels can be determined by taking a blood sample from an earlobe. The relative simplicity of the tests makes them an ideal aid during pre-season as the players undergo fitness training.

Felix Magath, who won the *Bundesliga* with Wolfsburg in 2009, has the same attitude to lactate tests as Klopp does to statistics: 'I don't need to do a lactate test to know whether a player is fit or not.' Klopp might agree with that sentiment, but thanks to the tests he knows 'where we need to place a player to do the right intensity of training. Because it would be foolish to go through a training session that was only perfectly tailored to three of them, when for the rest it's either too intense or not intense enough.'

Such personalised training regimes were also made easier by the increasing resources available to coaches. Klopp offers one small example: 'You used to have one heartrate monitor for twenty players, now you have forty heartrate monitors for ten players. That opens up new possibilities and it's also easier working that way.' Together with the new scientific methods, then, there's also a much deeper well of information to draw from than earlier generations of coaches enjoyed. This greater depth of knowledge is ultimately of great benefit to the players, who are able to push the limits of their fitness.

Klopp is clear on the difference between training practices now and those he experienced as a player: 'I think that many of my generation of players were definitely trained a bit too hard. It was unbelievable how much we did in training. It was crazy how long we spent on the pitch, how much running we had to do and how hard we had to run. One of the main indicators as to whether the training session had been hard enough was when at least one of the players threw up on the pitch. In contrast, the current training model has a much more nuanced understanding of effort and rest, of tension and relaxation.'

That Klopp is particularly focused on stamina training can come as no surprise. After all, stamina is crucial to the pressing style that is fundamental to his system. The importance of running was confirmed in Klopp's mind right at the start of his time at Dortmund: in July 2008 at the T-Home Supercup match against Bayern Munich, which Dortmund won 2–1. Klopp observed later that, 'As a team we ran a total of 121 kilometres. That didn't say all that much to me at the time, because I hadn't used these values as part of my work before.' Yet during the course of the 2008–09 season, when Dortmund failed to win a single match from the first seven games that followed the winter break, Klopp brought the statistic back into his calculations: 'I discovered that we hadn't got further than 113 kilometres in these games.'

Klopp had some time to work with the squad at a training camp: 'I made a deal with the players there: if you can manage to run more than 118 kilometres in nine out of ten games, you'll get three extra days' holiday. And the players actually went out and did it.' Freshly motivated, the players finally broke their bad run against Werder Bremen. Alexander Frei's spot-kick gave the Borussians their first win of the *Rückrunde*, the second half of the season. This was just the beginning: those seven winless games were followed by seven victories in a row as Dortmund chalked up twenty-one points.

At the start of his tenure, Klopp was concerned with doing 'more' than the opposition, with literally running them ragged. As time went on, the 'how' became more important: 'We've started being much cleverer with our runs now. We have more of the ball and we don't need to run so far when the opposition has it.' The chances of winning a game aren't derived from the number of kilometres the players have put behind them alone. Dortmund went on to have some great performances without particularly impressive running stats, and they also had poor performances with enormous distances run. Nevertheless, it's a piece of information that Klopp is still fond of turning to, especially when the team is going through a bad patch.

It's a statistic some other managers have commented on to humorous effect. During the International Coaching Congress in Bochum in 2011, Hannover 96 manager Mirko Slomka offered a different reason for Dortmund's high mileage – suggesting that the Dortmund numbers were being massaged by the addition of the mileage generated during their collective goal celebrations. After all, they had sixty-seven occasions to celebrate in the 2010–11 season compared to a 'mere' forty-nine for fourth-placed Hannover. Klopp responded to the suggestion in kind: 'That's right, against Hannover alone we scored four goals on two occasions, that's an extra 400 kilometres …'

Managerial banter aside, the emphasis on running at Klopp's Borussia Dortmund is made clear by a look at the numbers. In the first game of the 2011–12 season, at home against Hamburg, the *Bundesliga* database IMPIRE[5] revealed the following interesting points: with 58 per cent possession, the Borussians ran a total 124.67 km – over 10 km more than their opponents (113.70 km). Running 12.9 km, Sven Bender proved himself once again a tireless worker bee. Klopp's team were also superior to the opposition when it came to sprints, with 193 compared to 150. The number of misplaced passes also reflected the one-sidedness of the encounter. While nearly a quarter of Hamburg's passes (23.6 per cent) failed to find their target, the home team's passes failed to find a teammate only 13.6 per cent of the time.

The revealing nature of this mountain of data – which was accessible not just to the clubs but also the media and hence the public – provoked some criticism at the start of that season. There were fears that players were being reduced to living spreadsheets who would be judged entirely on their 'km run' – leaving less mobile players to be 'singled out', although how much a player runs is very much dependent on their position and role in the team. As such information has become more commonplace, it feels as if a more nuanced and realistic appraisal of such statistics has become the norm.

* * *

Jürgen Klopp is open-minded in the best sense of the word: always ready to listen to new ideas that might give him and his team that extra advantage. One of the most effective pieces of training equipment that Borussia Dortmund possess is the 'Footbonaut' at their Brackel training complex. During Klopp's appearance on ZDF *Sportstudio* in September 2012, a computer animation demonstrated how the piece of kit works. Similar to a tennis-ball machine, balls are fired at the player inside the Footbonaut cube. He then has to shoot it as quickly as possible into one of seventy-two target squares that light up. There are two football guns in each wall, meaning the ball could come from one of eight possible places. Speed and swerve can be adjusted. As a result, it's possible to closely simulate a real playing situation, training reactions, precision, control and placement. At the time of the TV appearance the device was still being trialled, but went on to be a permanent and flagship addition to the training facilities.

Another part of Klopp's training regime at Dortmund came about by chance. Klopp was watching TV when he came across Life Kinetik, the mental training system developed by sports instructor Horst Lutz. And he was clearly enthusiastic about the system: 'Life Kinetik is incredibly exciting, it's a real eye-opener. For managers, it's something you really need to look into.'

Life Kinetik is a training system designed to improve brain function by challenging the body to complete complex tasks. According to its website, 'Life Kinetik is a fun exercise program based on motion to enhance mental capabilities. Life Kinetik training forces all brain areas to actively take part and master the given movement challenges and therefore it creates new connections in our brain. The training works by simultaneously combining exercises of different movement patterns, visual tasks and cognitive elements. Life Kinetik accomplishes this with the help of ever changing exercises that scale the difficulty level to the ability of each person.'

Employing training methods like Life Kinetik helps Klopp to increase his players' (mental) flexibility. A practical exercise might look like this: a ball is thrown towards a player while at the same time he's told a certain colour. Each colour stands for a particular action: trap the ball with your left or right foot, head the ball back, or control it on your chest. More demanding exercises such as juggling the ball or catching it with crossed arms are also part of the programme. The tasks are hard to come to grips with, and that's intentional – this forced coordination is a learning process designed to generate new synapses.

The added value for footballers lies in sharpened perception and faster reaction times – qualities that are essential in modern high-tempo football. The first improvements should be noticeable after two to eight weeks of training for an hour a week. Life Kinetik has another bonus for professional footballers as well. As Klopp says, 'How can I work with the lads without asking too much of them physically? I'd like to conduct training sessions eight hours a day, but that's not possible … so we think about things we can do with them off the pitch.' It's a low-intensity programme that allows for additional training without overloading the players.

Klopp is convinced that you have to keep improving all the time, as his use of such innovative methods shows. 'It's all about keeping informed. That's my job as a manager. You get bombarded with huge amounts of information, and most of it you can happily discard right away. But if there's 20 per cent among that that's really worth working with, then it's completely worth the effort.'

* * *

Good ball control: Jürgen Klopp in a blue Mainz 05 jersey from the 1999–2000 season.

A happy reunion: Klopp greets his mentor Wolfgang Frank on his return to Mainz in April 1998. Behind them is sporting director Christian Heidel.

Not afraid of a challenge: Klopp
duels with Uerdingen's Hasan Vural
during the 1997–98 season.

Dance partners Jürgen Klopp
and midfielder Antônio da Silva
celebrating promotion in 2004.

Jürgen Klopp fires up Mainz fans in May 2004.

Visibly moved, Klopp says goodbye to Mainz in May 2008.

Title celebrations with two games to go: Borussian bumps for the gaffer in April 2011.

The party bus on the road again: Dortmund celebrates its double-winning heroes in May 2012.

Sporting director Michael Zorc, manager Jürgen Klopp and chairman 'Aki' Watzke show off the *Bundesliga Meisterschale* and DFB Cup trophy in May 2012.

With a smile on his face despite defeat: Klopp with wife Ulla at a post-match dinner.

The final game of the 2014–15 *Bundesliga* season. The Yellow Wall pays tribute to their iconic manager with a signature banners 'Thanks Jürgen'.

Arriving at Anfield, Liverpool,
9 October 2015.

Unveiled at Anfield as the
new manager of Liverpool FC
standing alongside chairman
Tom Werner and chief executive
Ian Ayre in October 2015.

With the Liverpool lads at a training session at Melwood in November 2015.

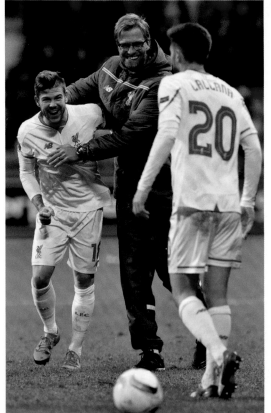

Celebrating with Alberto Moreno at the end of the 2015 UEFA Europa League match between FC Rubin Kazan and Liverpool FC.

Man of the people, Klopp, greets supporters before the
UEFA Champions League first-leg quarter-final between
Liverpool and Manchester City, 2018.

Celebrating as Liverpool qualify for the 2018 Champions League final.

Comforting Mohamed Salah as he leaves the game through injury in tears during the Champions League final.

A dejected Klopp walks past the Champions League trophy as he collects his runners up medal.

Thanks to his multi-faceted approach to training, Klopp managed to achieve at Dortmund what Jürgen Klinsmann had stated as his ambition when he took charge of Bayern Munich in 2008: 'To make each player a little better every day.' The evidence can be found in analysis of a selection of players from his 2011–12 squad.

Take Kevin Grosskreutz, who returned to Dortmund in 2009 from the second division team Rot-Weiss Ahlen. He was initially viewed primarily as a squad player – warming the bench and stepping in if needed. Yet as it turned out, Grosskreutz, who as a kid had been no stranger to the South Stand, worked the left flank assiduousy, fighting his way into the first eleven through tenacity and desire. His well-earned reward was to be an ever-present in the league during the 2010–11 championship season. Klopp's management had improved the native Dortmunder both tactically and technically, and in May 2010 he celebrated his first cap in Germany's 3–0 win over Malta.

Another success story was Sven Bender. It's true that Bender wasn't exactly a blank slate when he arrived from second division 1860 Munich as a twenty-year-old in 2009. As an Under-17 player, his outstanding talent had won him the DFB's bronze Fritz Walter Medal for the *Bundesliga*'s rising stars of 2006. But how many players have shown tremendous promise only to stagnate in their development because their manager lacked the courage to put them in the team and give them pitch time? No one could ever accuse Klopp of not having courage. When a long-term injury to captain Sebastian Kehl offered Bender an opportunity in midfield alongside Nuri Şahin, he took it, cementing his place in the side. Like Grosskreutz, tough-tackling defensive midfielder Sven also went on to be capped for Germany.

Mats Hummels and Neven Subotić were two other players who became full internationals under Klopp's guidance. Subotić was part of the Serbia team that beat Germany 1–0 in South Africa in 2010. Klopp had shown complete faith in the two nineteen-year-olds when he arrived at Dortmund and made them his central-defensive partnership. Although lacking in experience, the pair made up for it by being strong in the tackle, having excellent technique, a great tactical understanding, and the ability to open up the game with the ball at their feet.

Dortmund's Brazilian defender Felipe Santana would probably have been a certainty for the first eleven at almost any other *Bundesliga* club – but there was no way past Hummels and Subotić for him.

Another player whose progress really excited Klopp was full-back Marcel Schmelzer, whom he brought into the senior squad from the Dortmund youth team: 'He has developed more than any other player I have ever known.' Repeating the pattern of other Dortmund players, Schmelzer also managed to break into the German national team.

That Klopp put great emphasis on promoting and developing youth players made him particularly valuable for the 'new' Dortmund. 'This manager is the best fit in Germany to help us make our concept of bringing through young players a reality,' chairman Hans-Joachim Watzke said of Klopp in 2011. Two years earlier, the Dortmund Academy had been opened, which was coupled with the extension to the training complex. This unified set up, according to the club homepage, had a target of 'optimising the footballing and personal development of BVB's players and coaches'.

The Academy offered a varied and forward-thinking programme: personal development was considered just as important as sporting progress; media training was part of the programme, as was sports psychology, nutrition and tactical analysis. The academy had support from psychologists at Ruhr University Bochum, who taught alongside Dortmund coaches. The courses were run in addition to the normal training schedule.

Within this school-like system, age groups were divided into Under-9, through Under-15, Under-17, Under-19, as well as Under-23 and the development squad. The aim is to have as many youth players as possible graduate to the full professional squad, or at least give them the best possible preparation for a life in football elsewhere. It was a talent production line reminiscent of Barcelona's famous La Masia youth academy.

It's not just here that Klopp and Dortmund had followed Barcelona's *Més que un club* ('More than a club') approach. Barcelona's playing style, too, was one of Klopp's key reference points. This was not so much because of their heady attacking fireworks, but because of their lightning transitions when they lost the ball. 'It's extraordinary how high up the pitch this team is when they win the ball back,' Klopp once noted. 'And the reason they can do that is because every player presses. I think Lionel Messi is the one who wins the ball back the most when he loses possession. If he loses possession, he's right back there the moment the opposition player takes a touch, to win the ball back. The players press like there's no tomorrow, as if the most enjoyable thing about football is when the other team has the ball. And what that does for them is for me the biggest achievement of all. The best example that I've ever seen in football.'

Under the guidance of Josep 'Pep' Guardiola, Barcelona won a total of twelve trophies between 2009 and 2011, including the Champions League twice – each time beating Manchester United in the final. In the 2011 final the Catalans were so dominant that the then United manager Sir Alex Ferguson conceded, 'They do mesmerise you with the way they pass it ... I would say they're the best team we've faced ... No one has given us a hiding like that.'

Perhaps the most fascinating aspect of Barcelona's success during this period is that they never seemed to lose their desire despite victory being almost run of the mill for them. The Barcelona players defined an era of almost unparalleled achievement in which each new trophy demanded yet another be won. 'They celebrate every goal as if they had never scored before. You get the feeling they'll never be satisfied,' said Klopp in admiration. It's at this moment that it became clear that the *Bundesliga* titles weren't going to change Klopp either: he was still hungry for more.

Klopp appreciated the fact that while Barcelona might have followed a set game plan, they were never robotically following orders: the reasoning of the tactics was always explained to them, as they emphasised themselves when interviewed. They weren't just following their manager's instructions, they were internalising them – one of Guardiola's greatest achievements. Klopp also noted the Catalans' selflessness, despite the fact that almost to a man they were fantastic individual talents: 'A Xavi or Iniesta has no joy in having the ball for the sake of it: that doesn't interest them at all, they keep the ball moving. Xavi once said in an interview regarding that: "I recycle the ball just before the opponent reaches me – for me, that's the most beautiful moment in football." That's what he does. And right now, that's the standard everyone in world football looks up to.'

The result was that Barcelona were able to dominate European football like no team had done since AC Milan twenty years earlier under tactical genius Arrigo Sacchi, and featuring the world-class Dutch trio of Ruud Gullit, Frank Rijkaard and Marco van Basten in the team. Klopp had no pretensions about reaching Barcelona's level: 'We aren't all going to get there, because even if we had exactly the same plan, we wouldn't have the same players.' But even if it wasn't possible to match Barcelona, they could still be beaten in one-off games, couldn't they? Klopp's recipe for beating Barcelona was as follows: a team that would back itself to 'defend high up the pitch' and be prepared to lose the 'small challenges'; his logic was to challenge for the ball intelligently, preventing Barça from settling into their *tiki-taka* game and running circles around their opponents. Even then he added the following proviso: 'Keeping that up for ninety minutes, that would be a feat of concentration that the world probably hasn't seen since Albert Einstein.'

For all Klopp's admiration for Barcelona, he remains far less enthusiastic about teams who don't try to play. Take Dortmund's match at Barcelona's *La Liga* rivals Sevilla in December 2010. It was the last game of the Europa League group stage, and with the scored tied at 2–2, Klopp's side needed to score one more to go through. Yet the hosts held on by using every trick in the book to waste time until the ninety minutes were up. Six months later, Klopp was still unable to conceal his anger: 'Last season we were in a Europa League group with Sevilla and Paris Saint-Germain. We gained a lot of useful experience. For example, how Sevilla parked the bus for sixty minutes at home and ran the clock down to such an extent that my players were lost for words at their cowardice afterwards.' As much as Klopp appreciates the skill of a Barcelona, he is equally less impressed by 'dirty' victories – for him, the end emphatically does not justify the means.

That Sevilla match taught Klopp a valuable lesson. In response to the opposition tactics, Dortmund stopped playing their own game. Instead of their usual fluid combinations, they started desperately humping the ball forwards – the young Dortmund eleven had allowed themselves to be rattled by Sevilla's negative tactics.

Keeping patient and playing their normal game would have been the better course of action.

It wasn't the first time that Klopp had been taught this lesson of maintaining your tactics: 'As a very new manager I was fortunate enough to come up against Peter Neururer, who was manager at Rot-Weiss Ahlen at the time [Klopp's Mainz played Ahlen in May 2001]. We played 4–3–3 instead of our usual 4–4–2, and he brought on a third central defender and started man-marking us. And then we thought, young and wild as we were: "Right, let's change the system," so we only had two strikers left on the pitch so we could escape the man-marking. That's all a load of rubbish. Always, always stick to doing your own thing.'

Klopp learned an important lesson from this experience: 'What's critical is finding stability, that comes way before flexibility. Stability gets you points and wins you games.' Flexibility gives you more options, it's a kind of 'bonus'. Klopp also put an emphasis on stability because football is a team sport: 'The willingness of the players to work together as a team is crucial. After all, that's why we started playing football and not an individual sport like tennis. We wanted to be part of a group, and that's something we need to accept as a golden rule until the end of our lives: I'm only as strong as my teammates let me be. Then it works beautifully. Thanks to stability.'

Klopp extends this belief in the importance of his team to his refusal to mollycoddle his players. When the subject of Italy forward Mario Balotelli, who while at Manchester City threw a dart at a youth-team player, came up, Klopp didn't mince his words: if one of his players pulled a stunt like that 'they would never wear this club's shirt again. He won't get a second chance to make a mistake like that: "Look, you might be able to play, but I don't want to see your face again." Not when we've got so many lads who are a joy to work with.'

10

THE BUSINESS OF FOOTBALL

At the very start of his time at Dortmund, Jürgen Klopp announced that his target was to help the club get back on the right track. By 2012, there was no doubt: his mission was accomplished – both on the pitch and off it. Klopp had proved himself the perfect man for the job not just in footballing matters, but also on the business side as well. It was Klopp who would phone wavering BVB sponsors personally and persuade them to continue their relationship with the club. He was every bit as capable of charming the suits as he had been the players and fans. For chairman Hans-Joachim 'Aki' Watzke, Klopp was worth his weight in gold with his support for the club's financial consolidation, which for all the success on the pitch remained the focus of the entire club hierarchy.

The hard work that went in to balancing the books was bearing fruit. In August 2012 the club announced that revenue had increased to €215.2 million for the past financial year and they had generated €34.3 million in pre-tax profits. This was not just a huge step forward on the 2010–11 financial year, when they had raised €151.5 million in revenue and made €9.5 million in pre-tax profits, but was also the best financial return in the club's history. It wasn't just prize money being added to the balance sheet: the transfer fees received for Shinji Kagawa (€16 million) and Lucas Barrios (an estimated €8.5 million) also made a healthy contribution. It meant the club was also able to take an impressive chunk out of its debt burden. In 2005, this had stood at around €180 million, with BVB buying back their stadium bit by bit. The new management's debt restructuring programme and tightening of the purse strings meant that by 2012 they could reduce their liabilities to €40.6 million.

The new financial strength made possible the purchase of native *Dortmunder* Marco Reus for a reported €17.5 million from Borussia Mönchengladbach in January 2012. While the club had made a tidy sum from the sales of Kagawa and Barrios, the capture of the German international was an indication that they were now in a position to spend money as well. With their debt under control, money could now flow back into the team. For the 2011–12 financial year, they were able to afford a wage bill of €74.5 million, with just short of €60 million of that going on player wages. At 35 per cent of revenue, this was still a 'very healthy ratio', in Watzke's estimation: in top-level football, wage bills of 50 per cent of turnover or more are common (Arsenal's wages, by comparison, were 55 per cent of turnover for the 2013–14 financial year).

'We aren't running a savings account,' Watzke said. 'Nevertheless, we will continue to follow our ultra-conservative, old-fashioned policy of not spending more than we earn.' Watzke's policy was also designed to prevent Dortmund getting soft in their hunt for young, hungry players. If you have the money, it's all too easy to buy ready-made stars instead of putting in the hard graft it takes to uncover a new Lewandowski or Kagawa – players who also have development and resale potential. Watzke remained on guard: easy money could prove a burden.

'I could never really enjoy the title we won in 2002,' he said in 2011, referring to Borussia Dortmund's then already perilous financial situation. Watzke had been the club treasurer at the time – except the 'treasure' he was supposed to guard was in the process of disappearing. Today, after the credit crunch and the crisis in the Eurozone, it's doubtful whether in similar circumstances a rescue package would be put together for BVB as it was then. The club's creditors were notably lenient. In a sense, the club was lucky to undergo a financial crisis when the economy as a whole was strong and the will and resources were available for it to be rescued. For Watzke, who describes himself as a 'football romantic', the league titles in 2011 and 2012 were nevertheless all the sweeter for this time they rested on solid financial foundations.

Football is a business that never stops. That meant it was critical to stick to the successful trail Dortmund had blazed and make it sustainable. After all, Stuttgart in 2007 and Wolfsburg in 2009 had surprised everyone by winning the title, but then they had dropped away. Sustainability didn't necessarily mean winning the league every year: given BVB's improved sporting and economic potential, a realistic target was regular participation in European competition – and that demanded improvement in their Champions League performances.

Despite everything that had been achieved, there was no question that there were more challenges to come, including fixing nagging weaknesses on the pitch. A better rate of converting chances still needed to be worked on. Klopp admitted: 'From time to time we struggle with maintaining our accuracy at the high intensity we play.' That applied as much to the team's passing game as it did to their shooting accuracy, where it seemed that too many chances were snatched at. This might have felt like quibbling for a double-winning team, but Klopp knew that if you stand still, you go backwards. They had to keep improving.

The press debated whether the squad would be able to keep up this 'all-out, all the time' intensity with the same success they had grown accustomed to, or whether they would be able to adjust their game. Could they learn to play within themselves on occasion, to be more economical – in the more tactical Champions League, for example? The squad was now big enough to make changes without losing too much quality, making 'all-out attack' possible in every game.

The disappointing failure of BVB's Champions League run in 2011–12 paradoxically gave Klopp an opportunity to motivate his players for better performances to come. Klopp and BVB's first year together in the Champions League was put down to experience, but in the second it was time to put that experience to good use. It was clear from Klopp's unrelenting drive, passion and elan in the first fixtures of the 2012–13 season that success hadn't stilled his hunger. He had won trophies, but he was greedy for more, and once again he succeeded in instilling that desire in his team. This time, it would be Europe who would discover what Klopp's brand of football was all about.

* * *

He was sat there next to Jürgen Klopp, the man who embodied creativity in the *Bundesliga*. At the training camp at Grand Hotel Quellenhof in south-west Switzerland, Marco Reus was being presented as a BVB player for the first time. He was Dortmund's biggest buy since €22 million Márcio Amoroso in 2001; the club had payed around £ 17.5 million to Borussia Mönchengladbach for the gifted attacking midfielder. At Mönchengladbach, Reus had impressed under manager Lucien Favre as a 'false nine'. At Dortmund, his role was to be central attacking midfield, usually with his friend and fellow Germany international Mario Götze stationed to his right. This was a further injection of quality for the already offensively formidable 2011–12 double winners. It meant a concentration of creative talent in midfield, ready to supply the bullets for Robert Lewandowski, who was in an incredible run of form, to fire home.

For all the interest of other teams, Klopp's side had largely been kept intact over the summer of 2012. Kagawa and Barrios may have left, to Manchester United and China's Guangzhou Evergrande FC respectively, but reinforcements had also been brought in: Julian Schieber and Leonardo Bittencourt in attack, and Oliver Kirch at full-back. 'Neither the individual players nor the team have reached the end of their development,' said Michael Zorc at the start of the season.

The sporting director's assessment was to be confirmed in impressive style in the Champions League group phase. They had finished a deflating fourth in their group the previous season, and now they found themselves in a 'hammer killer group of death', as the *Süddeutscher Zeitung* subtly put it. They had to face Manchester City, Ajax and Real Madrid – a tall order – but this time they topped the group. At home, they beat Ajax 1–0 and Real, convincingly, 2–1. By the end of November they had already secured progress to the last sixteen with a pulsating 4–1 win in the Amsterdam Arena. Just eight minutes were gone before Reus put them in the lead, with Götze and Lewandowski each adding to the tally before the break. Lewandowski got his brace in the second half to put them four clear. It was a humiliation for Ajax. European football had to sit up and take note now: they had seen the Borussian attack in action that evening, an offensive unit that worked together in perfect harmony.

If their group-phase performances had been characterised by naivety against savvy European opponents the previous season, the *Dortmunders* seemed more in control this year. 'We can meet the challenge in the Champions League with much more confidence now,' Klopp was never tired of repeating. Along with the benefits of experience, it was obvious to anyone watching that Dortmund were playing with much greater flexibility. İlkay Gündoğan was the wily strategist who ran the midfield, while Reus added unexpected variety to their attacking phases. In addition, his goalscoring prowess was starting to approach Lewandowski's level. The *Dortmunders* had developed into a feared dark horse in the Champions League. It was a role they had grown accustomed to playing during the past two *Bundesliga* seasons.

As impressive as Dortmund's European nights were during the first half of the season, Klopp's team found itself stumped on more than one occasion in the *Bundesliga*. The champions' undefeated run was brought to an end after thirty-one games by, of all teams, Hamburg, who hadn't won a game for five months. Klopp justified the unlucky 3–2 away defeat with the not unreasonable remark that Hamburg had defended their advantage with their fantastic keeper 'René Adler, luck, and skill'. Once again, as had been characteristic of their two championship seasons, BVB struggled to convert the host of chances they created. What was unusual was that the Hamburg attack – admittedly with Rafael van der Vaart back pulling the strings – managed to score three times against the Dortmund back four.

These defensive frailties were to make themselves felt throughout the season, with Dortmund conceding forty-rwo times in the league. Compare this with the previous season: then, they had conceded just twenty-five in the *Bundesliga*.

Alongside the early unnecessary defeat in Hamburg, the Dortmund were particularly frustrated by their 2–1 away loss to Schalke. Finding themselves 2–0 down at half-time, Lewandowski had managed a consolation but no more. Fortunately, their home Champions League tie against Real Madrid was only four days away, and they were able to make good the derby loss by beating *Los Blancos* 2–1.

Instead, it was a revitalised Bayern who set the standard during the first half of the season. Manager Jupp Heynckes had returned from Leverkusen in 2011 and put them back on track. After just fourteen games they celebrated the *Herbstmeisterschaft* – the unofficial title for the team leading the table going into the winter break. It was the earliest anyone had ever done it. The title rivals faced each other fifteen games in, with BVB third and already eleven points behind the leaders. As far ahead as the Bavarians were in the table, the match was finely balanced. However, a 1–1 draw left the points gap as unchanged.

By this point, football journalists such as Peter Hess had long been contrasting the way Bayern and BVB were playing: 'Bayern have learned from BVB's run of victories last season. Thirty-three shots on goal after quick counter attacks and ten goals scored on the break are the best numbers in the league. The foundation of Bayern's success is their defence – just six goals conceded in fifteen games shows just how accomplished they are defensively. Another bonus is their high level of discipline in defensive midfield: so far, they haven't conceded a single goal from a counter-attack. The time has come to discard old assumptions and prejudices, the old story of fresh and cheeky Dortmund and stuffy Bayern. Bayern Munich have much more in common with Borussia Dortmund now than most people would ever have imagined.'

Nor were the *Dortmunders* blind to how well Bayern had integrated Klopp's *Gegenpressing* into their own system. In March 2013, Munich's new style of play led to Klopp firing allegations of plagiarism in their direction. The breaking point had been Dortmund's 1–0 defeat in Munich in the DFB Cup quarter-final, Bayern taking convincing revenge for their defeat in the final the previous summer with an Arjen Robben goal.

In a press conference two days after the cup exit, Klopp went on the offensive: 'Bayern are just like the Chinese in industry, they see what others are doing and copy it so they can follow the same plan with more money and a different set of players.' The controversial accusation of 'industrial espionage' could be taken as a signal towards Dortmund's own fans that they wouldn't roll over and take Bayern's tactics lying down. Klopp's choice of comparison struck a chord: in the Ruhrgebiet, the traditional industrial centre of Germany with Dortmund at its heart, they had undergone the painful experience of having blast furnaces disassembled and being shipped to the Far East, where they were rebuilt and run with lower operating costs.

Neutral observers, however, were less enamoured by the attack on Bayern boss Jupp Heynckes. Klopp looked like a sore loser who wasn't able to deal with Bayern's dominant position. Heynckes refused to let himself be provoked by his younger managerial colleague, answering the criticism with a piece of fatherly advice: 'If Jürgen ever has the good fortune to manage a team like Bayern Munich or Real Madrid, he'll realise what it means, that it's a completely different world. I suspect he might have something else to say about it if he ever has that experience.'

* * *

The copycat debate soon faded into the background as attention turned to Dortmund's continuing progress in Europe. The team reached the quarter-finals of the Champions League comfortably with a 5–2 aggregate win over Shakhtar Donetsk. In the first leg of the tie in Ukraine, Robert Lewandowski and Mats Hummels put them in a favourable position with two away goals in a 2–2 draw. The job was completed with a 3–0 win at Signal Iduna Park, Felipe Santana, Mario Götze and Kuba all getting on the scoresheet.

Dortmund's opponents in the quarter-finals were Spanish surprise packages Málaga, and once again the first leg was played away from home. The match ended goalless, with Dortmund strong in defence and having enjoyed the balance of the play. There were frustrations, however, that they failed to finish off golden opportunities from Lewandowski and Götze. If they were hoping that the home leg would nevertheless see them cruising into the next round as they had done against Donetsk, they would soon find that they were sorely mistaken.

It would be a mistake to call the return leg on 9 April 2013 dramatic – the word fails to express the true intensity of that night. 'This game,' said Michael Zorc after the final whistle, the effects of the adrenaline rush still visible, 'staked a place in BVB history.' For long stretches, BVB had put in what was probably their worst ever performance in the Champions League, as Klopp would confess afterwards. His team were tense, 'showing their nerves for the first time'. Joaquín took advantage of BVB's hesitant showing to put the Spaniards 1–0 up after twenty-five minutes. In response, Klopp switched the Dortmund formation from their usual 4–2–3–1 to a 4–3–3. Dortmund started to get back in the game and five minutes before half time levelled it through Lewandowski, who put the finishing touch on their first decent move of the game.

The starting gun for an unforgettable finale was fired in the eighty-second minute when Eliseu restored Málaga's lead from an offside position that went unnoticed by Scottish referee Craig

Thomson. Thanks to the away-goals rule, Borussia Dortmund now needed to score least twice to reach the semi-final. Klopp brought on Mats Hummels and Nuri Şahin, the latter having returned from Real Madrid in January. The two took up position in front of the defence, which now pressed high up the pitch. Their task was to target Málaga's centre-backs and ply emergency strikers Neven Subotić and Felipe Santana with long balls. Klopp had turned to the 'brute force' strategy and tirelessly urged his players forward from the touchline. 'We had to make our luck,' said Klopp.

In three minutes of injury time the brute-force method proved its worth. First Marco Reus equalised, then a minute later Felipe Santana scored at the second time of asking to give them the 3–2 scoreline they needed – even though, in fairness, he too had been offside. But Dortmund had never given in and this was their reward. It was 'unbelievable how this team can defy the world,' said Zorc, summing up the magical *Schwarzgelbe Nacht* – a crescendo in black and yellow.

Klopp celebrated going through by jumping for joy towards the South Stand together with his assistant Željko Buvač.

Klopp, however, was not to have long to enjoy the memorable victory. The next morning, Michael Zorc visited him at the training centre. 'He looked like someone had died,' Klopp recalled. 'He said, "I have to tell you something. There's a good chance that …"' And that was how he heard the news of Mario Götze's transfer to Bayern. Götze was taking advantage of an escape clause in his contract. According to press reports, he would be moving to Bayern that summer after they triggered his €37 million release clause. 'It was like a heart attack.' Zorc asked Klopp if he wanted to talk. He said: 'No. I've got to get out of here.' That evening, the Klopps were invited to a film premiere in Essen, but Klopp told his wife that he couldn't go, that he needed to be alone. It was the next day before he was halfway back to his old self. 'I know just how difficult it's going to be to find a player who can replace Götze. But next year we will set up differently. It will take time.'[6]

Götze's departure was doubly hard because not only was he a crucial component in how the side played, but he was a local boy the supporters identified with. Although he had been born in Memmingen in Bavarian Swabia, Götze's family had moved to Dortmund when he was five. He had progressed through BVB's youth teams to become a firm fan favourite. As recently as March 2012, he had signed a contract extension to 2016, just over a year before he announced his decision to leave. The fans weren't the only ones in a state of shock: the players were completely blindsided too. Mats Hummels didn't hold back in describing the feelings in the dressing room, telling *Sport Bild* magazine that he found the move incomprehensible: 'You could see the progress the team was making, and Mario got on fantastically well with a lot of the lads. That's why I find it so perplexing that he felt the need to leave so soon.' And Götze wasn't the only player thinking of pastures new: Robert Lewandowski had also repeatedly made it clear that he did not want to remain until the end of his contract in 2014. Bayern Munich's interest in yet another of Dortmund's key players didn't go down well, and threatened to cause unrest in the dressing room.

But there was little time for the club to dwell when they had a Champions League semi-final against Real Madrid coming up. In the aftermath of the shock announcement of Götze's impending departure, Dortmund played out of their skins to thrash Real Madrid 4–1 thanks to four Lewandowski goals. Klopp's side were well worth that scoreline and Madrid could count themselves lucky to have left Signal Iduna Park with a crucial away goal, scored by Cristiano

Ronaldo shortly before the break, giving them a faint glimmer of hope going into the return leg. The then Real manager Mourinho could find no answer to Dortmund's lightning transitions: 'Dortmund were stronger, more focused, and more aggressive,' he had to admit.

Dortmund were in control for much of the return leg in the Bernabéu. With fifteen minutes to go, Lewandowski could even have given them the lead, but unlike the first leg he didn't have his shooting boots on and the chance went begging. The game turned with eight minutes to go. First substitute Karim Benzema put Real ahead. Then Sergio Ramos smacked the ball into the roof of the net from the midst of a huddle of players in the box five minutes later, making the final outcome much less certain. Dortmund needed a fair slice of luck to survive the final minutes without conceding a third, which would have put Real through on away goals. But they did it, and Borussia Dortmund had reached the Champions League final for the first time since 1997. Their opponents in Wembley on 24 May? Given the way the last few months had gone, it couldn't be anyone other than Bayern Munich, setting up the first all-German final in the history of the competition.

* * *

In the run up to the final, Jürgen Klopp did his best to drum up support for Dortmund in a series of interviews with the British press, attempting to get the neutrals on their side. He wasn't afraid to make his appeal emotional, if that's what it took. 'We're a club, not a company,' he told the *Guardian* on 21 May, 'but it depends on which kind of story the neutral fan wants to hear. If he respects the story of Bayern, and how much they have won since the 1970s, he can support them. But if he wants the new story, the special story, it must be Dortmund. I think, in this moment in the football world, you have to be on our side.' In response to the question of whether he would be staying in Dortmund or saw his future elsewhere at some point, perhaps in the Premier League, he replied that for the moment, he had no interest in any other club. Dortmund was 'the most interesting football project in the world'.

Certainly, Borussia Dortmund won a lot of fans among the 86,000 spectators in Wembley and the 200 million watching on TV. If resolute defending had been the order of the day when Chelsea triumphed in Munich the previous season, the 2013 Champions League final was a different vintage, with both teams serving up attacking and often spectacular football this time round. It was Dortmund who got off to the better start, with Klopp's plan to disrupt Bayern from the beginning showing early results. When Munich attacked down the right through Arjen Robben, the Dutchman was double marked by Kevin Grosskreutz and Marcel Schmelzer; Łukasz Piszczek and Jakub Błaszczykowski did the same job on the other flank against Franck Ribéry. İlkay Gündoğan was looking very comfortable in the middle against fellow Germany international Bastian Schweinsteiger. Before Bayern even got a sniff at Dortmund's goal, Dortmund had already forced Manuel Neuer into saves from Reus, Błaszczykowski and Sven Bender.

But as the game wore on, Bayern gradually began to free them-selves from the shackles of Dortmund's pressing, getting some joy from long cross-field balls. It looked like Roman Weidenfeller was going to have some work to do after all, and shortly before the break Robben wriggled free twelve yards out, but fired straight at the keeper. Fifteen minutes in to the second half, Weidenfeller was left with no chance. Ribéry slid the ball through to Robben in the box; he took it to the goal line and put in a cross-cum-shot that Mario Mandžukić nudged home.

Dortmund were down, but they weren't out. Within eight minutes, they were level. Dante fouled Reus in the area, and Gündoğan slotted the penalty home. With both teams pressing for a winner, the chances were coming thick and fast now. When Weidenfeller couldn't hold onto the ball, Subotić scraped it off the line. This was spectacular football, and as full-time neared thirty minutes of extra-time seemed to be on the cards. Until, that was, a long ball from Alaba dropped on the edge of the Dortmund area in the eighty-ninth minute. Ribéry managed to backheel the ball into Robben's path, and he raced through the middle at top speed, leaving three defenders in his wake, to take control of the ball and roll it gently into the corner of the net. The final whistle blew: Bayern had won 2–1.

It was an agonisingly close-run thing, but Klopp put a brave face on it. 'It was a close game that was decided late on. We've left everything we had on the pitch again at the end of a long season. But they earned it. Congratulations Bayern, congratulations Jupp.' Unlike the preceding two seasons, his team had ended the season potless, but they could look back on a magnificent Champions League journey.

Klopp, too, could take pride from the fact that the Champions League run had now established him as an internationally respected manager. The former second division manager was now frequently on the phone with José Mourinho, and kept in touch with Sir Alex Ferguson. *Gegenpressing* was now part of the international football lexicon in the German original thanks to Klopp, and the term was used in one breath with any description of the Dortmund style of play. That was – leaving the plagiarism debate to one side – a sign of recognition and respect for the manager who had been the first to bring the tactic to perfection.

11

KLOPP'S RIGHT-HAND MEN

The days when a manager's assistants were widely seen as glorified ball boys and training-cone monitors are long gone. When Jürgen Klopp was named manager of the year in 2011 by the football magazine *11 Freunde*, he made sure to point out how much of his success was thanks to his assistants. Klopp has often referred to the vital support he receives from Željko Buvač and Peter Krawietz in public: 'The three of us together make one really good *Bundesliga* manager. That's what's important. It's not important for me to be omniscient or my assistant or my second assistant. Ideally, we work together and that spits out the perfect result at the end. Because I can't be so sure of myself as to say: What I say, goes.' Klopp has the last word – as the manager, the buck stops with him – but before he makes a decision he gets input from his assistants.

The extent to which the Klopp, Buvač, Krawietz trio understand themselves as a team is soon clear: 'Željko Buvač and Peter Krawietz know exactly how much they mean to me – I couldn't do it without them. Not one of us would go somewhere else without the others,' Klopp has emphasised. The relationship with Buvač, whom he has known since they played together at Mainz, is particularly close: 'I've made a lot of good decisions in my career as a manager, but the best one was appointing Buvač coach – he's the best coach I've ever known. He's the one I've learned the most from these past few years. We're like an old married couple, and that's sensational.'

When he was appointed manager of Mainz 05 in 2001, Klopp only had his DFB 'A' Licence – technically, he wasn't qualified for the job. (Klopp has only been permitted to call himself *Fussball-Lehrer* – with German equivalent of the UEFA Pro Licence – since 2005, when he finally completed the required DFB courses. Prior to that, Buvač had always been listed as manager on Mainz' team sheets.[7]) So Buvač was brought in to help out – a stroke of luck, as it proved. But even after many years of their relationship, the publicity-shy Željko Buvač is still relatively unknown. He has not given a single interview, so uncomfortable is he at taking centre stage. Indeed, in some ways he's seen as the polar opposite to Klopp – helping them to complement each other perfectly.

Željko Buvač was born in 1961 in what is now the Republic of Srpska in Bosnia and Herzegovina. His first club in Germany as a player was Rot-Weiss Erfurt before he moved to Mainz 05 in 1992. There, he strengthened the midfield with his strategic play for three years, during which he developed a close friendship with Klopp. Although Buvač had to overcome a language barrier at first as he needed to learn German, the pair hit it off straight away without much needing to be said.

In 1995 Buvač moved to the *Regionalliga* team SC Neukirchen in Hessen, where he played until the end of his career in 1998 – before starting his coaching career there, first as assistant and later as head coach. He earned his DFB *Fussball-Lehrer* licence in 2000, which qualified him to coach professional football in Germany. Buvač had kept in touch with Klopp over the years, and when Klopp went overnight from player to manager at Mainz, he brought Buvač back as his assistant coach. The pair had agreed that if one of them were to secure a coaching job in professional football they would bring the other on board. Klopp kept his word, just as Buvač would have done.

'We have an identical understanding of football,' Klopp said in 2011. 'We've got 200, 300 special drills, training exercises, 200 of them are his and 100 are mine.'

Together, Klopp and Buvač guided Mainz through a memorable era until 2008, the highlight being promotion to the *Bundesliga* in 2004. And together, too, the two of them took on the new challenge of Borussia Dortmund in 2008. Buvač has two nicknames – 'Chucky' and 'The Brain' – and a Klopp quote from the BVB homepage makes the reasoning behind the second one clear: 'Željko is football expertise made flesh and a master of all forms of training.' As he was as a player, Buvač is a strategist as a coach too. Whereas once he pulled the strings in midfield, today he moulds the tactics from the dugout. Buvač is quick on the uptake: when something's going wrong during a game he's the first to spot it and starts discussing a remedy with Klopp at once.

Buvač feels completely at home in his role as 'second-in-command'. He was never a fan of the media work that is obligatory for managers. His motto is: 'I only speak when I have something to say.' This is further proof of how the two complement each other perfectly, given Klopp's palpable enjoyment of the media spotlight.

He might not talk to the media but Buvač is not a silent partner in the relationship. 'When he does say something, you know it's going to be right. It'll be bang on and we'll be acting on it,' said Peter Krawietz. Krawietz is the third member of the Klopp triumvirate. His nickname is 'The Eye', derived from his skill in video analysis. It was thanks to him that the Dortmund players could see selected scenes from the first half of a match during the half-time break, making it possible to adjust their game 'live'. Krawietz also acted as the link-man at Dortmund between the professional squad and the amateur and youth teams, ensuring the whole sporting unit developed along the same lines.

Krawietz was born on New Year's Eve in 1971, and also knew Klopp from Mainz. His relationship with Mainz 05 started in the mid-1990s as part of a university sports science project in video analysis. Krawietz's work was so convincing that Mainz 05 'kept' him and put him in charge of the scouting department. Until Dortmund came calling in 2008, that is. And it wasn't just at Bruchweg or Signal Iduna Park that Klopp put his trust in his assistant – Krawietz was also his best man. He is a tall man – like Klopp and Buvač well over six foot – resulting in a coaching trio of equal standing in more ways than one.

* * *

Other members of Klopp's coaching staff have played an important role over the years. A key component of Klopp's Dortmund coaching team was goalkeeping coach Wolfgang 'Teddy' de Beer, a member of the 1989 cup-winning squad. Roman Weidenfeller and the other keepers benefited from his innovative methods, one example of which was 'the ramp'. Teddy built a special ramp he would blast the ball at, deflecting the ball at all sorts of angles and putting the keepers' reactions to a real test. When his reflexes schooled like this, you could understand where some of Weidenfeller's impressive saves have come from.

As a player who was promoted directly to the managerial hot seat, Klopp is used to working with a team of coaches. The extent to which Klopp relied on his staff is made clear by the story of the discovery of defender Marcel Schmelzer. 'Our former youth coach at Mainz, Willi Löhr, was going round the area looking for new talent. At some point he rang us up and said, "Here in Dortmund there's Marcel Schmelzer."' When Klopp and his team made the switch to Dortmund themselves in 2008, Klopp asked, 'Who's the back-up left-back behind Dedê?' 'We don't need one, he's never injured,' was the response. 'But what do we do if we play a game of ten versus ten in training – who's the second left-back then?' Klopp asked.

Florian Kringe – the versatile midfielder – can do it, was the response. Then Klopp asked about Schmelzer to the bemusement of the staff, before explaining, 'Yes, he's with the amateurs, Willi told me ...'

It was a strange twist of fate that Dedê was to suffer a cruciate ligament injury that would keep him out for months during Klopp's league debut as Dortmund manager, a 3–2 win away to Bayer Leverkusen. The injury opened the door for Schmelzer, who went on to appear twelve times in the *Bundesliga* in his first season as a senior professional. Schmelzer's performances were so encouraging that he kept his place even when 'Mr BVB' Dedê returned to fitness. In the 2009–10 season, Schmelzer made twenty-eight appearances, while in the subsequent title-winning season, he was an ever-present in the league.

What Klopp took from this episode was that it's crucial to have a competent team working for you – and to trust them. He's well aware that while he can coach, he can't do everything, so he has to delegate in areas such as scouting, for example: 'I'm not going to travel all over Germany and unearth gems because I'm checking out every single sports field in the country, that's nonsense. If you're sending the lads from the scouting department to games and you can't say to them "Keep an eye out" but feel the need to drive down there four times yourself, you're just throwing money out the window. You really need to say: "This is what we're looking for, and if you find someone, call me."'

That's how it was with Shinji Kagawa, who came to Dortmund in 2010 for a €350,000 development fee from Japanese club Cerezo Osaka. Klopp didn't personally take a flight halfway around the world – he left the matter in the hands of his staff. 'They absolutely love it. They love it when at the weekend one of these lads they spotted is playing in the *Bundesliga* and maybe he's getting some positive reviews.' And it wasn't to be long before Kagawa was getting glowing praise – the attacking midfielder was soon lighting up the *Bundesliga* with his excellent technique, his ability to take on players, his burst of pace and speed of action. And he wasn't shy of taking a shot either, with eight goals to his name in the first half of the season.

Sporting director Michael Zorc was another to benefit from the transfer coups such as Kagawa set up by Klopp's team. Although the club's near financial meltdown had left it in a weakened position when it came to transfers, Dortmund was still considered a big club with the concomitant big expectations – even if the club sought to broadly define sporting success in order to keep expectations realistic. A subject of public criticism for his transfer policy in 2008, Zorc is now celebrated as one of the canniest sporting directors in the *Bundesliga*. But it was Klopp and the scouting team who were able to run with this policy and make it work on the pitch.

* * *

Brackel, September 2011. At the BVB training complex, a typical Klopp practice session is underway. The sun is out and it looks as though Germany might enjoy an Indian summer before the nights draw in. The mood in Brackel is similarly buoyant. The first game of the Champions League campaign during the week went well: a 1–1 draw at home to Arsenal, with a performance reminiscent of the heady days of last season, even if with the same number of missed opportunities as well.

'Come on Kuba, you've got to bury that,' sighs one of the fans watching the session, as Jakub Błaszczykowski blasts the ball over the net from close range. It doesn't take long for him to silence his critics, his next attempt booms into the net; sub keeper Mitchell Langerak has no chance. Klopp grins. 'Believe me, we're going to wipe the floor with Hannover this weekend, 4–0. You mark my words, 4–0!' says one of the onlookers. That's how quickly the mood of supporters can change.

Klopp calls the players over. He and his assistants stand in the middle of the training ground, with the players forming a circle around them. The manager explains the drill he wants them to practise, then steps aside to watch proceedings from behind the goal and leaves Buvač in charge. For someone so reserved in public, Buvač is in his element here, calling out instructions in a powerful voice: 'Come on Kevin, faster! Kuba, over here, hup hup hup!' With his long dark hair, he's easy to spot from a distance. A real character, who gets the job done.

Buvač demonstrates the drills himself, showing he's still got top-drawer technique, even if his playing career ended more than a decade ago. It's immediately apparent he isn't happy when the players can't follow his clearly self-explanatory instructions. This is a perfectionist at work. Klopp, by contrast, doesn't take part in training as a player himself anymore. He's given up on that. He wouldn't want to get wound up like he did as a player – if he couldn't manage to do something, couldn't understand why the body wouldn't do what the brain commanded, that probably wouldn't look too good in front of the players.

The training drills come with a set of rules: no weak passes, get your foot behind the ball. Buvač makes clear that the gaps between defenders, midfield and attack are important too: they have to be kept tight, leaving no room for the opposition. Now it's time to practise quick, direct play. Pass out wide, cross back into the middle, shoot. Langerak is in great form, making one save after another. On the other side, Mats Hummels bangs the ball into the top corner just beautifully. Florian Kringe, despite being kept out of the first eleven by Dortmund's array of midfield talent, also shows he's no slouch when it comes to finding the back of the net. From close range, Marcel Schmelzer and Mohamed Zidan drag the ball wide of the net. Buvač urges them on: 'Again, get on with it!'

Not long after, Klopp stops the drill he has been watching in silence. He demands more concentration: too many shots are missing the target. It's serious business, but there's still time for a bit of a laugh. Zidan challenges Klopp to nutmeg him from a good ten yards' distance. He doesn't need to ask twice. His first attempt hits the striker's left leg, the second is a good 'un. The old fox hasn't forgotten all his tricks.

Nearly all the training drills involve working with the ball. Intensity levels are high, and in the next exercise too. Three goals are set up in a triangle, so each goalkeeper can see the other two. Three teams are chosen, one with a red bib, one with white and one with yellow. Each team has to defend its own goal and try to score in either of the other two. Three teams of five or six players playing at the same time in a cramped space: the entire 'triangle pitch' is smaller than half a football pitch. If someone passes loosely, one of the players from the other two teams is quick to profit and uses the involuntary assist to their own advantage.

Klopp has an eye everywhere: '12 to 9 to 3,' he says, announcing the score. What's it all in aid of? The quick and constant movement and switching of situation trains one-touch passing, quickness of action and reaction, passing accuracy and awareness – that is, spatial awareness in fractions of seconds. Agility and quick transitions, the hallmarks of Klopp's system team, are being drilled here.

* * *

One of the supporters watching on at Brackel is Thorsten Birgel, a Dortmund fan since childhood and now in his mid-thirties. Very, very early on he was a fan of the other Borussians, the ones from Mönchengladbach. Why? 'I couldn't really say anymore.' For him, having Klopp as manager was a real stroke of luck for Dortmund. Or as they say in the colourful local phrase: 'He fits like an arse in a bucket.'

'Klopp is the manager as fan,' says Birgel. 'He kicks every ball and feels the emotions just as intently as the man in the stands. Klopp's also completely convinced that he knows exactly what he's doing: he's the consummate professional. Klopp is very meticulous during training, always correcting and making adjustments. If three corners aren't hit as cleanly as he wants, he gets hold of the players and makes them do it over and over until they get it right. They have to be able to do it without thinking.' Klopp never resorts to hot air to get his point across: when he says something, it's calmly explained. He's about substance not passion.

Birgel explains who does what in the coaching team: 'The assistant runs the drills and Klopp steps in only when it's really necessary. He consciously pulls back from training so he can keep an overview, so he can take the whole thing in. But he doesn't just delegate everything, he'll give it to them straight. If someone's not getting it right, he's right onto them.' Birgel also finds the way in which Klopp always manages to keep his players motivated remarkable: 'There's thirty-four games a year just in the *Bundesliga*, and you always have to think of something new to say; there must be a danger you're going to wear yourself down.'

If there's something to criticise, then Birgel feels a little more composure might not go amiss. 'After the game in Leverkusen [an early season goalless draw] there seemed to be a bit of a lack of critical self-awareness, like his blood pressure was still 180. As the boss, he has to be more in command of himself than that. The way I see it, when he loses his cool he's opening himself up to attack, especially when we aren't winning.' In a TV interview with Sky, Klopp had become worked up over something interviewer Ecki Heuser said regarding 'retaliation' after Mario Götze was sent off: 'Just you listen to me, for fuck's sake!' was his response to the TV man's analysis.

During more than two decades as a fervent Dortmund supporter, Birgel has seen a lot of managers come and go. For him, Klopp is one of the best, close behind an icon who won the Champions League with the Black and Yellows in 1997: 'If I go through all the managers who've been here since I've been a *Borusse*, then Jürgen Klopp comes directly behind Ottmar Hitzfeld. I put Hitzfeld a little ahead of everyone else because of his aura. But Klopp knows what he's doing too, while with a lot of managers I got the impression they were experimenting a lot without having a guiding philosophy.'

12

A CHALLENGING SEASON

With the domestic double in 2011–12 and the Champions League final against Bayern Munich in 2013, along with the other emotional highpoints like the matches against Málaga and Real Madrid, the pinnacle for Borussia Dortmund had (almost) been reached. And once the pinnacle has been reached, there's no other way but down. It was a gradual process at first for Dortmund in the 2013–14 season, but in 2014–15 it accelerated.

As painful as losing in the Champions League final to Bayern had been, what really hurt was the loss of Mario Götze to the club sometimes disparagingly known as FC Hollywood. The shock transfer had robbed the team of something of its innocence – and a critical component of its style of play. The naive yet beautiful dream of a forever young team of underdogs who could bloody the establishment's nose and tear up Europe on the *Bundesliga*'s behalf, throwing in their lot together like eleven Ruhrpott musketeers, was over. The team had already lost Nuri Şahin from their band of brothers in 2011 (he returned in January 2013 after unsuccessful spells at Real Madrid and Liverpool), but his departure to Spain had been understandable at the time. But to jump ship to your biggest rivals? Only moving to Schalke 04 would have been more unforgivable for *die Schwarzgelben*.

It was through no fault of his own that Götze missed the Champions League final against his future employers with a thigh injury. Unfortunately for him, in attempting to get fit for the Champions League final, Götze returned to training too soon and aggravated the injury. The minor muscle tear that had been diagnosed after the semi-final return leg in Madrid turned out to be a more serious hamstring problem that would keep him out for weeks and continued to give him problems even after his Bayern debut. None of this reduced the intense disdain that Dortmund fans now felt for him. Indeed, when the versatile attacker fired home the extra-time goal that won Germany the 2014 World Cup in Brazil, there were many in Dortmund who didn't know whether they should celebrate or not.

Götze was replaced by the relatively unknown Henrikh Mkhitaryan from Ukraine's Shakhtar Donetsk. Mkhitaryan had come to the club's attention partly as a result of his performances against them on their road to Wembley, after 2–2 and 3–0 scorelines against Shakhtar Donetsk put them through to the quarter-final. He was an aesthete on the ball, a virtuoso, a wily fox, yet the Armenian rarely seemed to fulfil his potential in two seasons under Klopp, perhaps because he overthought things, perhaps because he put himself under too much pressure, something that he himself admitted was a problem. That pressure could come as no surprise, given that he had the club's record transfer fee, €27.5 million, to live up to. Yet being aware of the problem didn't seem to help solve it.

Mkhitaryan wasn't the only new signing. With the first Gabonese player in the *Bundesliga* in the shape of Pierre-Emerick Aubameyang, brought in from France's Saint-Étienne, BVB had at least by appearances an extrovert player, who drew attention not just with his outrageous haircuts and Batman-mask goal celebrations. Aubameyang was also noticeable for his quick start in German football, the striker hitting a hat-trick in the first game of the season away to Augsburg, where Dortmund triumphed 4–0. The two newcomers presented the fans and the press with a tongue-twisting test that they solved tactfully, transforming Mkhitaryan and Aubameyang into 'Micki' and 'Auba'.

There was a third addition to the team as well: Greek centre-back Sokratis Papastathopoulos was brought in from Werder Bremen to provide competition to Neven Subotić as to who was to partner the firmly established Mats Hummels in the heart of defence. Unfortunately, the battle was decided not on performances but by injury, when Subotić suffered a cruciate knee-ligament injury that ruled him out for six months in November 2013. When Hummels suffered a ligament injury soon afterwards, Dortmund suddenly found themselves acutely short in defence.

At first glance, the 2013–14 season seemed to have been a decent one for Dortmund. Klopp's side had secured second place again, yet looking at the points totals, it was clear that Bayern had left them for dead – they were nineteen points behind (a small improvement on the twenty-five points gap in 2012–13). Bayern could have stayed in the team hotel eating their Nutella for six of their games and they would still have won the league. The Bavarian side had lived up to its self-inflated reputation and taken revenge for the – by their standards – humiliating series of second-place finishes in 2012: in the *Bundesliga*, in the DFB Pokal and in the Champions League. They had responded with a transfer offensive and a total focus on success that had put them back on top.

But when the season had kicked off, it had still looked as if Dortmund had what it took to mount a proper title challenge, leading the table from the second to seventh matches. After that, Bayern seized top spot and held onto it for the rest of the season. It was an outcome that seemed ominously likely as early as

23 November, when Bayern visited Signal Iduna Park to take on their title rivals. While the teams were evenly matched at first, Bayern eventually ran out clear winners, putting three past Dortmund to no response, and leaving them trailing by seven points.

To add insult to injury, who else but Mario Götze opened the scoring for Bayern? Fearing the reaction of the Dortmund faithful to their new recruit, Bayern had Götze warm-up indoors instead of on the pitch, before he was subbed on to the accompaniment of an ear-piercing apocalypse of boos and whistles. Then he left the stadium in perplexed silence by putting Bayern 1–0 up, but refusing any celebration more extravagant than apologetically and diplomatically raising his arms in the air.

In fairness to Dortmund, the 2013–14 season was one where the club were plagued with injuries, particularly in defence. Absent against Bayern were not only Subotić and Hummels, but also left-back Marcel Schmelzer. His counterpart on the opposite flank, Łukasz Piszczek, was only back in the squad for the first time that season after injury problems of his own, and appeared only as a substitute in the final few minutes. In other words, the Dortmund defence that started against Bayern featured not a single one of their title-winning back four.

Indeed, the club had turned to a free agent in the form of recently signed Manuel Friedrich to combat their defensive shortfall and hurled him into the fray against Munich. Yet this makeshift solution did little to ease the situation. Klopp had turned to a player who had been a solid, reliable defender for him over many seasons at Mainz 05, whom he felt could now once again do a job for him. On his debut in a black and yellow shirt, Friedrich seemed to be coping well at first, but a lack of match sharpness soon showed as he faded badly. As Dortmund opened up in the search for an equaliser, late goals from Arjen Robben and Thomas Müller put the game and arguably the season to bed.

Over the winter break Dortmund regrouped. The team were subjected to pressure to make the title race more interesting than the previous season, but Klopp acted to relieve this added onus on his side, responding to the *WAZ* newspaper in his usual off-the-cuff style: 'If we end up second come the summer, then I'll fetch a bus and drive around my garden and party. If no one else can celebrate second place, I'll do it alone ... Take a trip round the world and tell me which team is certain to be champions in the same league as Bayern Munich. Is there any team who could? There aren't many. Manchester United, no chance. Manchester City, no chance. Maybe Barcelona. Real Madrid, no chance. And that's where we are, and we're supposed to do it? If anyone still has these kind of expectations, they're being completely unrealistic ... We have to win every game or people get on our backs. That's an attitude we earned. The air's thin up here.'

Having dropped as low as fourth in the table, Dortmund climbed back up to second place. They were to maintain their hold on the runner-up position until the season's end, once again ensuring direct Champions League qualification. The team also achieved a satisfying revenge for their defeat by Bayern when they travelled to Munich in April – reversing the scoreline from November with 'Super Micki' Mkhitaryan putting in an all-round performance that showed just what he was capable of, not least by scoring the opener.

Unfortunately for Klopp, the league win in Munich didn't turn out to be a harbinger for the subsequent DFB Cup final against, yes, Bayern. After a difficult season, it seemed as though things had finally tilted in Dortmund's favour: the *Dortmunders* being back in form on the one hand, with Bayern, already crowned champions, seemingly sated on the other. On top of this, the Bavarians had also been unexpectedly easily knocked out of the Champions League by Real Madrid, 5–0 on aggregate. Their winning run was over, and in the public's perception at least, the role of favourites was now occupied by the Westphalians once again. Such confidence was burgeoned by a run to the final without conceding a goal: winning 3–0 away to SV Wilhelmshaven, 2–0 after extra-time at 1860 Munich, 2–0 at Saarbrücken, 1–0 over Eintracht Frankfurt and 2–0 in the semi-final against Wolfsburg – their sole cup fixture played in front of their own fans.

The final delivered the expected evenly matched battle between the two dominant forces in German football. After an hour, Dortmund should have taken the lead through a Mats Hummels header, which was cleared by Bayern defender Dante only after it had crossed the line. The refereeing team, however, failed to spot what the TV replays proved, and denied Hummels what was clearly a legitimate goal. Having ridden their luck to get to extra-time, Arjen Robben and Thomas Müller then got the goals to given Bayern the trophy.

Klopp's fury at the disallowed goal was clear after the match. 'All of my subs were in a worse position than the linesman, and they could see that the ball was in,' he told ARD TV. He made his incomprehension for the failure to award the goal plain in the official post-match press conference as well: referring to the fact that Dante already had his right foot on the goal line as he cleared with his left. Klopped added that, 'If he could clear that ball before it went over the line, he must be a member of Cirque du Soleil.'

The criticism of the officials after the DFB Cup final was not an isolated incident in Klopp's managerial career. While Jürgen Klopp has won the sympathy of much of the football world with his open and charismatic personality, many referees aren't quite so keen on the manager's behaviour: when he attempts to influence the fourth official on the touchline, when he screams at officials, when he gets sent to the stands. On 18 November 2013, Lutz-Michael Fröhlich, the head of the refereeing department at the German FA, said the following on Deutschlandradio: 'Even if this Mr Klopp always comes out and says: "Oh, sorry" ... at the end of the day, there's still something hanging in the air. The kind of behaviour that we have seen from him on many occasions shows such a capacity for aggression that we could see violent excesses at the grassroots level taking their cue from it.' The Berlin amateur referee Gerald Bothe then reinforced what Fröhlich had said on the radio show, arguing in an interview that whatever happened in the *Bundesliga* would be copied 'blow-by-blow' by Saturday- and Sunday-league players the next weekend. Bothe's comments were given prominence because in 2011 he had been assaulted by a player and knocked out, suffering serious head injuries.

When he learned of Fröhlich's reproaches, Jürgen Klopp expressed his 'shock' at the accusation. He admitted that on occasions watching back his behaviour during a match left him painfully embarrassed. Nevertheless, he refused to see any link between violence on the pitch and his own behaviour: 'Professional football has a lot of problems, and I don't believe I'm the worst,' he said.

Fröhlich, however, has not been the only official to comment on Klopp. In his 2015 book *Ich pfeife!* (*I'm Blowing the Whistle*), the amateur referee (and literary critic) Christoph Schröder criticised Klopp, whom he had got to know personally years before at Frankfurt: 'He was a friendly guy with a smile on his face and generally behaved very professionally out on the pitch, although he did have a tendency to lose his temper.' Schröder went on to ask, 'What happened to this friendly, funny Klopp that makes him spend

ninety minutes raging on the touchline with a grimace on his face?'
In Schröder's opinion, the role and job description of managers and
coaches have undergone a fundamental change. Today, the majority
of them are not football intellectuals but rather 'Firestarters, fuel,
motivators', who spread that fire to their team, fans and the public.

* * *

Back in the 2013–14 season, Klopp had another public confrontation
with officialdom, this time during their run in the Champions
League. At the group stage, Dortmund found themselves drawn
against a tough group of opponents: Arsenal, Napoli and Marseille.
It was to be the match in Naples, which Dortmund lost 2–1, where
events became heated. This turn of events was something of a surprise
to European football fans. While Klopp's occasional outbursts were
part of the scenery in the *Bundesliga*, they came as something of a
shock in Europe. Up to this point, Klopp had been feted abroad,
perceived as a personable and eloquent manager, sophisticated
and collected.

Not so in Naples. Following a supposed refereeing error, Klopp
stormed up to the fourth official on the touchline and, getting right
in his face, screamed at him with his features distorted by such rage.
So fearsome was his appearance that it was as though the meta-
morphosed manager was about to swallow the poor official whole.
As a result, Klopp found himself dismissed and sent to enjoy the
rest of the game from the stands. Klopp claimed afterwards that his
extraordinary facial expression had not been one of rage but rather
letting off steam – an argument that didn't quite seem to tell the
whole story.

Even so, Klopp was prepared to admit that he had stepped over
the line: 'What happened with the fourth official in Naples was

completely beyond the pale. There's no excuse. If you do something like that, there needs to be a sanction, and that's absolutely the right course of action,' he said to Sky, referring to his ban from the dugout for the next two competitive matches. Showing self-awareness, he acknowledged that he needed to keep a better grip on himself in future, but without taking anything away from his passionate coaching style. 'I went too far in Naples. I didn't know where to draw the line. I don't want to change the way I am, but I need to know when to draw the line.'

The incident that had sparked the outburst followed Neven Subotić being treated on the touchline for a cut to his eyebrow. After a short wait, he was allowed back on the field – a wait that was too long in Klopp's book. Having just sprinted back into the box, and likely not quite having found his bearings yet, both Subotić and the opponent he was marking missed a cross that fell to Gonzalo Higuaín directly behind him, who made no mistake to score for Napoli. The manager lost his cool because in his opinion the goal could have been avoided if Subotić, normally unbeatable in the air, had been allowed back on the field earlier. Klopp later had to admit that however he felt about it, everything had proceeded according to the rules.

After the game Klopp apologised for his behaviour, both to the officials and to his players, on whom he had imposed 'unnecessary stress'. As for being given his marching orders, Klopp watched the second half of the match on TV from inside the belly of the stadium, sitting with the caretaker in his hideaway. Sitting in the stands with the Napoli fans was too much even for the outgoing Klopp: 'There were too many fans there who were happy to see me being unhappy.' With a glass of water at hand and cake to nibble, Klopp and the caretaker Vincenzo Gerrone watched the rest of the match in peace. The delighted caretaker told *Bild* afterwards that 'Klopp was very nice. He was the best visitor since Diego Maradona.'

The Napoli match showed the two sides of Klopp's character, switching back and forth from a hearty, jocular, upstanding and easygoing coach, into a terrifying 'monster' manager. There was even speculation that his unbounded ambition and inability to accept being wronged, which drove him to such outbursts, would one day cause him to lose control completely, unleashing physical and not just emotional aggression. Naples, however, was to prove a watershed: Klopp took note of what had happened and there was to be no repeat during the rest of his time with Dortmund.

Even without Klopp in the dugout, Dortmund managed to regain their European form. With Željko Buvač, Klopp's publicity-shy assistant, thrust into the limelight, Dortmund won both at home against Olympique Marseille 3–0 and against Arsenal at the Emirates, 2–1. After the Marseilles match, Klopp commented on watching the game from on high that 'this isn't something I want to make a habit of. You get a better view, but otherwise it's crap.' Almost inevitably, when Dortmund lost in Klopp's first game back – going down 1–0 at home to Arsenal – the joke did the rounds that the manager should should go back to watching the game from the stands. But even with the chastened manager back on the touchline, Dortmund managed to take revenge against Napoli, winning 3–1.

The final group game in Marseille would thus decide who would go through to the last sixteen: Marseille, on no points, were the only team in the group who had no chance of qualifying; one of Arsenal, Dortmund or Napoli would join them in not making it through, depending on the night's results. When Napoli beat Arsenal 2–0 in the Stadio San Paolo, they thought they had done enough, especially with Dortmund being held to a 1–1 draw in

France. But then, with just three minutes of normal time left, Kevin Grosskreutz finally converted one of the guests' many chances to give Dortmund the game. He celebrated directly in front of the travelling fans who were congregated at the bottom of a stand near the pitchside. It was a goal that was worth millions: the result left Arsenal, Dortmund and Napoli all level on twelve points, but with Klopp's side having the better head-to-head record against the other two, it was Dortmund who went through as winners and Arsenal as runners-up, with Napoli ending up in third.

In the last sixteen, BVB were rewarded for winning their group by being drawn against the Russian side FC Zenit St Petersburg. Following a 4–2 win in Russia, Dortmund made it unnecessarily exciting in front of their home crowd by losing 2–1. This set up a quarter-final against Real Madrid, who were desperate to avenge their defeat to Dortmund the year before. Without the suspended Robert Lewandowski, who had scored a fabulous four goals in the first leg of the 2013 semi-final, Dortmund found themselves lacking the necessary cutting edge in the first leg at the Estadio Bernabéu. A dominant Real won 3–0, all but making the second leg redundant.

But in comparison to the last sixteen against Zenit, now it was Dortmund who were the team taking advantage of a side too sure of itself. After Roman Weidenfeller kept out a penalty taken by Ángel di María in the seventeenth minute, the keeper seemed to have given his team the signal to attack. With two goals before half time, Marco Reus unleashed dreams of another historic evening in Signal Iduna Park. Yet despite further good opportunities, the third goal – and with it the equaliser to the first leg result – simply didn't want to come. Dortmund were out, but with their heads held high – the fans giving them a standing ovation for their efforts at the end of the match. As it turned out, Dortmund had been beaten by the eventual European champions, Real beating their Madrid rivals Atlético in Lisbon.

The applause for Dortmund's efforts was well-deserved. Klopp's team selection was still hampered by injuries, and required second-string replacements like Erik Durm, Manuel Friedrich, Oliver Kirch and Miloš Jojić to play with aplomb. Following the match, Klopp was visibly excited by his team, telling Sky: 'You should preserve that game, make a video out of it, say to all the clubs who have lost the first leg 0–3, something can still happen … Unbelievable. Among the million different ways to bow out, this was the best.'

Dortmund had ended the season trophyless, but at least there was a small fillip in the form of an individual award: Robert Lewandowski left Dortmund as top *Bundesliga* scorer with twenty league goals before joining Bayern. A year before, BVB had been able to fend off approaches from Bayern, even disregarding a high transfer fee – a decision which had some economic sense, with Watzke arguing the absent transfer fee needed to be set against the missing Lewandowski goals if Lewandowski had gone – and with them the millions gained by staying in the Champions League. This was an admittedly difficult calculation to make because the numbers of goals, and with them the monetary rewards, couldn't be foreseen – not to speak of the risk of Lewandowski not being able to play due to injury. But what Dortmund's decision did show was to send a sign of regained strength to the competition. It said, 'Look, we don't have to sell our players to our greatest rivals if we don't want to.'

A year later, however, Lewandowski's contract expired and Dortmund were forced to watch as he left for Bayern on a free. But unlike the episode with Mario Götze at the end of the previous season, Lewandowski's departure lacked a similar sense of vitriol.

While Götze left with the fans' curses ringing in his ears, the BVB supporters applauded Lewandowski, even after his transfer had been sealed. They didn't hold a grudge against him because Lewandowski had always been upfront about his intentions. His transfer had already been building over months and Lewandowski had never given the impression that he had wanted to stay with Dortmund forever, instead regarding it as a stepping stone on the path to his next career move.

Despite the more positive mood music, Lewandowski's departure left Klopp with a difficult challenge. From a sporting perspective, Lewandowski was one of the five best strikers in Europe, and would be even harder to replace than Götze. In the following season – Klopp's last with the club – his goals would be sorely missed.

13

KLOPPO!

Anyone who has watched Jürgen Klopp run up and down the touchline celebrating his team's goals – his hair tousled and arms whipping like windmills, his face betraying an outpouring of tension – can be in no doubt that he is something of a live wire. The double 'saw', where Klopp rotates both of his arms while keeping his torso ramrod straight, is another favourite celebration. The ritualised performance with Dortmund goalkeeping coach 'Teddy' de Beer was no less beautiful – the two keeping their arms to the side and jumping into a chest bump: 'head up, chest out' as a symbol of strength, self-confidence and success. This is a man who lives and loves his sport, as if he were playing on the pitch himself.

That bubbling enthusiasm, the energy and impulsive passion that Klopp radiates, is in stark contrast to many of his fellow managers. But what is the driving force behind this charismatic man, who even wears some of the pieces from his own fashion collection Übungsleiter K., and has a fan club in Dortmund that was founded in his honour? What is the origin of his driving ambition, which he transfers on to the teams he coaches? Where does that mixture of easy-going fellow and natural authority come from? How is he a figure who fills a room as soon as he walks through the door?

The first thing to say about Jürgen Klopp as a character is that he is always himself, always genuine. It's probably the most remarkable part of who he is. He doesn't play a role, indeed in his own opinion 'can't act at all'. This is to the extent that he doesn't consciously use the media for his ends; he doesn't think about how his words could be interpreted publically – meaning his press interviews don't always correspond to a book on etiquette. 'Regarding the public, I'm super lucky because I really don't care at all what they think,' Klopp has said. 'That keeps me completely relaxed. Some might think "there's a real nice bloke, always in a good mood" and the others might say "that smug git has been getting on my bloody tits for years". But I don't have to worry about one or the other. I have to worry about what's important to me: making sure that my immediate surroundings benefit from me – whether that's my family or my job. I've long been considered a windbag. But ultimately work and quality asserts itself and what you say publically isn't so important.'

Klopp has always stayed true to his coaching style – and in doing so, there is no contradiction in the fact that he's continued to develop. He is also somewhat more distanced from his players than was the case at the beginning of his time in Mainz. At the time, he was barely older that several of the players who had been his teammates. Today, Klopp the coach has long cut the cord to his time on the pitch, though his understanding and memory of being a player informs his managerial style. As Wolfgang Frank said: 'In my opinion arrogant football coaches don't stand a chance today. Young players expect you to live alongside them, engage with them, and be creative … you can also admit your own failures, and still make demands of them. It's a constant give and take – and I believe Jürgen does it very well. He melds objective discussion with a certain kind of emotionality.'

Klopp's players have also profited professionally from the fact that he's in tune with the coaching zeitgeist. His team talks chime with a new generation of pros who don't just smile and nod their head at decisions, but also want to have them explained. They want to understand them first, rather than just having tactics barked at them. Klopp is convincing by making his decision-making process transparent, by listening to outside opinions, even if in the end he makes the final decisions himself. After all, as the manager, he has to answer for them: 'You can talk to me, but players still don't have any influence on my decisions. We don't do group discussions and then I just go with the majority, that's not what happens. So there's no reason to ask a team: "How would you like to play? More attacking, or defensive, more on the left or on the right?" I have to make the decisions because I'm the only one who sees the whole picture.'

* * *

Those who know Klopp well speak highly of his people skills: he is an emotionally intelligent manager who is also extremely intelligent and, at times, highly emotional.

Dortmund chairman Hans-Joachim Watzke has called Klopp a 'fisher of men, who puts people under his spell'. Klopp is someone who places an emphasis on doing things his way, as does his kindred spirit, second wife Ulla: 'Everything had to follow certain rules, which drives me crazy,' she said in an interview with *Focus* magazine, explaining why the trained educator quit her job at a special needs school with 'old-fashioned methods': 'I'm like my husband in that respect. We Kloppos need our freedom in order to realise ourselves,' said the children's book author.

Yet if something threatens to limit that self-realisation, or something rubs Klopp up the wrong way, then that trademark smile disappears. A second, irascible face appears: his lips become thinner than usual, a distant look appears on his face. If Klopp really loses his temper, then he pulls himself up to his full height, his head occasionally drawing within nutting distance of his interlocutor. An extreme example of this took place in November 2010 in the course of a 2–0 defeat to Hamburg. Klopp became worked up about an unacknowledged foul against his team, and pressed the peak of his cap into the fourth official's forehead. The DFB handed Klopp, who was subsequently apologetic, a fine of €10,000.

It's a tightrope Klopp walks. He makes no bones about what's in his heart and acts the same in front of the camera as away from it. If he crosses the line, the stereotype of the 'impulsive loudmouth' is soon doing the rounds. But Klopp cares little about his image. He is a 'fan among coaches' as Dortmund supporter Thorsten Birgel put it: Klopp not only celebrates the goals as hard as the season-ticket holders in the stands, he is just as passionate about supposed injustices. Klopp is even somewhat proud of the first time he was sent off as a coach, as he likes to repeat in interviews: during his days in Mainz, he asked the linesman how many mistakes he was allowed – if it was fifteen, then he had one left.

Klopp is indeed aware that on occasion he is in danger of over-stepping the mark. But even then, as an emotional man, he doesn't believe he'd change his habits: 'I've already made a lot of stupid mistakes in public I'm not proud of. But the next time, when I've just browbeaten a reporter, then I might be able to tolerate the next three stupid questions and think: "Come on, you messed up just last week." But with the fourth stupid question I know without a doubt I'll be on fire again, code red, and the boiler starts overheating. That's who I am and it's not so easy to change.'

For some commentators, there is method behind these emotional outbursts.

Thomas Hennecke, who writes regularly for *Kicker*, is convinced that Klopp intentionally draws attention to himself when he believes he needs to protect his team: 'His [Dortmund] team is still very young and not very experienced in dealing with setbacks. That's why I believe that he consciously gives them breathing space when they're going through a bad moment. Eyebrow-raising statements or wording that get a reaction from the general public are only tolerated in exceptional cases or due to spontaneous emotions. An intelligent man such as Klopp is well aware of the impact of his words.'

As an expert on Borussia Dortmund, Thomas Hennecke has frequently interviewed Klopp, with the discussions often having a 'gloves off' feel. Hennecke describes Klopp's relationship to the media as 'unbelievably professional' but also 'downright direct': 'When Klopp feels he has been misquoted or he just doesn't agree with the gist of a story, then he sometimes takes the journalist to task personally, and then he eschews niceties. But he doesn't hold a grudge, even when something rubs him up the wrong way. He vents, blows off steam, and then it's over the next day. I like that. With him, you know where you stand.'

However, according to Hennecke, not all of his colleagues can handle Klopp's approach: 'Sometimes Klopp talks a little condescendingly, in two senses of the word, when he's sitting up there on the podium at the press conferences and is looking down at his audience. It's not pleasant to be his target then, when he makes no bones about his displeasure regarding a question he considers superficial or just dumb. In spite of that, Klopp is valued by media reps for his communicative nature.'

Hennecke understands the fact that Klopp can get annoyed when he has to answer the same question for the thousandth time. 'Then, he can get a little short-tempered. I remember a press conference two months after the start of training, where he was asked about his season goals, obviously not for the first time. Then he thought about it for a second, shook his head, and asked the journalist if he'd been in a cave for the past couple of months. In moments like these he lets off steam unchecked.'

Hennecke has enjoyed the professional jousts with Klopp, which are often controversial, but fair. The journalist offers an example from the 2010–11 season: 'Poor chance conversion is a repeated narrative in the media. One that Klopp is unable to understand, because his approach is completely different. He regards it as a positive sign for BVB's play that so many great chances are being produced – and considers focusing on how many are converted to be too negative.'

Hennecke and Klopp also reached differing positions at the beginning of the following season: 'I wrote a long piece about the slow start to the season, why Dortmund were playing differently than the year before, why they were no longer playing so effortlessly. He didn't like that methodical approach in the least, and we had a full and frank discussion. His position was that one couldn't compare the first five matches with the entire previous season. And he remained very tenacious in defending his position. He very clearly communicated that I was barking up the wrong tree.'

* * *

With his five-o'clock shadow, thick blond head of hair, glasses, baseball cap and hoodie, Jürgen Klopp certainly knows how to makes a visual impact: he is one of the most instantly recognisable managers in world football today. So much so that he changes his wardrobe only for Champions League appearances, for which UEFA imposes a dress code and he is forced to suit up. Early in his managerial career, Klopp sported wire-framed glasses and shorter hair and briefly had a Harry Potter nickname. Since then, Klopp has outgrown such names to very much define himself – as a person, as a manager, he is, to borrow from marketing speak, a brand in his own right.

But what exactly makes a brand a brand? How is it formed and what is at its heart? The first prerequisite in business is product quality, which has to be convincing. Translated to football, this almost always means: attractive, entertaining and as successful as possible, and something the fans can identify with. If a club disappoints the expectations of the fans too often, then the product's not right. Just like the goods in a supermarket, consumers of a football match have very specific expectations for the 'product' – which can be intensely emotional in the case of football.

'The best brands are those that are successful. The others lack credibility,' Bayern Munich's sporting director Matthias Sammer said. In Sammer's dictionary, 'success' is adding as many stars as possible to the club badge – winning trophies. This definition fits Klopp's career in Germany. He's credible as a footballing brand because his teams play with an identifiable style and because he's successful. That's been true since he added the *Bundesliga* to his CV in 2011 at least, but also way before then, when he first saved Mainz 05 from the danger zone, and then ultimately led the club back to the *Bundesliga*.

Does success in football exclusively mean winning titles and surviving relegation battles? Or can Sammer's definition be expanded. After all, success for a smaller club such as St Pauli is not identical to that of Bayern Munich. As a brand, St Pauli stands for happiness, being relaxed, humour and non-conformity. For its fans, being in the *Bundesliga* is already a gift, relegation isn't dramatic. For St

Pauli fans, it would be worse for the *Kiezklub*, the 'little local club', to betray its identity than to go down. Such belief made it possible that even after a 8–1 debacle against Bayern in the penultimate match of the 2010–11 season, sealing their relegation, the team was still applauded by its fans. And so was the departing coach and St Pauli cult figure Holger Stanislawski.

The situation is different with Bayern Munich, whose yearly aim is winning the *Bundesliga* title as well as playing a central role in the Champions League. Based on this approach, a loss carries much more weight because the brand demands regular victories (a self-understanding that only emerged after their triumphant seventies trophy haul). Therefore, a loss proportionally has more consequence than is the case for St Pauli. Accordingly, success and its influence on brand formation are a question of definition: what does the club represent and what are its goals?

In addition to demonstrations of success, further factors have an effect on brand viability – even with professional football managers. Their realm of responsibility has greatly increased during the last ten to twenty years. They are no longer mere coaches whose work is restricted to training sessions and match management. Public relations have become increasingly important. Managers represent not only themselves, but their clubs. The combination becomes ideal when the manager embodies values and convictions that match the ideals of his employer. Where there are shared values, it eases working together in the same direction. In this vein, Klopp identified with the Dortmund concept of emphasising young talent from the beginning.

Frank Dopheide, a leading expert on branding, argues that the strength of Klopp's brand comes from him being down to earth: 'He speaks the language of the people and also makes appearances in a tracksuit. His external appearance is not a means to an end. He's actually the way he presents himself. He always remains similar and has changed little over the years, from the perspective of appearances, language or habits. He's true to himself and that's also what makes his brand so valuable. The fact that Klopp keeps his own sense of style is something that gives him great power. Just look at the way he parts his hair in the middle, which he persistently retains – regardless of whether it's in style or not. Klopp stays steady!

'He's very convincing rhetorically, and what he says fits with what he embodies. This leads to credibility that is very decisive for brand formation. He has a big mouth, speaks metaphorically and understandably so that you don't have to be a football pro to follow him. He doesn't beat around the bush, which is also good for the BVB brand, because Klopp's down-to-earth, honest appearance overlaps with the mentality of the Ruhr region. In addition, I believe Klopp is very attractive to women and has great power over young people. You just have to look at the young and powerful squad he's formed.' (For the full interview with Dopheide, see the Appendix.)

* * *

A brand needs a brand manager and, in Klopp's case, this comes in the form of his long-standing agent Marc Kosicke. Born in 1971, Marc Kosicke is an athletic north German with close-cropped hair, and is today head of his own agency, advising football managers. His clients include Michael Oenning, Bruno Labbadia, Holger Stanislawski, Viktor Skripnik, André Schubert and Jürgen Klopp. In 2007, Kosicke established Project B together with his friend and German national team general manager Oliver Bierhoff. These days Kosicke is the sole man in charge and has moved the firm's headquarters from Starnberger See in Bavaria to Eltville in Hesse, and finally to Bremen in the summer of 2013.

The friendship between Jürgen Klopp and Marc Kosicke began many years ago in Nike's German headquarters with a simple question. At the time Klopp was still at Mainz and Kosicke was head of marketing at Nike. Klopp asked the then head of marketing if he could sign a shoe contract with the sports-kit manufacturer. 'It fits me,' Klopp said. When they grabbed a beer together the same evening, the manager murmured to him that he didn't want any money, just the kit.

Kosicke speaks warmly of Klopp. They trusted each other from the off and sealed the deal on their partnership in 2007 with a handshake. It must have been a very firm handshake. Kosicke squeezes very tight when he greets a business partner. He makes a strong impression, yet seems pleasantly grounded in the notoriously excitable football business. He works in an industry in which even the most experienced professional has their agent or their staff take care of the most routine tasks. Modern football players expect that much will be taken off their hands. Klopp as a client, however, is not like that: he knows what he wants and that's true for most managers who are used to making decisions. 'That makes working together quite pleasant,' says Kosicke.

Kosicke is undoubtedly one of the best in the business and his Project B, as a result, has many of the most coveted managers in the *Bundesliga* in its portfolio. Many of these famous faces are frequently seen in television advertisements. Jürgen Klopp, for example, has been in campaigns for products from car company Seat to wallpaper-paste manufacturer Metylan (he was the 'Metylan Face of 2011'). The slogan 'enjoy', which Klopp had to say four times in one Seat advert, might seem slightly excessive even to the most generous of critics, but such endorsements are a proven means to profit from Jürgen Klopp's high popularity.

There was another advertising contract, however, that Marc Kosicke did have to cancel. Klopp had been holding motivational seminars for young talent and leading managers since summer 2010 for the Ergo Insurance Group, which belongs to Hamburg-Mannheimer International. In spring 2011, it came to light that a trip for insurance reps belonging to Hamburg-Mannheimer in Budapest in 2007 had included an organised orgy with prostitutes. 'One can only have the strongest condemnation for what one reads about that trip,' Marc Kosicke stated in *Handelsblatt* in May 2011. In order not to damage Jürgen Klopp's good image, Kosicke cancelled the contract.

There was also a change that took place that summer when it came to trainers. The choice of trainers can be of enormous importance for the fashion conscious – wearing something other than a favoured brand is a recipe for a ruined reputation. Marc Kosicke and Jürgen Klopp are past that age and not at all sentimental when a chance for an attractive new sponsorship contract arises. That happened in August 2011 when Puma entered into a long-term partnership with the title-winning manager, starting at the beginning of the new season. 'Having the right boots is of enormous importance for athletes. Puma and football – it's true love, it just fits,' Jürgen Klopp was quoted in the accompanying press release.

* * *

One of the reasons that Klopp is in such demand with advertisers is his easy and relaxed manner in front of an audience. Speaking freely is second nature to Klopp, regardless of whether it's in front of his team or a wider public. It's a characteristic Klopp believes he inherited from his father. The eloquence is a gift, not trained. Klopp is quick-witted and thinks fast, in part because he not only speaks well, but also listens well. That's why it was logical that Klopp started an additional career in 2005 as a TV pundit. Together with the presenter Johannes Kerner, he analysed Germany internationals, supported by Franz Beckenbauer and Swiss referee Urs Meier.

With the help of an electronic tactics table, Klopp was able to explain decisive phases in the game in an attractive, easy and clear manner – allowing complex issues to become understandable even for football novices. This form of tactics table was new in Germany. Using the technology, Klopp made a show of virtual marking on the screen, pointing out where a player should have been standing or which running lines would have been better. It was an instrument that he used effectively during his convincing explanations, leading to the TV audience considering Klopp the 'TV Germany Manager', elucidating tactics that were otherwise obscure. This helped increase his popularity and made him a well-known name far beyond Mainz, where he was managing at the time.

In honour of their entertaining and informative match preparation during the 2006 World Cup, Klopp, Meier and Kerner received that year's German Television Award for Best Sports Show. Klopp would receive the same honour four years later for the World Cup 2010 coverage, this time with RTL, alongside presenter Günter Jauch. Klopp, however, did not accept the award in person, explaining that 'I don't want to go down in history as the football manager who won a television prize twice but nothing important with his team' (a situation that changed when he won the *Bundesliga* the following year).

Klopp's reticence to accept the award was understandable in light of the fact that he had been forced to deal with public criticism during the 2006–07 relegation season with Mainz, that he was 'The manager who explains football to television viewers but doesn't understand his own team.' Klopp ended his activity as a TV football expert upon taking the helm at Dortmund in 2008 – and, according to his own statements, would have stopped even if he'd stayed on in Mainz because he feared the perception of him as a media expert had grown too dominant.

But while Klopp cut back his regular TV work, he remains a natural media darling: someone whose presence on TV is always welcome due to his natural charisma, high entertainment factor and way with a catchy soundbite. In 2011, for example, he was nominated for the best quote about football by the German Academy for Football Culture: following the first Dortmund victory at Bayern Munich in twenty years, Klopp said, 'Most of my players were still being breast-fed the last time we won in Munich.' Yet despite his excellent public image, those who worked with him day-in and day-out, Dortmund sporting director Michael Zorc and chairman Hans-Joachim Watzke, know that there is always substance behind the style: 'First and foremost, Jürgen Klopp is an excellent football coach.'

14

LEAVING DORTMUND

Jürgen Klopp's last season as manager of Borussia Dortmund began with a trophy. With their 2–0 win over Bayern in Signal Iduna Park, BVB secured the German Supercup (a contest between the winners of the *Bundesliga* and DFB Cup winners, with the cup runners-up taking part, as here, if a team had won the double). It was Dortmund's fifth Supercup win and their second in succession, making them the record holders in the competition: Mkhitaryan and Aubameyang scored the goals for a refreshed-looking Dortmund.

But as with the Charity Shield in the UK, the result of the Supercup isn't always a useful guide to the season ahead. Indeed, Dortmund's start to the 2014–15 *Bundesliga* was not successful, beginning with a home defeat to Bayer Leverkusen. The fact that Dortmund were behind after just nine seconds of the season – Leverkusen's striker Karim Bellarabi moving like greased lightning and putting the ball away in front of the South Stand – was not the most auspicious of league starts. With the game ending in a 2–0 defeat, Jürgen Klopp didn't beat around the bush after the final whistle: 'I take the blame for us not being alert out of the starting gate.'

The Dortmund side for the season saw a familiar face returning to the club: in an echo of Nuri Şahin's return after a disappointing spell at Real Madrid, Shinji Kagawa had also found the grass wasn't greener at Manchester United. Like Şahin, Kagawa had failed to hold down a starting place, and spent much of his time in the UK on the bench. But while Klopp and the Dortmund fans were delighted to see him return, the lack of playing time over those two years abroad had left its mark on the Japanese player. He wasn't helped by returning to a team performing below their full potential, but Kagawa never came into the sort of form that had caused him to become a celebrated star during his first stint at the club. Here again, there were parallels to be made with Şahin, who after long being hampered by injuries, struggled to regain the level that had made him the *Bundesliga* Player of the Season.

It wasn't just Kagawa and Şahin who disappointed, however. Many more *Dortmunders* were not able to reach their peak performance levels of previous seasons. Five consecutive losses led the club to drop from eighth to seventeenth in the table: the worst standing they'd had since Jürgen Klopp had been at the helm. Time and again, Dortmund were finding themselves struggling to break down teams who were (successfully) attempting to stifle their tactics through parking the metaphorical bus in front of goal. Bayern and Borussia Mönchengladbach were almost the only teams not to attempt this, being confident they could beat Dortmund their own way.

Thomas Helmer, ex-Dortmund defender and television pundit for *Spieltaganalyse* on Sport 1, made the following analysis: 'It seems the opposition have figured BVB out, they've adapted their game.' Like many other observers, Helmer also believed that Robert Lewandowski's transfer to Bayern had left a hole that Klopp was unable to fill. Ciro Immobile, *Serie A*'s reigning *Capocannoniere* (the winner of *Serie A's* Golden Boot for top scorer), had been brought in from Torino at the start of the season for an estimated €18 million. But for all his strengths as a striker, he wasn't able to convert the chances as Lewandowski did, or to link up with the attacking midfielders in the same way. According to Helmer, Immobile was a 'pure penalty box player and doesn't participate in combination play as much as Lewandowski'. A second signing, Adrián Ramos, who was purchased from Hertha Berlin for some €10 million, struggled just as much as Immobile. From the start, the Colombian made only infrequent appearances. Overall, he only managed two goals in eighteen matches during the season.

But it wasn't just the loss of the Polish international that made Dortmund's form stutter. Jürgen Klopp also had to cope with the loss of several important players from the beginning of the season: Nuri Şahin, İlkay Gündoğan, Jakub Błaszczykowski and Oliver Kirch were all out for several months. Then in November 2014, Marco Reus suffered a serious injury for the third time that year. He was carried from the pitch at Paderborn with torn ankle ligaments – the match that ended in a 2–2 draw against the recently promoted side.

Throughout the course of the *Bundesliga Hinrunde* – the first half of the season – a depleted Dortmund were unable to compensate for their missing players. It was the same for all teams, of course, but the 2014 World Cup and the success of Germany in particular had reduced the time Klopp had with his players pre-season. The team's lack of success wasn't through a lack of trying: no team ran more than Dortmund in the first half of the *Bundesliga* season, logging an average of 120 kilometres per match. However, despite the distances put in, the running at opponents no longer had the incisiveness of previous years' *gegenpressing*. The sobering result was that Dortmund were exerting a lot of effort for very little reward.

* * *

Dortmund's Champions League campaign initially went far better, which was only surprising at first glance. There, Borussia met opponents who, in contrast to the *Bundesliga*, didn't just park the bus, but also wanted to influence the match. The result was that Borussia won all of their first four group matches: winning against Arsenal 2–0 at home, Anderlecht 4–3 away, and defeating Galatasaray twice (4–0 in Istanbul and 4–1 in Dortmund).

'I feel like I'm on holiday – it's only Champions League,' Klopp had said in the press conference before the home match against the Gunners in light of their *Bundesliga* struggles. Against Arsène Wenger's Arsenal, Dortmund's '*Bundesliga* holiday squad' were afforded far more chances to counterattack. Klopp used a 4–4–2 formation with Aubameyang and Immobile as dual strikers to great effect: both scored shortly after the start of the second half and were praised by Klopp for their defensive work in particular: 'A rock solid performance in addition to their two goals.'

Despite the return match in London being a considerably weaker performance (Arsenal won 2–0), the *Bundesliga* club remained tied at the top of the group with Arsenal after a final 1–1 draw against Anderlecht in Signal Iduna Park. 'First place, maximum target achieved. All good,' was Klopp's staccato summary. Almost more importantly, it was the first match back after injury for Nuri Şahin after seven months out, Jakub Błaszczykowski after nine, and Oliver Kirch after four.

But away from the Champions League 'holiday', the daily grind in the *Bundesliga* continued to prove difficult despite newly increased depth. In the last match of the *Hinrunde* before the winter break, Borussia faced off against Werder Bremen. Even though Mats Hummels pulled back a goal to make the score 2–1, an equaliser wasn't on the cards. After seventeen *Bundesliga* matches Dortmund stood in seventeenth place. Following the match, Klopp told Sky: 'Any criticism levelled against us is justified. It's all correct. We have to take it. The only good news is that 2014 is over, the first half is over. I wouldn't write us off but we deserve the fact that we're standing here now like complete idiots.'

Such a run of results wasn't new to Klopp. He had previously endured a similar series of losses at Mainz in the first half of the 2006–07 season. Mainz sporting director Christian Heidel recalled that his friend had been briefly 'beaten down' by the relegation fight, but the next morning 'he came back and could have torn the stadium down with all of his pent-up energy'.

At Dortmund, the expectations – and accompanying pressure – were considerably higher. The goal at the beginning of the season had been qualification for the Champions League: this now seemed quite unrealistic for a club mired in a relegation battle. After the Bremen match, Michael Zorc, Hans-Joachim Watzke and Jürgen Klopp sat down together for eight hours to thrash out what had gone wrong. At the end of the analysis session Klopp emerged upbeat: 'If we'll finally be able to work hard with fifteen, twenty men during the winter break, we'll experience a different BVB. We'll get there.'

* * *

But after the winter break, Dortmund's start to the second of the season showed few immediate signs of improvement. The team played very cautiously during the 0–0 draw in Leverkusen and produced a surprising number of missed passes. The following match against Augsburg ended in a 1–0 home defeat, leaving Borussia bottom of the league.

This, though, turned out to be the nadir of a season to forget. Dortmund didn't remain bottom for long, as finally both the team's performance and their league position started to improve. Klopp guided Dortmund to victory in their next four league matches: away at Freiburg (3–0), at home against Mainz (4–2), away at Stuttgart (3–2) and a satisfying home derby win against Schalke (3–0). 'A relegation battle can be so simple, you just have to go about it like Borussia Dortmund,' said Christof Kneer, reporter for the daily *Süddeutsche Zeitung*, praising the fans and club leadership for never calling the manager into question. Following the enthusiastic performance against Schalke, which was reminiscent of the 'old' BVB, Dortmund had leaped up the table to tenth. The Champions League might still have been a tall order, but at least qualification for the Europa League was once again a realistic goal.

The ship had been steadied, but still virtually no one had a plausible answer as to where this remarkable sporting crash, from title contender to relegation candidate, had come from. The stress caused by the World Cup was limited for Dortmund: of the German world champions, only Mats Hummels had been consistently deployed as a starter. In contrast, Bayern contributed a far greater number of players to the national team but still had no problem starting the new season. So that couldn't have been the reason.

Klopp attempted to provide an explanation in an official illustrated book put out by the local daily *Ruhr Nachrichten*, *Jürgen Klopp – Meine Sieben Jahre in Schwarzgelb* (*My Seven Years in Black and Yellow*): 'I believe I was able to assess our situation during the sporting crisis in an increasingly realistic way: fragmented preparation, many injuries, and above all: no fit players. The ones that at some point were no longer injured, were still not completely fit in the *Hinrunde*. We frequently had six, seven players on the pitch who weren't at a 100 per cent personal fitness level. Naturally, that changes everything. And if you play increasingly poorly after a decent start, then it obviously has grave effects on the lads' self-confidence.' Klopp also argued that the team had frequently wrung out the last drop of effort in the Champions League, 'only to suffer in the *Bundesliga* three days later as a result'.

The Champions League wasn't so much of an issue in the second half of the season, with Dortmund going out in the last sixteen to Juventus. The first leg had seen Dortmund lose 2–1 in Italy, giving them a realistic chance of going through. But in Dortmund, the Italian champions were ice cold in exploiting the space offered to them by Klopp's side: Carlos Tévez scored after a mere three minutes; Álvaro Morata added a second in the seventieth minute, with Tévez putting the result beyond doubt nine minutes later. Dortmund had nothing to counteract the compact and ruthless strategy of the Italians. 'We were abysmal during the second half,' Matt Hummels said afterwards, 'so the scoreline was completely correct.' Jürgen Klopp was equally disappointed: 'That was a game to forget about. The early goal was the worst thing that could happen. We hardly got a shot off.'

Back in the *Bundesliga*, Borussia Dortmund found themselves up against the two top teams in the league. First, Bayern prevailed in a tight game at Signal Iduna Park by a solitary goal. Despite a solid display on Dortmund's behalf, Munich combined a concentrated defensive performance with a winning goal scored by Robert Lewandowski (who respectfully eschewed any celebration). Away at Borussia Mönchengladbach, meanwhile, Dortmund suffered a comprehensive 3–1 defeat. For all the improvements since the winter break, the two matches clearly demonstrated the still significant distance from Dortmund in tenth place to the top teams. Even so, what happened next was a surprise to everyone.

* * *

On 15 April 2015, a Wednesday, Borussia announced that there would be a short-notice press conference. Since November 2014, Michael Zorc and Hans-Joachim Watzke had been fearing that 'Klopp, well-known as being emotional, would resign'. Now, that decision had been made. On the podium in front of the media sat a pale Watzke to the left of Jürgen Klopp and Zorc. Watzke began his statement with the introduction that 'following Jürgen Klopp's initiative, we have conducted several intense conversations over the last few days and then reached the mutual decision that the path that we have been travelling on for seven long years with unbelievable success will come to a conclusion at the end of the season'.

Watzke gazed sorrowfully at the floor. The chairman then made clear how much he respected and admired Jürgen Klopp, not only as manager, but most of all as a person: 'It really hit the three of us, Jürgen, Michael and me. You can be sure of that. These were conversations where you could once again see that we at BVB have a focus on the big picture. Because this club is something very special, there's no doubt about that. But also that it was especially difficult for us, because we once again could see that we have a very special relationship, characterised by extreme trust and friendship. And to that extent, overall it's very difficult for us.' Watzke had to swallow, his voice faltering from time to time. 'Jürgen, you can be sure that you will have the eternal thanks of all Borussians after these fantastic successes we've achieved together and the incredible work together. The only thing that is a slight comfort to me is the fact that our friendship will surely remain.' Watzke grabbed Klopp by the shoulder. Both stood up and hugged each other.

Michael Zorc also expressed his great appreciation: 'Over the last seven years we have written a modern football fairy tale, with Jürgen Klopp playing the main role. In 2008, we weren't in good sporting condition, but you gave this club a huge amount of optimism.'

In response, Klopp took a deep breath before starting his remarks. 'This decision feels absolutely right,' he said with a firm voice. He explained there wasn't another club involved, and that he wasn't tired either, 'even if I sometimes look that way'. Rather, the club needed a new start: 'I believe that BVB needs a change. There will be other influences on the team, which will be positive.'

Without getting caught up in minutiae or naming the reasons for the unfortunate course of the season, he explained the steps professionally, saying he 'was no longer the perfect manager for this extraordinary club, which deserves to be managed by the coach who is 100 per cent perfect for it'. He argued that the club could use the great potential available without being constantly blocked by the memory of past successes. 'But then a big head has to go. And in this case it's mine.' At the end of this momentous press conference, during which he largely kept his feelings about his resignation to himself, Klopp didn't even forget to mention the next scheduled press conference, before the home match against Paderborn.

Klopp's analysis that he was no longer able to help the Dortmund squad 100 per cent was a result of the preceding months, which were difficult from a sporting perspective. He and his staff increasingly had the sense that it was difficult to further develop the team tactically. 'Within BVB there had long been differences with Klopp,' wrote Dortmund expert Freddie Rockenhaus in the *Süddeutsche Zeitung*. Rockenhaus explained further: 'Attempts to modernise were usually blown off after tentative attempts. To the end, Klopp's creed remained: "*Gegenpressing* is the best playmaker."' Correspondingly, working with the players hadn't been as seamless as before: 'With Klopp, the symptoms of fatigue were far more significant than previously indicated.'

* * *

Klopp had expressed one particular wish in parting: to 'go one more time round Borsigplatz ... that'd be pretty cool'. He wanted to give the fans one more occasion such as the title win in 2011 and the double victory in 2012, when almost the entire city had been on their feet and celebrated their heroes. From the ashes of a disappointing season, there was still a chance to make this possible. For while Dortmund had lost out in Europe and the *Bundesliga*, the DFB Cup offered Klopp a final shot at silverware.

Away from the drudgery of the league, the DFB Cup had been a source of optimism for Klopp and the club. That had been clear right from the second round match against second division St Pauli, which Dortmund won 3-0. The post-match press conference had been interrupted by a feisty woman, who with her yellow apron appeared to have scurried straight out of a stadium souvenir stall. The woman was there to encourage Jürgen Klopp, which she then proceeded to do at length in front of the assembled press: 'You carried us to victory and now we will carry you through this crisis. For me there's nothing I love more than my BVB!' 'Thank you,' a surprised Jürgen Klopp had replied, awkwardly massaging his scruffy stubble before getting up, hugging the woman and signing the books she'd brought along. 'You could say that when those types of declarations of love are necessary, then the shit's starting to get real!'

Dortmund hadn't had any problems dealing with the second division club at their Millerntor stadium, even if Jürgen Klopp had received a particularly loud chorus of boos while the teams were warming up. 'Because I mowed over Bernd Hollerbach here once?' Klopp pondered (Hollerbach and Klopp had had a coming together during Klopp's playing days at Mainz). But he took the jeers in his stride, just as Borussia did with the match itself. In fact, it had been one of Borussia's best performances of the season to date. St Pauli were as easily dispatched as third division Stuttgarter Kickers had been in the first round (4–1), and Dynamo Dresden were in the third.

The subsequent rounds proved to be more dramatic, however. In the quarter-finals, Klopp's side were drawn at home to 1899 Hoffenheim. The 80,000 fans that filled Dortmund's stands witnessed a fabulous cup game that BVB won in extra-time 3–2. Neven Subotić's opener was cancelled out by Hoffenheim's Kevin Volland. Then Aubameyang's strike was almost enough to seal it, until Roberto Firmino forced an extra thirty minutes with a goal in stoppage time. When Sebastian Kehl hit what turned out to be the winner in the 107th minute, Signal Iduna Park erupted. It was a fitting moment for another Dortmund icon nearing the end of his time at the club: captain Kehl was set to bring his career at Borussia to a close at the end of the season after nearly thirteen years of experiencing all the club's great ups and downs, front and centre. Together with Jürgen Klopp he would be given a lap of honour in front of the fans after the final home *Bundesliga* fixture against Werder Bremen.

The semi-final saw Dortmund drawn away against Bayern in a repeat of the previous year's final. It was a close match that was eventually decided by penalties. Oddly enough, both Philipp Lahm and Xabi Alonso had their standing leg slip when taking their kicks in a nearly synchronised and (for Dortmund fans) highly amusing fashion. With Mario Götze, of all people, and Manuel Neuer also missing the mark, Bayern remained without a goal from the spot, negating the miss by Mats Hummels thanks to İlkay Gündoğan and Sebastian Kehl converting. After the decisive spot-kick Klopp sprinted across the pitch in Munich's Allianz Arena to celebrate the coup with his team.

For the third time in Jürgen Klopp's era, Borussia Dortmund had reached the cup final, this time facing off against *Bundesliga* runners-up VfL Wolfsburg – the club that had taken BVB's place as the current 'second force' in German football.

All seemed set for a triumphant finale to Klopp's Dortmund career, with another victory parade to follow defeating Wolfsburg in Berlin on 30 May 2015.

Certainly, Dortmund had an excellent start in Klopp's last game as manager: Pierre-Emerick Aubameyang scored the opener in the fifth minute, before Marco Reus squandering a huge opportunity to put them two clear. But then the game turned: BVB had to watch as Wolfsburg netted three goals before half time, with Luiz Gustavo, Kevin de Bruyne and Bas Dost scoring. Although the game swung back in Dortmund's favour after half time, they couldn't convert their dominance into goals, and Wolfsburg ran out 3–1 winners.

After the final whistle, Klopp stood alone on the pitch in his trademark yellow cap. The 25,000 Dortmund fans kitted out in black and yellow cheered him on with songs, constantly calling out his name. Klopp waved back in sadness. In contrast to his emotional exit from Mainz in 2008, it seemed he didn't want to well up in public. In an interview with the television broadcaster ARD he said: 'I'm tearful every time I hug my players and think it might be the last time. It's a wonderful story that's coming to a close. But I have to process everything in order. And I'd like to sort through this when the cameras are off.'

* * *

During the party that evening in an old Berlin power station, Klopp seemed sadder than a week before during the official farewell in Signal Iduna Park at the last *Bundesliga* match against Werder Bremen. Dortmund had won 3–2 and with the resulting seventh place in the table had at least met the minimum target of Europa League qualification. In his farewell to the fans, Klopp had not been set up with a microphone in front of the South Stand as expected. Instead, he used video screens to play a speech he'd recorded before the match, repeatedly accompanied by the fans' applause.

'I didn't want people not being able to understand me with my blubbering,' Klopp explained this decision. It was self-protection after the experience of the tears leaving Mainz. Although he wasn't embarrassed after the fact, Klopp did seem to feel it was an excess of emotion aired in public. Even so the departing manager was clearly moved when the South Stand called out to him after the match, cheered him for minutes on end, with the team lining up behind him with solemn respect.

In Berlin, Watzke presented the outgoing manager with the season tickets that Klopp's wife Ulla had requested for the family. Yet in that moment it was little comfort for her husband: 'I just noticed that the pain of parting was coming. And it ruddy hurts. I hugged the lads and noticed that it was so unbelievably difficult to let them go.'

Full of gratitude, Klopp turned his attention to the people in Dortmund who had grown dear to him over the years: 'We were here for seven years. And today I can say: it's never important what people think of someone when he arrives. What's important is what people think of someone when he goes. I'd like to thank everyone for what they think now. We'll take that with us, pack it up. And regardless of where we'll land in this world: we'll never forget this.'

15

KLOPP FOR THE KOP: OFF TO NEW SHORES

In spring 2015 Jürgen Klopp announced that following the DFB Cup final against Wolfsburg, he would be taking a break from football. Regarding his time in Mainz and Dortmund, his agent Marc Kosicke said: 'Jürgen has two great loves in his past, and it's difficult to jump right into the next relationship. He wants to feel like a "single manager" and experience things with his wife that he hasn't had time for in a while. That need became increasingly strong.' Klopp's assistants Željko Buvač and Peter Krawietz also treated themselves to time off. Wherever Klopp was destined to go, it was already agreed that his faithful and wonderfully harmonious team would join him in the new task.

Before taking time off – it turned out to be a four-month break, considerably shorter than expected – Klopp had already been a manager for fourteen years. In that time, he had coached only two teams, an impressive achievement given the often-dizzying rate of churn managers now undergo. A new, exciting chapter awaited in the form of Liverpool. Would Klopp be able to continue his success story on Merseyside? The prospects seemed good: Klopp and his 'new love' looked to be a perfect match.

* * *

Jürgen Klopp and Borussia Dortmund. From the very beginning it had been something special, a flame that has yet to die. It wasn't long before the club expressed its faith in the coaching team – regardless of the position in the table. In March 2009, Dortmund extended their contracts, ahead of schedule, until 2012. It wasn't just the fact that less than a year had passed since Klopp & Co. had taken up their positions: BVB was suffering a seven-game winless streak at the time. The signal from the Dortmund board was clear: 'We're going places with this manager – and his team.' The decision was typical of the Ruhr mentality: Klopp now knew that the club would stick with their man through hard times as well as good, as long as the fundamentals were right and he was putting in an honest shift.

Sharing their conviction that hard work is the key to success, Klopp was the perfect fit for Dortmund. In a city of hard graft, gritty defensive midfielders were appreciated just as much as glamour players. Battlers like Günter Kutowski and Murdo MacLeod, two BVB legends from the 1980s and 1990s, have traditionally had a special place in the fans' hearts. Anyone who 'gets' that is all the more welcome.

The next surprise came in 2010, when the coaching staff's contracts were extended again. There were rumours that Dortmund wanted to head off potential interest from Bayern Munich. After all, Germany's top club had considered appointing Klopp in 2008 before plumping for Jürgen Klinsmann. 'We would have signed practically anything,' Klopp said about the new contract extension, his youthful grin on display as he put on record how close the relationship between the coaching staff and the club had become since 2008. 'From day one we've felt that something big is happening here and we want to stay on that track.'

The triumvirate of Chairman Hans-Joachim Watzke, sporting director Michael Zorc and coach Jürgen Klopp presented an impressive picture of professional solidarity for their entire time together. It was a relationship that symbolised: 'You couldn't get a sheet of paper between us.' Making contradictory statements and internal debate public? Not in Dortmund. All three were committed to a common club line. On a personal level, too, the relationship between the club's leaders was sound.

By summer 2014, Klopp had been in the Dortmund hot seat for six years – just as long as Ottmar Hitzfeld, without doubt one of the greatest managers in the club's history. Hitzfeld had held the club record for longest serving manager. He was at the Westphalians' helm from 1991 to 1997, in which time he reached the final of the UEFA Cup, brought home the league trophy twice and won the Champions League. Klopp went on to exceed even his longevity.

But then came the big bang: Wednesday 15 April 2015. Klopp gave a press conference with Watzke and Zorc and revealed that he had asked Borussia Dortmund to release him from his contract, which was due to run until 2018. They had agreed, and he was set to leave at the end of the season. Sure, the season following the World Cup in Brazil in 2014 hadn't been the greatest for BVB, and speculation that Klopp was running on fumes had been rife. But still, the timing – just as Dortmund were starting to find their feet again – came as a shock. It seemed as if the entire city needed a couple of days to gather itself, so inseparably close had the bond between club, city and coach been for the past seven years.

Klopp and his team seemed to be more motivated than ever after his departure had been announced. When the apparent car crash of a season hit the final straight, Dortmund gathered momentum and finished high enough to qualify for next season's Europa League, and reached the DFB Cup final.

But what was Klopp's future going to look like after his self-imposed timeout? Would he follow Hitzfeld's example and follow his successful era at BVB with a switch to Bayern Munich? Take charge at an elite Italian, Spanish or English team?

Liverpool was soon in the running as a possible employer. It was a cult club not unlike Borussia Dortmund: down to earth, passionate, steeped in tradition. And its manager Brendan Rodgers was increasingly in the firing line thanks to disappointing results.

* * *

All was quiet on the Klopp front during the 2015 summer break. Following his emotional departure from Dortmund, he took a break as planned, went on holiday and bade the headlines farewell. One thing that didn't go away was speculation about the next chapter in the Klopp saga. What was the right club for him – the right challenge? A manager in the Premiership has more responsibility for paperwork than a German coach would be used to, but a position in England still seemed more logical than a move to glamour club such as Real Madrid. With staff turnover akin to a call centre and no patience for team building, did Real really sound like Klopp's cup of tea? Not to mention that his Spanish-language skills didn't exceed 'Una cerveza, por favor.' Or should he take the Germany job if Joachim Löw decided to throw in the towel after Euro 2016?

The buffet was open, and Bayern wasn't the only team looking tasty in the *Bundesliga* section – he was especially interested in other clubs that would provide a real challenge. Taking a down-on-its-luck club back to the top, like he had done with Borussia Dortmund: that was what turned Klopp on. And, much earlier than expected, that desire was going to lead him to Liverpool.

Suddenly everything kicked into motion. The in-demand German had just turned down the Mexico job when Liverpool let Brendan Rodgers go at the beginning of October 2015, after a shaky start to the season. Klopp was presented as the new manager within days, to the excitement of the supporters, who had practically longed their 'saviour' into office. His charismatic and entertaining press-conference performance before Champions League ties against Arsenal, along with his almost fluent English and that hearty laugh, had won English hearts as much as his tactics had won minds. After all, his unforced, spontaneous, jovial style stood in stark contrast to the buttoned-up reserve of some of his fellow managers.

Klopp had won the hearts of Liverpool fans in particular when, in 2014, he had placed his hand on the famous 'This is Anfield' sign in the tunnel, almost caressing it, before a friendly match between Liverpool and Dortmund. He was expressing his respect and esteem for the club – just like the home players do before walking onto the pitch. Delighted Pool fans started a Twitter trend, #KloppForTheKop, to bring their man home. Clearly, it worked.

* * *

After successful negotiations with Liverpool FC and signing a three-year contract, Klopp was presented as the Reds' new manager on Friday 9 October in an instantly legendary press conference that distilled the essence of the Klopp legend: 'The first one I've ever really prepared for,' the improv artist revealed. Full of good humour, it soon became clear that even after four months out of the game and speaking a foreign language, he had lost none of his easy charm. He was asked how he would describe himself, compared to José Mourinho, the self-ordained 'special one'. His answer: he was from the Black Forest, had been an average player, then he had started out as an average coach in Mainz. 'My mother may be sitting in front of the television and watching this press conference and understand no word until now. But she is very proud.' Recalling José Mourinho, he then added a trademark Klopp comment: 'I am the normal one.' The assembled press fell about laughing.

The man at the press conference not just the standard, carefree Klopp. He looked more like the thinner, athletic golden boy of the past, and one could well believe that he had already fully recovered from the stresses and strains of fourteen intense years at the helm of Mainz and Dortmund. 'I'm forty-eight, yes, most of the time in my life I had no money to make holiday, and on next day I had no time, and now I had four months. So it was really cool.' Plenty of time to play tennis and watch football all over the world.

He had chosen Liverpool not for its similarities with Borussia Dortmund, he claimed, but simply because it was a 'great club'. Klopp promised 'emotional football' – which would perfectly suit the spirit of Anfield – and the kind of full-throttle 'heavy metal' game he was known for in Dortmund. He revealed that he had looked up the translation for *Umschaltspiel* – 'transition game'. It was a core component of his playing philosophy, and one to which he was going to stay true at Liverpool. Klopp disclosed his weakness for romantic football: 'Anfield is one of the best places in the football world, for sure ... now I'm here. It seems to be I'm a real lucky guy.'

Although Klopp made no secret of the fact that he was there to win trophies, he was careful to try to keep expectations realistic and claimed not to be a miracle worker: 'Does anyone here think that I can do wonders?' Klopp's ability to mix humility, energy and hype makes him continually fascinating. He added, to the sound of laughter from the assembled journalists, 'Everyone has told me about the British press. It's up to you to tell me they are all liars!'

Praise for Klopp's first official appearance as Liverpool's manager was fulsome. Champions League-winning legend John Arne Riise captured the euphoric mood via Twitter: 'Never ever seen a better press conference from a new manager! The energy, how he speaks, everything! Give this guy time! What a man!'

* * *

Like Klopp, Karl-Heinz Riedle he has worn both colours: the black and yellow of Borussia Dortmund and the red of Liverpool. A BVB player from 1993 to 1997, the aerially dominant 'Air Riedle' won the league twice and scored twice in the 3–1 Champions League final win against Juventus in his final season. He then switched to Liverpool until 1999. Despite being somewhat overshadowed by Michael Owen's emergence, Riedle's vast treasure trove of experience made him a mentor to the young superstar. Now fifty-one and an international brand ambassador for Borussia Dortmund, Riedle is still in touch with Owen, Steve McManaman and other Liverpool stars of the day. With the new manager in place, Riedle was the perfect man to turn to for an opinion.

On Klopp and Liverpool ... 'A perfect fit. Klopp stands for passionate, emotional football, direct and high tempo. That's what Liverpool wants to see.'

On Liverpool and Dortmund ... 'Equally passionate about football: people feel the same, football is like a religion.'

On the dreaded transfer committee Klopp would encounter at Anfield ... 'Klopp will have insisted on having the final say. After all, as far as results are concerned, it's his head on the line. It would be counterproductive to give him players against his will who might not even suit his system.'

On Klopp's first season ... 'Difficult, simply because the team isn't at the same level as it used to be. They don't have the quality to challenge for the title, and they've missed a lot of injured players.'

On managing with managing ... 'Klopp will have to be more of an organiser than he was in Dortmund, where Michael Zorc and Hans-Joachim took a lot of the off the pitch work off his hands. Given the large size of the coaching team though, this shouldn't be a problem, they can divide the workload in training among them.'

On adopting Dortmund's style of 'full-throttle football' and pressing high up the pitch ... 'Klopp will show restraint and modify his tactics, because the season is longer in England than in Germany and there's no winter break. So he'll have to find a compromise to avoid burning his players out with too much intensity. But I'm sure he knows what needs to be done.'

* * *

Klopp and Pool: a promising combination. For starters, he already spoke English – an elementary requirement for coaches in general, but Klopp in particular is known for his close relationships with his players. Also, Liverpool is like Dortmund in that both clubs are known for their highly emotional fans as well as their legendary football – a match made in heaven for a man as passionate as Klopp. He would be able to enjoy that emotion at close hand in a stadium where the fans are practically on top of the pitch. Both Dortmund and Liverpool are big businesses with corporate interests, but both are also classic workers' clubs (miners in Germany and dockers in England) and offer a comparable sense of family and belonging. They share a romantic, emotionally driven football culture, fuelled by the unshakable devotion of their supporters – epitomised by the *Südtribune* (South Stand) in Dortmund and the smaller but no less legendary Anfield Kop.

Both clubs value the development of their own local talent rather than relying on buying readymade stars. Klopp proved in Dortmund that he was capable of developing talented players into internationals such as World Cup-winner Mario Götze. Robert Lewandowski, Klopp's former number nine whom he turned into a world-class striker, summed it up: 'Klopp recognises talent and he backs talent. He doesn't just want to buy players; he has an eye out for youngsters who can help him put his ideas into practice.'

In terms of the league, the situation facing Klopp was similar too. Liverpool were bobbing along in tenth place at the time Klopp took over. When he moved to Dortmund, they had been drifting aimlessly in the mid-table doldrums. Within three years, they were champions. If he could manage the same for Liverpool, he might be even more idolised than he was in Dortmund. The supporters had been longing for their nineteenth title since 1990 – an eternity for a team that had dominated football in the 1970s and 1980s. Worse, in terms on the number of league titles, they had been overhauled by arch-rivals Manchester United in 2011. So there was a similar job to accomplish at Anfield as there had been in Dortmund – and that's exactly why Klopp wanted to be there: to wake the sleeping giant and make it great again.

Wherever expectations are high, the fall back down to earth can be fatal if things don't go according to plan, which is why Klopp lost no time in injecting a note of realism at his first press conference. Probably in vain. The question was, how much time would the fans, the club and the media give him if results didn't match up to expectations straight away? In Dortmund, two years of mental and physical toil had preceded the harvest in terms of honours. There, it was understood that tiny acorns do not make mighty oaks overnight, but what about Anfield? Three draws in his first three matches in charge – two in the Premier League, one in the Europa League – weren't exactly the dream start everyone had been hoping for. The performances were just as disappointing as the results.

Already, questions were being asked about how long the process of getting Liverpool back on course was going to take. Had it really been fair of him to question his players' 'bravery' after conceding a late equaliser to Southampton in the league? That was never his intention, Klopp said, but his team's body language had bothered him. He felt misunderstood, admitting that his English vocabulary wasn't yet extensive enough to express every single nuance. The honeymoon had quickly given way to reality. 'I'm sorry,' he said, unusually subdued. However, he was right to point out, 'If you are new in a club, normally you have more time, but if you don't you have to accept that the way is hard.'

As he'd said from the very beginning, not even he could work miracles. Especially not with the unsettled squad he had taken over with the season already well underway. The number of injuries also made life more difficult. He needed to get to know his players and transmit his ideas – a process that would have to be done progressively.

* * *

Ex-pro Thomas Helmer, fifty-two, who appeared nearly 400 times for Borussia Dortmund and Bayern Munich, wasn't surprised that Klopp was having teething troubles on the other side of the Channel. 'Klopp took over the team without any preparation and without knowing the players well. Nevertheless, I still believe it will be a successful collaboration as long as they give him time to make the team in his image. Sure, there is an enormous amount of hype surrounding Jürgen Klopp. Still, as far as mentality is concerned he's a good fit for LFC. Everyone will tell you he's a solid bloke, who's easy to get along with. And he really knows how to market himself.'

For all the similarities between Klopp's two latest clubs, Helmer could see differences too: 'The connection between the fans and the club is even more intense than in Dortmund, if that's possible. The expectations are also significantly higher in Liverpool than they were when Klopp took over at Dortmund in 2008.' Indeed, while BVB had been on the brink of total financial breakdown just a few short years before, Liverpool had been in an increasingly powerful financial position – thanks to American investors Fenway Sports Group and a slice of the Premier League's enormous TV revenues.

Helmer, who was a European Championship winner with Germany in 1996, played out the autumn of his career in England: the 1999–2000 season with promoted Sunderland. 'That's when I got to know the unique atmosphere in British stadiums: you'll often hear a murmur running round the stands, and there's always a massive cheer when the teams run on the pitch. It's the sort of atmosphere that an emotional kind of guy like Klopp should thrive on.' Helmer only ever played twice in the league for Sunderland. 'Peter Reid told me that I had the best attitude he'd ever seen in a professional footballer, but he hardly ever let me play. He never told me why.'

During Helmer's time 'the manager was hardly ever on the training pitch. He used to delegate instead and gave a lot of responsibility to his coaches.' It was common practice both then and now, because in comparison to the German model, a manager in the Premier League has much more responsibility. Helmer speculated that Klopp would have asked to be allowed to concentrate purely on sporting matters.

Helmer pointed out that Klopp would face another difference in football culture, at least at the beginning: 'In the past there was a question mark over Klopp and his ability to deal with top stars and their egos.' Not that Dortmund had been a team without stars, but the 'Klopp Doctrine' of focused play and a shared team mentality had been drilled into his players for years, which made the team and not the individual the star.

* * *

Klopp's first victory with the Reds came with a 1–0 win over Bournemouth in the fourth round of the League Cup, and there were already signs that he was making his mark. The manager was living up to his reputation for blooding young talent: both Cameron Brannagan (nineteen) and Connor Randall (twenty) made their full professional debuts. 'I had seen these players train for two weeks and I knew I would play them the first chance I had,' Klopp told the *Daily Mail*.

As a skilled psychologist, Klopp eased the pair's nerves before the match by telling them that he was playing them because he wanted to win. The youngsters paid their coach back with convincing performances. After the game, Brannagan was thrilled by Klopp's human qualities as well as the footballing faith shown in the pair: 'He trusts us.' The 'normal one' can be special too.

The 3–1 away win on 31 October – satisfyingly, at José Mourinho's Chelsea – was interpreted as the first significant step forward in the process of learning Klopp's playing philosophy. 'Stamford Bridge is falling down,' sang the Liverpool fans. The press picked up on the chants and the manager's wild gesticulations on the touchline. Gesticulations that drove Chelsea assistant coach, José Morais, so far up the wall that he jumped up and swore at Klopp, who cooly recommended that he 'Take a timeout.'

As cool as he was on that occasion, Klopp's effervescent temperament didn't remain hidden in England for long. Ian Doyle wrote in the *Liverpool Echo*: 'It's Klopp who is the new people's favourite. The normal one has usurped the special one. There's something honest and endearing about the manner in which the German bounces along the touchline, kicking every ball, living every challenge and celebrating a goal as if it was the last one that will ever be scored – although any more going almost nose-to-nose with the fourth official, as he did yesterday, will probably be more than frowned upon.' Klopp is Klopp, even in England.

However, while the success at Stamford Bridge was hailed as a turning point, it proved to be nothing of the sort. The reigning champions were a shadow of their old selves and Mourinho would soon be out on his ear. Interim manager Guus Hiddink managed to drag them away from the spectre of a relegation battle to finish tenth.

Liverpool – classic Liverpool – started to drop points against the 'little teams'. Particularly bitter for Klopp was the 2–1 home defeat to Crystal Palace just a week after the triumph at Chelsea – it was Klopp's first defeat, in his seventh game in charge. It wasn't so much the loss itself as the circumstances: after Scott Dann headed Palace into the lead in the eighty-second minute, the fans started to leave in droves. Klopp wasn't happy: 'I turned around and I felt pretty alone at this moment ... between eighty-two and ninety-four you can make eight goals, if you want, but you have to work for it.' The message had got through. 'That is what we have to show and we didn't, and things are like they are. We decide when it is over.'

That Klopp, a new manager in unfamiliar surroundings, had the balls to call a spade a spade and even criticise Liverpool's own fans, cleverly packaged as feeling abandoned, earned him a lot of respect. Klopp had touched a nerve and challenged the Liverpool supporters' pride – after all, you'll never walk alone.

The next matchday made it clear that, under Klopp, Liverpool were on a rollercoaster. At least in the first few months he was in charge, the only certainty was uncertainty. The 4–1 win over league leaders Manchester City was a textbook example of the effectiveness of the 'Klopp press', but also proof that Liverpool had a much easier time of it against offensive teams that left space behind. Liverpool often seemed to lack a strategy when it came to breaking down teams that chose to sit and concede space to them, especially at Anfield. As a result, Liverpool often seemed to be bogged down at home, while away, where as a rule the home fans weren't prepared to watch their team defend for ninety minutes, they seemed to have the wind at their back.

Such was the case in their 6–1 thrashing of Southampton in the League Cup quarter-final, the hosts' worst home defeat since 1959. As the BBC noted, they just didn't stop pressing all match. The funny thing was that Southampton had scored after just forty seconds. It was like a red rag to a bull. After seeing his team putting on a goal festival, a grinning Klopp quipped that you don't come to Liverpool for the weather.

At the same time, he was keen to dampen down the euphoria and point out that there was nothing magical about the mini four-game winning streak of the past few weeks – it was hard work paying off. The proof that there really wasn't any magic at work came sooner than he would have hoped. Four days later, Liverpool lost 2–0 defeat to second-from-bottom Newcastle, followed a week later by an equally sobering 2–2 draw with West Bromwich Albion at Anfield. At least Belgian forward Divock Origi, who Klopp had once wanted to bring to Dortmund, had managed to rescue a point in the sixth minute of injury time.

Yet that wasn't the most memorable thing about the match. England's football community got to taste raw Klopp for the first time: emotionally unrestrained to the point of explosive rage. What happened? West Brom's Craig Gardner caught Liverpool defender Dejan Lovren, who had already missed a month of the season with an ankle injury. The Croatian international screamed in pain after the blow to the knee and, bleeding, had to be treated on the pitch before being stretchered off and taken to hospital. No laughing matter for Klopp. His face distorted by righteous anger, he hurled a few choice words at West Brom boss Tony Pulis.

When Origi's deflected strike from distance managed to find its way into the net deep in injury time, Klopp erupted. Provocatively close to the away dugout and Tony Pulis, he didn't hold back on his celebrations and fired up the crowd. Funnily enough, Origi had replaced Lovren in the seventy-ninth minute. In the end, Lovren could count himself lucky: his injury proved much less severe than first feared and he missed only one game before being able to play again.

Many found Klopp's behaviour immediately after the final whistle difficult to swallow: not only did he refuse to shake Pulis's hand, he also celebrated the win ... err, draw ... by jollying the entire team along with him to salute the Kop. It might have been par for the course in front of the South Stand in Dortmund, but here it came across as utterly foreign. A home draw against a mid-table team was hardly a champagne moment.

The chastised manager couldn't understand what all the fuss was about. In his eyes, he and the team had only wanted to thank the fans for some fantastic support and the best atmosphere since he'd arrived. Sometimes, an honestly earned point said more about a club's development than a win. 'It was only one point but it felt like three. This moment, it was an explosion,' Klopp explained at the post-match press conference. Regarding the infamous snubbed handshake: 'Usually I shake hands. I did not today because it was not a friendly game.' He had exchanged a few words with Pulis and needed more than just a couple of seconds after the final whistle to calm down.

The volcano had erupted once again. On the one hand, it was understandable: the style of play that West Brom indulged in affronted his sense of fair play. Many of the fans had nothing but praise for Klopp – they could see that their manager was just as passionate about Liverpool as they were. Seen in a different light, though, it was hard to quantify the 'normal one's' reaction as 'normal'. A few days later, Klopp apologised to Pulis for his choice of words during the match. 'I can only say sorry for what I said during the game ... I am emotional during the game and sometimes during the game you say things you would not say in normal life.' However, he stuck by his management style: 'Up until now I couldn't stop it. Not my coaching, I don't want to stop my coaching.'

* * *

Klopp may have been having a little wobble, but he was about to receive a tremendous vote of confidence from Steven Gerrard, the

Liverpool legend who, including youth teams, spent twenty-six years in red and won the Champions League in 2005. 'I had coffee with him and when I came out of the room I just felt happy. I felt taller,' Gerrard, another victim of the manager's huge charisma, told the *Evening Standard*. 'The atmosphere at the club is brilliant. I love the way he handles his team and I am all over his tactics.' The long-time Liverpool captain regretted not being able to play under him. 'If I was a player at Liverpool – either a young player or one at my peak – and Jurgen Klopp walked through the door I would be licking my lips.' Stevie G had discovered Klopp in the same way as many other English football fans: 'I loved how charismatic he was on camera, I loved his tactics and I always appreciated Borussia Dortmund, who I watched quite closely in the Champions League.'

Speculation as to Gerrard's future role at Liverpool FC started before he even hung up his boots with LA Galaxy at the end of 2016. With the youth team? Or assistant manager? Klopp made it clear that the door at Anfield was open. It didn't take long. In February 2017, Gerrard joined the academy coaching staff. By May, Klopp was telling the *Times*: 'It's perfect that we can involve Steven. What a guy, he's fantastic!'

* * *

Klopp's first months in Liverpool didn't reach rock bottom with the draw against West Brom, but a week later away to promoted and on-form Watford. At 2–0 down with just a quarter of an hour gone, Liverpool put in an abject performance and conceded again shortly before full-time. Beaten three-nil and three games without a win in the league, it left them in ninth place five days before Christmas. When Klopp had taken over in October, they had been tenth. Stagnation. Nothing very jolly about that. Klopp had spiked critics' guns by warning that it would take time to put his ideas into practice. It was doubtful that he was happy about being proved right.

The inconsistency of Liverpool's performances remained the only constant. Just a week after that disappointing setback, Liverpool defeated Leicester, the side that would miraculously become champions that season. It was confirmation that Klopp's side had an easier time against forward-thinking teams. A shadow was cast over the Boxing day win by an injury to Divock Origi – yet another hamstring problem. They had been piling up since Klopp had taken over. 'Hamstring is the shit word of the year for me. It's always hamstring, hamstring, hamstring,' he complained. And there was no end in sight: by January 2016, ten of his players had picked up hamstring injuries.

The litany of injuries drew criticism of Klopp's possibly too demanding, energy-sapping pressing game. According to the naysayers, the Premier League was just too tough for it to work for any length of time. Club legend and Sky pundit Graeme Souness warned against wearing the players out: 'All the talk was "we're going to be energetic, we're going to be high press at every opportunity". That demands real fitness.' A balance had to be found between training the Klopp way and playing two or three times a week. 'The sports medicine people, they'll be tearing their hair out. They've got to manage that better because that can ruin your season.'

Klopp took responsibility for the frequent injuries and announced that he would re-evaluate the intensiveness of his training sessions. The Premier League turned out to be a learning experience for him and his coaching staff, after all. Repeated moaning about the pressure caused by the packed playing schedule – especially during the *Bundesliga*'s winter break – came across as an excuse. The grand old man of English football, Arsène Wenger, advised him to adapt to the circumstances: demands might be big nowadays, but so were the squads. Klopp soon learned to adapt more and lament less.

Liverpool's position remained unsatisfactory in January. Yes, they were just two points off a Europa League spot, but they seemed incapable of putting together the winning streak that would actually get them there. They were stuck in ninth. But that didn't imply any lack of drama – especially not when facing another newly promoted club, Norwich City. When they were 3–1 down at Carrow Road in the fifty-fourth minute, it looked like the Reds were heading for another defeat. Yet Jordan Henderson immediately struck back and with quarter of an hour to go, goals from Roberto Firmino and James Milner had put Liverpool in the lead, only for the Canaries to equalise in injury time. Game over? In injury time of injury time, Adam Lallana volleyed home to have the final say – unleashing celebrations so wild that Christian Benteke knocked Klopp's glasses off. Klopp: 'It's difficult looking for glasses without glasses!'

There was more sensational games to come that season, and not just in the league. Anticipation was already building for the later rounds of the Europa League.

* * *

February 2016 wasn't proving to be the best of times. Klopp had to have his appendix removed, but he wouldn't let emergency surgery stop him, discharging himself from hospital and quipping: 'I have a few holes in my body so hopefully the water will stay in!' With their manager missing the match at home to Sunderland, the Reds surrendered a 2–0 lead to draw 2–2, accompanied by another early rush for the exits. Around 10,000 supporters left the stadium in the seventy-seventh minute, but this time not because of anything happening on the pitch: they were protesting against a planned increase in ticket prices. Season tickets were set to be priced at more than £1,000 for the first time and the most expensive matchday seats in the new Main Stand would cost £77 – hence the protest in the seventy-seventh minute. Angry supporters chanted, 'Enough is enough you greedy bastards,' at the club's owners. The banners read: 'Football without fans is nothing.'

Klopp returned to the fray only three days after his operation, and he must have been asking himself what surgery he needed to perform on his team after West Ham knocked them out of the FA Cup. 'Liverpool in this moment is not the most sunny side.'

Still, the supporters could pat themselves on the back for getting their message heard. Before any more protests could take place, the owners conceded and called off the price increases. There would be no premium price for matches against top clubs, and the most expensive tickets would remain £59. The owners announced penitently: 'It has been a tumultuous week ... part of the ticketing plan we got wrong ... Message received.' The people had spoken. Klopp had been unusually quiet during the ticket-price controversy and kept any mention of it diplomatic to avoid complicating the situation any further. Besides, the manager didn't want to place himself in any crossfire between the owners and the fans.

Before February could spring another disappointment, a 6–0 Valentine's Day drubbing of Aston Villa at Villa Park joyously confirmed the Reds' prowess on the counter in away games. Still, the two-point gap to the European places remained. A longed-for win in the Merseyside derby would have done nicely, but that would have to wait, postponed because of the League Cup final, in which Liverpool would face Manchester City. Liverpool had reached Wembley by beating Stoke on penalties.

For the German, the Wembley final meant returning to the spot where he had lost the 2013 Champions League final against Bayern. And City were having the best of this match, too, taking the lead shortly after the restart through a Fernandinho goal. Yet Pool had discovered some bounce-back-ability under Klopp, and Coutinho equalised in the eighty-third minute to take the game into extra-time. Goalless. Now it would come down to penalties again. Lucas, Coutinho and Lallana all missed as City won the shootout 4–2. The loss was to prove doubly annoying for Liverpool as it meant losing out on automatic qualification for the Europa League.

Revenge was a dish best served warm for Liverpool, because their very next league fixture was against City. It was a completely different game with Liverpool running out clear winners by three goals to nil. 'Only silly idiots stay on the floor and wait for the next defeat,' Klopp had said defiantly after the final – a lesson his players had been quick to learn.

The Reds were doing well in the Europa League that spring. In contrast to many Premier League managers, who looked on the Europa League as a competition fit for giving the reserves a run-out, Klopp's line-ups left no doubt that he was taking the competition seriously: he was in it to win it. A wafer-thin margin saw them progress through the round of thirty-two against Augsburg (0–0 and 1–0). It was Klopp's first trip to Germany as Liverpool manager, but it was thin gruel, and they'd been lucky to keep a clean sheet in Augsburg.

The Europa League really got going in the round-of-sixteen tie against arch-rivals Manchester United, led by Louis van Gaal, which Klopp dubbed 'the mother of all games'. He was familiar with the Dutchman from his days managing Bayern Munich. Liverpool took the tie with surprising ease, winning 2–0 at Anfield, fired on for the full ninety minutes by a fantastic atmosphere, before closing it out 1–1 at Old Trafford. The first leg had left its mark on an effusive Klopp: 'The atmosphere tonight was unbelievable. It was really great and I want to say thank you to everyone who was involved in this atmosphere. It was easy to enjoy from the first to the last second. That was Liverpool how I knew it before I came here, so that was really, really great. Thank you for this.' Little did he know at that point how intense the famous Anfield atmosphere was going to be in the next round, for the scriptwriter wasn't afraid of being too obvious: coming up next, Borussia Dortmund.

* * *

Liverpool headed for Dortmund for the first leg of the tie at Signal Iduna Park, where the fans gave Klopp a warm but restrained welcome. It was the first time since 2006, when he was at Mainz 05, that he had sat in the opposition dugout. A chill was about to run down everyone's spine as both sets of fans gave their all to 'You'll Never Walk Alone'.

In a comparatively unspectacular game, which provided little justification for the enormous media circus of the previous weeks, the guests took the lead through Origi with the first half starting to draw to a close. Milner beat Mats Hummels in the air to set the Belgian up to shrug off Łukasz Piszczek and fire into the bottom-left corner from the edge of the box. Just before the end of the half, Origi almost latched onto the ball to add a second, only to be denied by an alert BVB keeper, Roman Weidenfeller.

Borussia Dortmund had dominated possession in the first half but hadn't put it to good. But the second half began promisingly for them: Hummels headed in after a short corner and a cross from Henrikh Mkhitaryan. Coutinho almost responded immediately but Weidenfeller made another fine save. The life went out of the game as it went on, both sides holding back, more afraid of conceding on the counter than they were interested in winning. The 1–1 scoreline meant that anything was possible in the second leg a week later – and how true that was to prove to be!

The evening began with a special, respectful moment: both sets of fans once again united in singing 'You'll Never Walk Alone', this time in memory of the victims of the Hillsborough disaster of 1989, when ninety-six fans lost their lives and hundreds more were injured. The return leg took place on 14 April 2016, one day before the twenty-seventh anniversary of the tragedy. The behaviour of Liverpool and Borussia Dortmund fans that night would later be acknowledged by FIFA, who gave them the FIFA Fan Award. Torsten Schild, the representative of the Dortmund fans, dedicated the award to the ninety-six.

As soon as the game got underway, Dortmund demonstrated the focus that they had lacked in the first leg and took a 2–0 lead through Mkhitaryan and Pierre-Emerick Aubameyang after just nine minutes. The match had barely begun and Liverpool needed three goals to reach the next round. With the hosts having to attack and leaving space for Dortmund to counter into, the game opened up. There were no more goals before the break, but one was to come just after the restart. Klopp had sent his team back onto the field early to show that they were ready to fight on. And indeed, Origi slotted the ball through Weidenfeller's legs in the 48th minute. Dortmund weren't slow to answer, though, and nine minutes later Marco Reus restored their advantage. Game over. Surely.

But then the Reds, as they had done in so many legendary European games at Anfield, pressed the turbo-charge button. Momentarily in a state of shock, Klopp reacted by bringing on Joe Allen and Daniel Sturridge for Lallana and Firmino. After a one-two with Milner, Coutinho struck to pull a goal back – a glimmer of hope with twenty-five minutes to play. Anfield awoke and ceaselessly drove the players forward. Dortmund were struggling to relieve the pressure now. In the seventy-seventh minute, Mamadou Sakho was left criminally unmarked at a corner and nodded in from the edge of the six-yard box. Level! Klopp was in fist-pumping mood now. Twelve minutes left and there was electricity in the air. 'You could feel it, hear it, smell it,' Klopp said. The storm was breaking on Dortmund and Liverpool were delivering the thunderbolts.

The ninety minutes were up. Injury time. Milner received the ball from Sturridge in the box and hustled to the byline before digging out a cross that powerful centre-back Dejan Lovren towered to head home: 4–3! Lovren ran towards the corner flag to celebrate with the fans, who were in ecstasy. The Kop went wild.

But it wasn't over yet. The last act of the game would come courtesy of Ilkay Gündoğan with a chance to score the crucial away goal from his free-kick. Klopp looked on with clenched teeth as the ball passed painfully close to the left stick. The referee blew his whistle. That really was it, and the adrenaline-soaked Liverpool fans sang, danced, screamed, hugged, all at once. It was an eruption of emotion. The away end was as quiet as a dodo. The fans in black and yellow couldn't believe what they had just seen.

After exhaustive celebrations with the Liverpool fans, Klopp turned to the away fans to acknowledge the Dortmund contingent as well. Some were applauding him, but others were so frustrated that their ex-coach, of all people, had twisted the knife that their raw disappointment was plain for him to see. Once he saw their furious, hostile reaction, he turned back again.

It was a match characterised by breathtaking pace and high drama. A compelling duel that ended as it had started, with a passionate rendition of 'You'll Never Walk Alone', this time, though, sung only by those wearing red. In the post-match interview, BVB boss Thomas Tuchel attempted to explain what had happened: 'We must be fair and admit that after going 3–1 up we no longer coped with how much risk Liverpool were playing with. At a certain point, they were completely driven by emotion.' Dortmund had lost faith in their own game as the momentum and emotional power swung away from them, and they had fallen to a 'lucky punch'. Captain Mats Hummels found the defeat equally hard to take in: 'We suddenly got the jitters. We gave it away.' Even Borussia Dortmund struggled to cope with the Kop.

Tuchel's predecessor was in quite a different mood: 'The best half hour that I've had in football.' He recalled the evening some months later in an interview with the *Liverpool Echo*. 'I'm a really lucky guy. I had wonderful atmospheres at Mainz and at Dortmund but the last half an hour at Anfield that night was the best I have ever had. It wouldn't have been possible, no chance, without the crowd. That's for sure. If the game happened again and you switched off the sound in the stadium, then no chance we win. It's not just about the noise, it's more, it's about the vibe, everything. You could catch it. It was outstanding. I loved it.'

Strangely, when the winning goal went in, Klopp had appeared almost detached from proceedings as if he couldn't believe what was happening. Only after a delay, in which he seemed to observe the chaotic celebrations around him, did he too let the emotion out. Divock Origi revealed to the TV cameras that Klopp had played his part on that magical night. His half-time team talk had clearly hit the right nerve: 'The manager told us we had to create the moment to tell our grandchildren and make this a special night here for the fans. We believed in it.'

That night, 14 April 2016, was when Klopp truly arrived at his new sporting home. The doubters, encouraged by Liverpool's stagnation in the league, had been silenced. The *Sun* wrote that it was 'the day Jurgen Klopp completed his journey from yellow to red'.

His success at Anfield was sweet, but there was a bitter aftertaste: it had come at the cost of his old love.

* * *

The rest of the 2015–16 Premier League season was an anti-climax for Klopp after his duel with Dortmund. Liverpool were still within touching distance of a European place, but could never quite close the gap. On 6 March, having beaten Crystal Palace 2–1 away and with a game in hand, the Reds were well-placed in seventh. But their attempts to build a solid foundation crumbled again when a 2–0 lead away at Southampton turned into a 3–2 defeat, and a 1–1 home draw with Tottenham produced just one point from a possible six. Hopes were revived gain with three wins, including a thumping 4–0 triumph in the Merseyside derby, so it looked like Europe might yet be within their grasp.

Or maybe not. When it came to the crunch, Liverpool choked, throwing away a two-goal lead to draw 2–2 with Newcastle and only managing a 1–1 draw with Chelsea. The Reds needed Southampton to slip up on the final day of the season – but their hope was in vain. Liverpool ended 2015–16 with another draw against West Brom and missed Europa League qualification by one place and two points. That left a mixed report card at the end of Premiership term. Klopp had taken over a team in tenth place and led them to eighth. His record in the league was thirteen wins, nine draws and eight defeats. Klopp's Liverpool took 1.6 points per game, whereas over the course of his tenure Brendan Rodgers had achieved 1.9.

* * *

One factor that stood in Klopp's favour was his team's performance in the cups. As well as reaching the League Cup final, Liverpool were still in contention in the Europa League in the last throes of the season, and Spain's Villarreal CF, the Yellow Submarine, awaited them in the semi-final.

There was no clear favourite. The Spaniards were undefeated in eleven games in the competition – since their opening group game – while Liverpool hadn't been beaten in their entire Europa League season, but that was to change in the first leg in Spain. The teams mostly neutralised each other, with few chances being created in a match lacking incident. A typical draw, then. But this time, injury time was to prove Liverpool's enemy. Adrian Lopez's ninety-second-minute winner meant that, if Villareal scored at Anfield in the second leg, the Reds would need to score three to reach the final. Still, if there was one thing Klopp's team was good at, it was comebacks. Klopp was quick to declare after the defeat: 'It's only the first half. It's 1–0, they have to come to Anfield and they know how strong we are.'

The Spanish visitors had the better start to the second leg, though they squandered two chances. They were soon to regret that profligacy when Bruno Soriano turned a Firmino cross into his own net; the tie was level after just seven minutes. From then on it was all red – *El Submarino Amarillo* had dived for cover – but it was to take until the sixty-third minute for Liverpool to add a second, with Sturridge putting them ahead. Villarreal's resistance was finally broken when Victor Ruiz received a red card, leaving them playing with ten men for the last quarter of the game, and Lallana scored a third.

While Villarreal clearly lacked the will to fight to the last on the pitch, that wasn't the case in the technical area, with Klopp and fellow manager Marcelino having to be separated by the fourth official. It got personal during the post-match press conference: 'Klopp is who he is,' Marcelino said. 'A great coach, but in the regards to the rest, I won't keep it to myself – I wouldn't want to be like him. Today, he went too far with his celebrations.'

What did he mean? The whistle had already blown, the players were already heading down the tunnel, and Klopp was celebrating with the fans. The Spaniard might have seen it as an insult, but as far as Klopp was concerned it was an expression of joy, a desire to share an emotional moment with the supporters. After all, it was his custom at Dortmund to celebrate big moments with the fans. Such was his excitement that he wanted to take all Anfield with him to the final: 'We go to Basel. We take 50,000, 60,000, 70,000 Liverpudlians with us – maybe 100,000 – not in the stadium, but in the city. Everybody is invited.' Sadly, Liverpool had been allocated a paltry 10,236 seats and Klopp had to urge only those with tickets to travel.

Klopp revealed his admiration for Liverpool fans to German TV before the second leg of the semi-final got underway: 'When we arrived on the bus we saw that everybody was in a great mood

Klopp celebrates with Andy Robertson, Georginio Wijnaldum and James Milner following Liverpool's last-minute victory over Paris Saint-Germain during the Champions League group stage in September 2018.

Georginio Wijnaldum wheels away in delight after scoring Liverpool's third goal against Barcelona during the Champions League semi-final second leg.

Liverpool players pose for a team photo ahead of the Champions League final between Tottenham Hotspur and Liverpool FC in Madrid.

Liverpool's Virgil van Dijk competes for the ball with Tottenham's Harry Kane.

Mohamed Salah celebrates with teammate Jordan Henderson after scoring Liverpool's first goal of the final.

Tottenham Hotspur goalkeeper Hugo Lloris is beaten by the shot of Liverpool's Divock Origi.

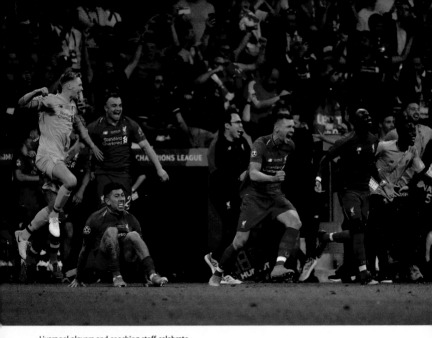

Liverpool players and coaching staff celebrate
their victory as the final whistle blows.

An elated Klopp holds the
Champions League trophy.

The team and coaching staff lift Klopp in celebration.

Klopp and Liverpool players celebrate on the packed-out streets of Liverpool during the Homecoming Parade.

Liverpool lift the UEFA Super Cup for the fourth time in their history after beating Chelsea on penalties in Istanbul.

Roberto Firmino heads the ball to score the winning goal of the FIFA Club World Cup final in Doha.

Liverpool, playing their first game at Anfield since the coronavirus pandemic, brush aside Crystal Palace 4-0 to move within two points of their first Premier League title. The Reds will be confirmed champions if Manchester City fail to beat Chelsea.

Liverpool supporters celebrate outside Anfield stadium after Chelsea's 2-1 win over Manchester City.

Jordan Henderson lifts the Premier League trophy after a match at Anfield against Chelsea.

Coronavirus restrictions mean that fans can't be present, but Klopp celebrates the Premiership victory with his team.

7

already.' Indeed, as the team bus drove to the stadium the streets were lined with supporters who formed a guard of honour for the team and sang 'We are Liverpool, tra-la-la-la-la, the best football team in the world, yes we are! Poetry in motion, tra-la-la-la-la!' at the tops of their voices, banged encouragingly on the side of the bus and set off flares in Liverpool red. Such were the crowds, the bus could advance only at walking pace. Villarreal's bus had taken the same route and been met with whistles and jeers. Perhaps this was why the Spaniards had appeared so daunted.

Even the hard-partying Kloppo, the opposite of a killjoy, seemed to think it had been a little OTT: 'There was bit too much flares because we couldn't see much so next time a little less of this,' he told BT Sport, not entirely jokingly after the game. As for the match: 'Wonderful night – a brilliant game from my side."

When he was first unveiled as the new manager, Klopp had said: 'In a special Liverpool way we can be successful.' With the prospect of a Europa League title looming, it looked like that might happen sooner rather than later. 'Kloppomania' would have reached boiling point in Liverpool in record time – but it wasn't to be.

'All or nothing' was the motto for the Europa League final against Sevilla at St Jakob-Park, Basel, on 18 May 2016. Only victory over the Andalusians would enable Liverpool to qualify for Europe next season – and thanks to new UEFA regulations, that would mean Champions League football. The pressure was on, but Sevilla were a hard nut to crack: the defending champions had won the UEFA Cup in 2006 and 2007 and its successor the Europa League in 2014 and 2015.

After a hectic start to the game by both sides, Liverpool started to find their feet and took the initiative, while remaining solid defensively and offering Sevilla no room to manoeuvre. Their boldness was rewarded in the thirty-fifth minute with the opener: Coutinho teeing up Sturridge for one of his classic outside of the boot finishes into the far corner. The travelling fans in St Jakob-Park were euphoric and starting to dream of their own fourth win in the competition (Liverpool had won the UEFA Cup in 1973, 1976 and 2001).

Liverpool pushed on for a second goal, but it remained out of reach. Just before the break Nathaniel Clyne whipped the ball across the 'corridor of uncertainty' with any one of three Liverpool players coming within inches of knocking it in. That was it for the first half.

Perhaps the Reds got a little complacent, having dominated so much of the first half, for it took just sixteen seconds from the restart for Sevilla to equalise, Kévin Gameiro putting away his eighth goal of the competition. Perhaps conceding in such a shocking manner simply stunned Liverpool for the remainder of the match. The defending champions were totally dominant. Liverpool managed to stave off a quick second, but they lasted only until the sixty-fourth minute before Sevilla's balletic combinations twisted Liverpool apart in midfield and captain Coke fired home from distance to give the now free-flowing Spaniards the lead. Once Coke got his brace six minutes later – helped in no little part by a series of individual errors, much like the first goal – there was no stopping them. The matched ended 3–1.

Klopp shared his analysis with German channel Sport1: 'After conceding we completely lost faith in our concept and were vulnerable defensively. That shows that we aren't as far advanced in our development as I would have hoped.' Liverpool were out of ideas and never came close to getting back into the game the entire second half. But the fans were as loyal and supportive as ever, and 'You'll Never Walk Alone' rang out across St Jakob-Park.

* * *

Since Borussia Dortmund's legendary 5–2 win in the German cup final against Bayern Munich in 2012, Klopp had lost five finals in a row: the Champions League 1–2 against Bayern in 2013; the DFB Cup against Bayern again, 0–2 after extra-time in 2014; the DFB Cup against Wolfsburg in 2015, 1–3; then in 2016 the League Cup against Manchester City on penalties and the Europa League 1–3 to Sevilla. It had taken Klopp until his third season with Borussia Dortmund to get his hands on some silverware – so perhaps it was just a matter of time before Klopp would be victorious in a final again.

The manager brushed off suggestions that there was a 'Klopp Final Curse' after the defeat: 'I don't think that God has the plan for me that I can go to the final and then always get a knock. Sometimes the way is a bit harder. I have a lot of luck in my life that I sit here and I am the manager of Liverpool FC.' That's not to say he had nothing to moan about: 'Today there were four decisive decisions I would say, maybe a few more, but very obvious decisions that went against us. In a final, when it's clear it is close, you need a little bit of luck. We didn't.' Still: 'All you have to do is self-criticism. Nothing else.' Liverpool, he implied, would learn from the experience and bounce back.

The denial of two penalty claims provided a particular bone of contention. Liverpool should have been awarded one in the thirteenth minute when Daniel Carriço clearly handled in the area, and there was a similar incident involving Grzegorz Krychowiak in the forty-first minute, but referee Jonas Eriksson judged this too to be unintentional. A reasonable decision. He had also made the right decision to disallow a Lovren 'goal' two minutes earlier for offside as, although Sturridge had not touched the ball, he had interfered with keeper David Soria.

Klopp was not alone in wondering whether Sevilla would ever have found a way back if they had gone 2–0 down. Yet it was too easy to pin the blame on the referee. Klopp might have seen four game-changing refereeing errors, but only the first handball could truly be called a mistake by the referee. The rest were defensible, at worst. The question that really needed answering was why Liverpool had been so passive in the second half, like a rabbit hypnotised by a snake and waiting for the inevitable. Had they burned themselves out in the first forty-five minutes? Had they simply run out of the energy needed to play the Klopp way at the end of a long season?

There it was again, the insinuation that had accompanied Klopp throughout his first months in charge: that he was pushing the players too hard. With the honeymoon period over and thoughts turning to the new season, it would soon be time to find out if Klopp's pressing game and passion could deliver silverware as well as headlines.

16

PRESSING, PASSION, PROGRESS

Two finals lost and a mediocre eighth in the league. So, had the new manager been a sporting success for Liverpool? The club was to answer that question after the end of the season with a clear vote of confidence. In July 2016, with the announcement of contract extensions to 2022, the club showed its faith not just in Klopp but in his team: assistant managers Željko Buvač and Peter Krawietz. After all, Klopp & Co. knew the value of teamwork.

Some felt expectations hadn't been met, but the club placed great value in the attractive, attacking football and distinct playing philosophy that the German was beginning to transmit to his team, and in the positive mood of the fans, who thanks to the 'normal one' dared to dream of a glorious future for their proud club again. Klopp's record wasn't judged solely on wins and sporting consistency. He was being given the patience he had asked for when he arrived, and given the chance to develop the team according to his ideas step by step. In his second season, after he'd had a summer transfer window and pre-season, these factors would no longer be enough. Wins would be expected.

During his first season with Liverpool Klopp had sized up the squad. Who was capable of following his vision of football? Who needed to go? The 2016 summer transfer window gave him an opportunity to make some adjustments. As expected, the transfers weren't box-office stuff, but – as at Borussia Dortmund – they all had a purpose. To strengthen the defence, he looked to the *Bundesliga*: central defenders Joël Matip from Schalke on a free transfer and Ragnar Klavan from Augsburg for £4.2 million, and keepers Loris Karius from Mainz for £4.7 million and Alex Manninger on a free.

Newcomers from the Premier League came with heftier price tags: lightning-quick attacker Sadio Mané from Southampton for £34 million and Newcastle midfielder Georginio Wijnaldum for £23 million.

The other side of the coin was a clearout of players who weren't Klopp's first choice: frontman Christian Benteke went to Crystal Palace for £32.5 million, 'difficult' striker Mario Balotelli to Nice on a free, winger Jordan Ibe to Bournemouth for £15 million, and midfielder Joe Allen to Stoke for £13 million. Luis Alberto, Teixeira and keeper Brad Smith also left, and it was time to say goodbye to Martin Skrtel (Fenerbahçe, £5 million) and Kolo Touré (Celtic, free). There were also numerous departures in the form of loans.

Perhaps the most prominent departure internationally was *enfant terrible* Mario Balotelli, but it can't have come as much of a surprise, Klopp having criticised his antics way back in 2011 at a coaching course in Bochum, long before he became his boss.

* * *

New signing Loris Karius missed the start of the 2016–17 season with a hand injury, but in October Klopp made him his new number one. A rash of errors, some of which led directly to goals being conceded, put him under the media spotlight and he suffered a barrage of 'expert' criticism. The manager shielded his new keeper from pressure and energetically defended him from critics, who included Phil and Gary Neville and Anfield legend Jamie Carragher. But Klopp didn't hesitate when he thought the time was right to take a tough decision – putting Karius back on the bench just two months after he'd made him his number one, and giving Simon Mignolet his place back. Klopp emphasised that the move was simply designed to lift some of the pressure off the German keeper. From then on, Mignolet played in the league and Karius in the cups.

This wasn't the only indication that Liverpool's performance was going to be judged by different standards this season. The probation period was over, expectations higher. Klopp had been able to buy the players he wanted and, without European football, finally had all the time he needed to work with the team – he now had a proper chance to instil his tactics. So when Liverpool suffered a shock loss to promoted Burnley in their second league fixture, the criticism wasn't slow in coming.

The season opener at the Emirates had showcased typical Klopp drama. Liverpool had fallen behind to Arsenal, only to come back to lead 4–1 with little more than an hour gone. Such were the celebrations, Klopp managed to lose his glasses not once but twice – his optician will have been rubbing his hands. But Liverpool were counting their chickens before they'd hatched and conceded twice. They hung on, relieved the scoreline stayed 4–3. Again, Klopp was self-critical. 'It's not allowed to celebrate the fourth goal like this with thirty-five minutes to go,' he told the BBC. 'At this moment, we switched off the machines. The game was not over. Arsenal lost, but we gave them a path back into the game.' The moment he was referring to was the piggyback ride he gave to Sadio Mané when he scored Liverpool's fourth. After that the team lost its focus, and almost the points.

There was no cause to celebrate a week later, with piggybacks or any other method, as Liverpool went down 2–0 at Turf Moor. Like an unpleasant itch, the pattern of the previous season of a high followed by a crushing low had returned. 'New faces but same old woes,' the *Liverpool Echo* lamented. A 1–1 draw at White Hart Lane left them with four points from a possible nine and a false start to the season. Worryingly, the defence was proving as vulnerable as ever.

The Reds, in order for construction work on the Main Stand to be completed, had to wait until the fourth match of the season to play their first home game. The stand added more than 8,000 seats and gave Anfield a total capacity of 54,074; as part of his preparations, Klopp had his team train in the remodelled stadium. When the christening of the newly extended cathedral of football finally came on 10 September 2016, it was a liberating moment for Liverpool. First, they brushed aside the stuttering champions Leicester 4–1; then they bested Chelsea 2–1 at the Bridge, Hull 5–1 at home and Swansea 2–1 away. Right on cue for Klopp's first anniversary on Merseyside, the team had put a winning run together and worked their way into contention. Liverpool continued to pile up the points and pummelled Watford 6–1 on 6 November to go top of the table – a position they forfeited in the next match with a goalless draw at Southampton. Rivals Chelsea had gone up a level after the home loss to Liverpool and just kept on winning – thirteen games in a row until 4 January when they lost to Tottenham.

Yet Liverpool stayed in contact throughout the first half of the season, losing just once in twenty games: 4–3 at Bournemouth, having led 2–0 and 3–1. They remained second with a bridgeable five-point gap to the leaders, and in the process enjoyed an away victory in the Merseyside derby, secured by Mané's injury-time goal. The team seemed to have found the stability that had been so obviously absent in Klopp's first season.

* * *

Klopp's ability to develop young talent is well-known, but as 2017 began he overdid it a little with what seemed to be his own version of *The Apprentice*. Liverpool kicked off their FA Cup campaign at home to League Two side Plymouth Argyle on 8 January. Klopp's starting line-up drew heavily on the reserves, and with an average age of 21 years and 296 days, it was the youngest side in the club's history – that is, since 1892. With Ben Woodburn (seventeen), Trent Alexander-Arnold (eighteen), Joe Gomez, Sheyi Ojo and Ovie Ejaria (all nineteen) starting, there were five teenagers in the first eleven. It was an understandable move: Klopp wanted to give the youngsters game time in a competitive match and rest the legs of the established players after the bruising Christmas schedule. The gamble didn't pay off, though: a 0–0 draw was both a minor embarrassment and meant adding an unwanted extra away trip to the schedule.

Klopp stuck to almost the same line-up for the replay, and Liverpool struggled again. Even Lucas's opener seemed to do nothing to settle the nerves of the clear favourites, and a bicycle kick almost brought Plymouth level but hit the post. It said everything about Liverpool's travails when Origi missed a penalty shortly before the final whistle. The Reds had bumbled into the fourth round of the FA Cup. Klopp: 'Job done, let's go home.' His youth policy was no mere whim, but carefully planned. He was attempting to make Liverpool a successful club, independent of spending huge amounts of money.

In the meantime, the signs were ominous before the match with arch-rivals Manchester United at Old Trafford on 15 January. Liverpool went into the match following three games without a win: 2–2 against Sunderland in the league, the FA Cup stumble in the first match against Plymouth, and a 1–0 defeat to Southampton in the first leg of the League Cup semi-final. The Red Devils, by contrast, were brimming with confidence after winning nine in a row. For Klopp, it was to be a reunion with his one-time protégé Henrikh Mkhitaryan, whom he had brought to Dortmund in 2013 to replace Mario Götze. In a boisterous encounter, Liverpool fought hard for a 1–1 draw that kept United five points behind them. Nonetheless, there some bitterness over the result: not only had Liverpool conceded very late, in the eighty-fourth minute, but the goal should not have stood due to an offside during the build up.

Those hoping that Liverpool would soon be back on the winning track were to be disappointed – in fact, the team was skidding out of control and into its biggest crisis since Klopp had taken over. A 3–2 defeat at home to bottom club Swansea City demonstrated once again that Pool had no answer to the 'little' teams; despite Firmino cancelling out Fernando Llorente's brace, Liverpool found no way back when Gylfi Sigurdsson put the Swans in the lead once more. If a 1–1 draw with champions-elect Chelsea, who were now ten points ahead of them, was an at least partial success (Simon Mignolet saving Diego Costa's penalty had secured the point), then the way they had crashed out of the cups was a new low.

Championship side Wolverhampton Wanderers dumped them out of the FA Cup, beating them 2–1 at Anfield. Wolves took a shock lead in the first minute and made it 2–0 by the break. Klopp had continued to put his faith in some of his fringe players, but his strengthened second-string team managed only a consolation despite creating a number of chances. 'I am 100 per cent responsible. I thought we were ready ... but we weren't,' Klopp said, downcast. Just days before, Liverpool had also been knocked out of the League Cup by Southampton, unable to overturn their 1–0 away defeat in the first leg. At Anfield, although they dominated for long stretches of the match, they were unable to make it count and conceded in injury time. A dream final against Manchester United would remain a dream.

With four games without a win in the league and their title challenge crumbling, January was a month to forget. Every major target for the season had already been missed. One-time England striker and current crisp salesman Gary Lineker didn't spare Klopp after the cup comedown against Southampton, tweeting the German the question: 'You're out of both competitions. That worth it?' With no European football, why play reserves in cup competitions you could win? The criticism was harsh: 'Shows a lack of knowledge of the depth in English football and respect.'

It seemed possible that the team would go into freefall and some saw storm clouds gathering over the manager. Yet Klopp wouldn't be Klopp if he couldn't find something positive in the situation. It may have been a low-point in his Liverpool career, but he saw that as the perfect moment to turn things around. Sadly, his team didn't seem to be listening. They lost 2–0 away to relegation-threatened Hull on 4 February. 'Unacceptable Liverpool need to wake up,' warned the BBC after the deserved loss. It was a performance to shatter dreams. Klopp himself admitted: 'I don't want to find excuses. It is hard to think of intelligent things to say after a match like this.'

He had much to think about. It was surely no coincidence that it wasn't until they faced a similarly offensive team, in the form of Tottenham on 11 February, that Liverpool finally found their feet again with a 2–0 victory after five league games without a win. Liverpool could then look forward to more than a fortnight off, thanks to their embarrassing departure from the FA Cup, and Klopp found himself preparing a 'pre-season for the rest of the season'. The terrible run of results had dropped Liverpool to fifth place and, whatever the disappointments, they still had to secure Champions League qualification – the bare minimum objective at the start of the season.

Even the luxury of the mini pre-season after the Tottenham game seemed to have no effect at first, or at least not one that could overcome the new-manager boost that Craig Shakespeare gave to Leicester after replacing Claudio Ranieri. Leicester were returning to the sort of form that had made them champions in the previous season, and they gave Liverpool a 3–1 hiding. That made Liverpool's 3–1 win over fourth-place rivals Arsenal at Anfield the following week almost a necessity to stay in the running. The points won against Burnley (2–1), Manchester City (1–1) and Everton (3–1) boosted Liverpool into third. The elevated position was deceptive, though, as the chasing pack – Arsenal and both the Manchester clubs – had games in hand that could give them the points they needed. A gripping mini-league developed between the four teams – Liverpool, United, City and Arsenal – fighting for third place (direct Champions League qualification) or fourth place (Champions League play-offs), with fifth and sixth place offering only the consolation of the Europa League. Chelsea and Tottenham were out of sight in a league of their own in first and second.

Liverpool had another setback in this neck-and-neck race on 23 April at home to their bogey team, twelfth-placed Crystal Palace.

It can't have come as too much of a surprise that Christian Benteke would come back to haunt Liverpool, with a brace that gave Palace a 2–1 win. If they wanted Champions League football, they daren't lose any one of the final four games.

They were up to the challenge: a spectacular overhead kick from Emre Can gave them a 1–0 away win over Watford, then came a dull 0–0 with Southampton (a team Liverpool had failed to score against in four attempts) and a surprisingly emphatic 4–0 away win over West Ham. It came down to the final day of the season, with Liverpool facing relegated Middlesbrough at Anfield and anywhere from third to fifth a possibility – the inconsistency of Manchester United and Arsenal aiding them in no small part.

Sunday 21 May 2017: the final showdown. Synchronised three o'clock kick-offs for all the matches. Arsenal and Manchester City both went ahead early to put Liverpool under pressure – Klopp's team would need to win to secure fourth place. The game against Middlesbrough was developing into a test of patience, but Georginio Wijnaldum settled the nerves with a strike in first-half injury time. Coutinho and Lallana each added to the tally for what was in the end a comfortable 3–0 win that gave Liverpool fourth spot and Champions League qualification. After warm embraces for all the players, Klopp was celebrating again.

If the Reds could make it through their Champions League play-off, they could consider it a successful season: since 2009, the five-time European champions had made it back into the elite level of European football only once. Klopp, visibly overjoyed after the match, was 'really happy'. But he wasn't satisfied: 'Liverpool needs to be there consistently,' he said of the Champions League.

* * *

Had Liverpool wrung every last drop out of the 2016–17 season? When they hit top spot in November, if only tantalisingly briefly, some of their fans were already dreaming of a first title since 1990. As the season drew to a close, Klopp claimed that if they'd had better luck with injuries Liverpool would have been in with a shout: 'I think we all agree that if we could have played our first twelve or thirteen for the whole season ... we are only six, seven, eight points away from the very interesting region of the table.'

Would it really have been that easy? Sure, core players such as Matip, Coutinho, Lallana, Mané and Henderson were missing for long periods. But of course, Liverpool weren't the only team to suffer from injuries. Would it not be more accurate to point to a failure of tactics, or perhaps an incapacity to implement them, which left Liverpool capable of hooking the big fish but incapable of bringing in routine points from relegation-threatened minnows? Liverpool looked good against direct rivals but had a very bad habit of dropping crucial 'easy' points. The defeats suffered when Klopp played his 'B team' highlighted a lack of depth in the squad. Did they truly have the resources to push for first place? And had Klopp's signings really caught fire?

The season was also accompanied by that keeper controversy. Were they missing a truly outstanding number one? And did they lack a 'hoover' in midfield like champions Chelsea's outstanding N'Golo Kanté? A twenty-goal-a-season man like Luis Suárez wouldn't have gone amiss either, with Coutinho (another player in Barcelona's sights) their top scorer with fourteen in all competitions.

* * *

It soon became apparent that Liverpool would not be winning their longed-for nineteenth league title in the 2017/18 season either. In his second year with Manchester City, Pep Guardiola had not just made canny reinforcements in defence, he had also impressively transmitted his playing philosophy to the 'Citizens'. Their dominance was as apparent on the pitch as it was in the league table: City won an incredible nineteen of their first twenty games (with one draw) and raced fifteen points clear at the top of the table. Liverpool, Manchester United, Arsenal, defending champions Chelsea – none of them could keep up with Man City. Not only were they the first team in Premier League history to reach 100 points, they also scored 106 goals, won 32 of 38 league games, and ended the season 19 points ahead of the runners-up, neighbours Manchester United. These were all new Premier League records.

Given that context, Liverpool had a decent if not spectacular league season, including dealing City one of only two league defeats – a rollicking 4–3 win at Anfield in January, with the Reds going 4–1 up and Liverpool's new signing Mohamed Salah netting from forty yards to send the crowd crazy. City keeper Ederson, racing out of his area to hit a misplaced clearance, had provided Salah with an unwilling assist to guide the ball into the empty net from distance. The one-nil loss away to bottom-of-the-table Swansea the week after confirmed once again the erratic nature of Liverpool's performances.

The season had been slow to get going: a 5–0 thumping away to City at the beginning of September, helped along by a red card for Sadio Mané, was an early sobering of any lofty expectations. They were in eighth place one week later after a 1–1 draw with Burnley at home, sixth place with ten games played, and fourth place with exactly half of the season gone after an entertaining three-all draw with Arsenal at the Emirates – Liverpool were making hard work of reaching the top table.

A less than fond memory from the first half of the season was the 4–1 defeat at Wembley at the hands of Tottenham in October – one of their worst performances since Klopp had taken charge, after which the manager was none too happy: 'We are ninth with the worst statistic since 1964, I can't believe it.' This time, Klopp departed from his otherwise firm principle of protecting his players. In fact, he was almost making fun of them, acknowledging some grotesque defensive errors during the game with derisive laughter, and adding in respect to Spurs' opener: 'The first would not happen if I was on the pitch.' Defender Dejan Lovren had such a shocker that Klopp took him off with just half an hour gone.

Klopp made another change in defence, unrelated to this game, in January 2018 when he swapped goalkeepers again, making Karius the new number one instead of Mignolet. There simply never seemed to be a permanent answer to Liverpool's goalkeeper debate.

The Reds defended the position they had secured at Christmas until the end of the season: with seventy-five points, one fewer than the previous season, twenty-one wins, twelve draws and five defeats, Liverpool once again crossed the finish line in fourth. They repeated another feat from 2017 as well: once more, qualification for the Champions League was only secured on the final day of the season, this time with a comfortable 4–0 home win over promoted Brighton. A happy twist: thanks to new rules introduced by UEFA, from the 2018/19 season the top four teams in the top four European leagues – England, Spain, Italy and Germany – qualified directly for the group stage. Fourth place now meant certainty for the coming campaign, without the diversion of a play-off tie.

Not that the play-off had been a particularly high hurdle in the summer of 2017, as Liverpool faced Hoffenheim and their highly rated young manager Julian Nagelsmann. Following a 2–1 away win, during the return leg at Anfield the Reds presented an appetiser of the offensive fireworks they were going to let loose later in the Champions League season. Klopp's team were three-nil up with barely twenty minutes gone, Germany international Emre Can making a decisive contribution with a brace. Roberto Firmino and Mohamed Salah contributed one each to the 4–2 final scoreline. It was a convincing entrance to the Champions League group stage, in which Liverpool's new signings would play a significant part.

* * *

Salah had arrived from Roma in June 1917 for a reported £37.8 million. The Egypt winger Salah was joined at Anfield by left-back Andrew Robertson from Hull (£8.1 million), striker prospect Dominic Solanke (Chelsea, free) and – just before the transfer window closed – England midfielder Alex Oxlade-Chamberlain (Arsenal, £34.2 million). With no deal completed for Dutch transfer target Virgil van Dijk, Klopp did without reinforcements to his vulnerable central defence. Departures included centre-back Mamadou Sakho, his loan to Crystal Palace being made permanent for £25.4 million, and striker Divock Origi, who went out on loan to Wolfsburg to gain more playing time.

While Klopp had been strengthening his team over the summer, he had been forced to contend with Philippe Coutinho making no secret of his desire to move to Barcelona, only to be denied by the club. Liverpool supporters were keeping a keen eye on how the Brazilian would react as the season began. Would he be ambling indifferently around the pitch from now on, to make his unhappiness at the lack of a deal clear? As it was, Coutinho received a warm welcome from the Pool fans as the season kicked off and he lived up to the reception, remaining as competitive, enthusiastic and dangerous in front of goal as ever. Klopp even gave him the captain's armband as January approached, but the Brazil star remained as determined to join Barcelona.

Klopp had to accept the weakening of his team in the January transfer window, when Liverpool finally agreed to Coutinho's switch to Barcelona. The monetary compensation for the move was reported to amount to a monstrous £105 million up front, rising to £142 million with add-ons. It was the second biggest transfer fee in history behind Neymar to Paris Saint-Germain in 2017, and a nice bit of business for Liverpool considering the mere £8.5 million they paid Inter Milan for him in 2013. Yet it seemed clear that the loss of their little magician would put a damper on the Reds' sporting ambitions, especially since no suitable replacement was available. For the time being, at least, the gap left by Coutinho would have to be filled internally.

That January transfer window was a record breaker for Liverpool in terms of outgoings as well as income: Netherlands central defender Virgil van Dijk, at six-foot-four and 92kg the epitome of the defensive 'unit', was finally landed from Southampton for a reported £75 million. As with Coutinho, this transfer too was the culmination of a saga. Much like the Brazilian, Van Dijk was vehement in making his wish for a move clear, regardless of his signature on a six-year contract. Yet at a time when contracts in professional football seem to be no more than letters of intent with no binding effect, at the end of the day here too it was only a question of the fee. Liverpool had officially apologised for their illegal approach in 2017, declaring that 'we have ended any interest in the player', but they got their man after all. It wasn't your typical Klopp transfer. As recently as 2016 he had responded to Paul Pogba's £89 million transfer fee with strong, moralising words: 'I want to do it differently. I would even do it differently if I could spend that money. If I spend money, it is because I am trying to build a team, a real team.' He didn't mince words about buying success: 'The day that this is football, I'm not in a job anymore.'

Clearly Liverpool's defensive weaknesses, which Klopp had failed to get a handle on in more than two years in charge, had brought about a change of heart. True to the cliché 'attack wins games, defence wins titles', Klopp was now banking on a defender who he didn't need to develop from a promising talent, as he once did with Neven Subotič and Mats Hummels in Dortmund, but could play at the very top level immediately. Questioned about the transfer fee, Klopp responded laconically that the price wasn't up to Liverpool, but rather the market. Double standards? Given Klopp's remarks about Pogba, it cannot have come as a surprise when Manchester United's José Mourinho spoke out to journalists in a pre-match press conference: 'If I was one of you I would ask him about his comments [from] about one year ago.'

A quite different reaction came from one LFC legend who for years had been the rock of the Reds' defence: 'He's better in the air than me, quicker than me, more composed & doesn't score own goals!' Jamie Carragher gushed on Twitter.

Weighing up the sporting significance of bringing in Van Dijk, independent of passing moral judgement on today's football business, the balance so far is positive: the team conceded twenty-three times before Christmas, and just fifteen times after. Admittedly this is not conclusive evidence on its own, given that

Van Dijk only played in fourteen of nineteen league matches, yet when the Dutch international was present, the Liverpool defence seemed more solid. His central defensive partner Dejan Lovren also seemed to be steadied by his presence. The record signing had soon become a stabilising factor who was happy to declare Anfield 'home' just months after arriving.

In the Champions League, Liverpool finished top of Group E ahead of Sevilla with three wins and three draws to their name – the same Sevilla that had defeated Klopp's team 3–1 in the 2016 Europa League final. This time too, the Anglo-Spanish clashes offered up some thrilling football: the 2–2 draw at Anfield was entertaining, but the encounter in Seville was particularly dramatic. The Reds were three-nil up with just thirty minutes gone before coming under increasing pressure after the break, and conceding in injury time to a Sevilla team driven on by frenzied fans. A boisterous 7–0 win in the final group game against Spartak Moscow made first place safe, though – with an exceptional goal difference of plus seventeen from six games.

The last sixteen provided another goalfest to enjoy: 5–0 away to Porto, with Sadio Mané's hat-trick helping to settle the tie in the first leg, before a 0-0 draw at Anfield sealed the quarter-final place. Waiting for them this time would be seemingly unstoppable Premier League rivals Manchester City, who would be clear favourites. Klopp: 'I knew it would be difficult. And that is difficult.' Yet once again the attacking trident of Sadio Mané, Mohamed Salah and Roberto Firmino demonstrated its outstanding form. In the first half, the team played exhilaratingly to send Anfield into ecstasy. The well-earned reward: an unexpected 3–0 lead, which Liverpool defended tenaciously until the final whistle, putting themselves in an enviable position going into the second leg.

Liverpool had been warned, though: they had conceded five without response to Manchester City in the league – and if that result was repeated, City and not Liverpool would proceed to the semi-finals. Indeed, City's goal hunt was not long in coming. With only two minutes gone Gabriel Jesus put them ahead, after Van Dijk of all people was put under pressure by the touchline and gave the ball away to give City an opening. Under constant pressure in the first half, Liverpool were struggling to create anything, but managed to limit their host's chances with tenacious and focused defending. Minutes before the break, perhaps the decisive moment in the tie: City thought they had made it 2–0, but the referee ruled the goal out for a supposed offside – overlooking the fact that the ball had come off Liverpool's James Milner, making it impossible to be in an offside position.

At the half-time whistle, City manager Pep Guardiola stormed onto the pitch to remonstrate, gesticulating towards the referee – and promptly getting himself sent to the stands.

Klopp had clearly sent his team out for the second half under orders to show more initiative, and their less cautious play was rewarded in the fifty-sixth minute with Salah's equaliser. City now needed four goals to go through, and without their manager in the dugout they didn't look like they had the fight left in them. Firmino's strike to give Liverpool the lead in the seventy-seventh minute was confirmation of the inevitable, and the match ended with the score still at 2–1.

Klopp was proud of his players, who had held their nerve despite going behind so early: 'We scored five goals against Man City and we conceded one – these numbers are usually not possible,' adding contentedly: 'We've matured constantly.' There was no doubting that in the Champions League, at least, Klopp's team was internalising his power-football mantra.

But what of the supposedly sorely missed Coutinho? Ironically, Barcelona suffered a shock quarter-finals exit from the Champions League at the hands of Roma, losing 3–0 in Rome after having triumphed 4–1 at the Camp Nou. Of course, upon his unveiling in Catalonia by his new club, Coutinho had stressed that the reason he had come to Barcelona was to win the Champions League. Now, cup-tied having already played for Liverpool in the competition that season, he was forced to look on helplessly as his new team crashed out. Insult was quick to follow and, by the end of their return tie against Manchester City, with a place in the semi-finals safe, some Liverpool fans were gloating, singing: 'We've got Salah, Mané and Bobby Firmino, but we sold Coutinho!'

In the semi-final, Liverpool stuck to their guns, again offering up an abundance of incident against Roma. The goal machine had been lovingly tuned and oiled, and was firing on all cylinders. In this replay of the European Cup final of 1984 (which Liverpool won in Rome on penalties), the Reds swept Roma away 5–2 – squandering an even better position in the process, having led 5–0 before conceding two away goals in the final minutes. Roma still had a slim hope of reaching the final. Another second-leg, 3–0 win, a repetition of their quarter-final against Barcelona, would see them through. But could lightning strike twice? One thing was for certain, despite what remained a healthy lead, there was no way Liverpool were going to underestimate their opponents.

The man of the match of the first leg was Mohamed Salah: the Egyptian attacker shone in the duel with his ex-club, who he had left in 2017 for Anfield, and contributed two goals as well as two assists to Liverpool's five. While boss of Borussia Dortmund, Klopp had already been struck by his quality during a friendly against Basel. At Liverpool, Klopp turned to the speedy, tricky winger, a dangerous dribbler with a sure eye for goal, who in his two seasons at Roma had made the breakthrough to international top-tier attacker.

Thirty-two goals in his debut season with Liverpool marked a new Premier League record for a thirty-eight-game season. Just recompense: selection as both the Premier League's and Africa's player of the year. Including the strikes contributed by attacking colleagues Sadio Mané (ten) and Roberto Firmino (fifteen), the triple threat bagged a massive fifty-seven league goals. It was the best attack in Europe in 2017–18.

The early hopes of the Italian fans in the Stadio Olimpico were quick to be punctured as Mané struck what seemed to be the nail in Roma's coffin in the ninth minute: a Liverpool away goal. After Milner's own goal in the fifteenth minute, Georginio Wijnaldum pounced ten minutes later to head the Reds back into the lead. It stayed 2–1 going into the break, and Liverpool clearly felt a little bit too confident thanks to their 7–3 aggregate lead. After conceding shortly after the restart, the Reds let another two in during the closing minutes to leave the score at 4–2 – too late, however, for Roma to score again and force extra-time. In this desolate second-half Liverpool had once again, as against Manchester City, enjoyed a bit of luck with refereeing decisions: this time, a foul by keeper Karius and a handball by Alexander-Arnold should both have been punished by the award of a penalty, although the penalty decision Roma did receive for handball in injury time was soft to say the least.

Including qualification, this was Liverpool's first defeat of a fourteen-game Champions League season – but it also meant that they had reached their first final since 2007, when they had lost 2–1 to AC Milan. With a jaw-dropping forty-six goals in a

Champions League season, Liverpool had set a new record even before the final, breaking Barcelona's record of forty-five goals from the 1999–2000 season.

* * *

Shock news broke at the end of April 2018 before the second leg of the semi-final against Roma. Željko Buvač, for seventeen years not just Klopp's assistant but also his 'tactical brain', left the coaching team with immediate effect and did not travel to Rome. The Liverpool FC website spoke of 'spending time away' from the club, not a permanent parting of the ways, but revealed nothing that might have explained the rupture.

There was speculation about tensions between the two. According to former Mainz 05 general manager Christian Heidel, rows were a regular occurrence, but they had always patched things up. Heidel revealed to German tabloid *Bild* at the beginning of May 2018: 'I could never picture them not working together. In fact, I only know the two of them together. But I also know that these are two really passionate guys. When it kicked off in Mainz sometimes, you thought, the door's going to burst open and only one of them's coming out, but instead they came out arm in arm and went to the pub across the road.'

Klopp himself had little to say about the reasons for the split, and that was less than revealing: 'We gave a club statement on that and that's all we're saying at the moment.' The said statement, however, did little to clarify the situation – apparently, Buvač was not leaving the club but 'spending time away from the first-team environment, between now and the end of the season, for personal reasons'. Klopp's other assistant, Peter Krawietz, the member of the coaching team responsible for video analysis, filled in for the rest of the season, with a decision on a permanent replacement presumably to be made during the summer break.

For Klopp, the break from Buvač, with whom he claimed to have a 'telepathic understanding', was no doubt a big personal as well as sporting loss. Klopp responded to the question of how much impact Buvač's absence would have on the tactical setup of the team with characteristic irony. Asked by a journalist before the Champions League final against Real Madrid what he thought of Zinedine Zidane, who some critics had accused of understanding little about tactics, Klopp rejoindered: 'If people think Zidane has no tactical knowledge – because people think the same about me – it would be really funny if two managers in the final had no clue about tactics.'

* * *

Kiev, 26 May 2018. The stage was set for the Champions League final, the crowning glory of an outstanding season in Europe for Liverpool, and the lifting of Klopp's 'cup final curse' after five lost finals in a row. Only one thing stood in their way, a certain Real Madrid, who seemed almost invincible in European competition, who the season before had become the first team to defend the Champions League title since it changed its name from the European Cup in 1992, and who had lifted the cup three times in the past four years. Yet their narrow, fortunate successes over Juventus in the quarter-final and Bayern Munich in the semi (both 4–3 on aggregate) gave some grounds for optimism that Liverpool's power football might just have a chance, even against Madrid. Wily, experienced Real or enthusiastic, passionate Pool, symbolised by the polar opposite characters of their respective managers – who would prevail?

At the international pre-match press conference before the final, Klopp showed how happy he was to be back on the summit of the Champions League five years after Borussia Dortmund's defeat by Bayern Munich: 'It's maybe once in a lifetime chance, that's how it felt that time ... Now I am here because my boys gave me that chance again.' And on their chances of pulling it off this time: 'I am pretty sure in the second before the game Real Madrid will be more confident than we are but that is not a problem because the game doesn't end in that second, it only starts.' Klopp felt that not only had his team risen to to the next level every time it was needed during the course of the competition, but that Real 'have played really strong teams but they never played us and we are Liverpool'.

The manager was trying as best he could to take the pressure off his squad. 'We had an early agreement when we started working together: I am responsible for defeats and the boys are responsible for the things we win.' However big the occasion might be, for a Klopp team the match should be just another football match: 'Shoot, cross, make headers, bicycle kicks if you want.'

So to the game. Liverpool began well and seemed to be making a genuine impact on the favourites with their lightning start. Quick into the tackle, rapid pressing, the first half-hour was quintessential Klopp football. Real Madrid were largely on the back foot, their only chance coming through Cristiano Ronaldo in the fifteenth minute. The Reds' best, missed, chances fell to Roberto Firmino and Trent Alexander-Arnold in quick succession in the twenty-third minute.

Then it began, the sporting drama, a drama in three acts.

Act I: Madrid captain Sergio Ramos dragged Mohamed Salah to the ground, who fell so awkwardly that he sprained shoulder ligaments and had to be substituted. With half an hour played,

Salah wept bitterly as he had to go off injured – as did Real Madrid right-back Dani Carvajal five minutes later.

Salah coming off had an instant impact on Liverpool's play. The poise they had previously enjoyed seemed to evaporate, as Klopp later conceded: 'Of course [the foul] was a big moment in the game. I know if you say something like that after a game you lost it's a little bit like you are a bad loser, but for me that was kind of a harsh challenge. The arm is there, it's like wrestling a little bit … The shock of the boys was obvious.' During the game, Klopp had thrust out his chest to signal to his players: 'Keep being brave!' Madrid were taking charge now, with Liverpool needing to recompose themselves after losing their outstanding goal threat. Half-time, 0–0. Time to work on Plan B. But it wasn't to endure.

Drama, Act II: Ramos's 'MMA move' against Salah was the object of heated discussion, which almost drowned out his later interference with Liverpool goalkeeper Loris Karius. During a Madrid attack in the forty-ninth minute, he struck the keeper in the temple with his elbow, sending Karius briefly to the ground. The referee chose not to take action. How much impact this blow to the head had on Karius' catastrophic blunder just two minutes later will remain an open question, but some days after the match, the goalkeeper was diagnosed with concussion. What followed was slapstick and disbelief: in the fifty-first minute, Karius picked up a through ball from Real Madrid playmaker Toni Kroos that had bounced harmlessly into the box and wanted to distribute it quickly to right-back Trent Alexander-Arnold, but he underestimated how close Madrid striker Karim Benzema had got. Benzema lifted a leg and Karius's throw rebounded off Benzema's right foot into an empty net. An unbelievable error coming in the biggest game of Karius's career.

Liverpool soon pulled back the completely unnecessary deficit. Only four minutes later, Sadio Mané made it 1–1: from a corner, Dejan Lovren beat Ramos in the air to guide the ball goalward and Mané poked it home for his tenth goal of the Champions League season. The Reds were back in business now, challenging for the ball as proactively as they had at the start of the game – until Madrid brought Gareth Bale on in the sixty-first minute and eased back into pole position. Just three minutes after coming on, the Welshman connected with an incredible overhead kick, goal of the season calibre, that slammed the ball unstoppably past Karius into the net. Even multiple world player of the year Zinedine Zidane, famed for his incredible technique, could hardly believe what a dream goal he was seeing from the touchline. It certainly wasn't the sort of bicycle kick Klopp had been thinking of before the game …

Drama, Act III: Perhaps Bale had sensed that Karius had lost his nerve after the howler that had gifted the opening goal to Madrid. Perhaps it was a reflection of tremendous self-confidence after the stunning bicycle kick. From around thirty yards out, Bale simply thumped the ball goalwards. The ball was coming straight down the middle – there was nothing blocking Karius's view. Yet the ball spilled from his gloves into the net – the decider, 3–1 to the defending champions. Some of the players in red sank to the ground in horror and disbelief. A long march through Europe accompanied by a unique flurry of goals had come to the most miserable end imaginable. Victory over the mighty Real Madrid remained nothing more than a beautiful dream. 'We would have deserved it,' Klopp said wistfully, looking back on the season.

Legendary Germany keeper Oliver Kahn, who had made a critical error in the World Cup final 2002 against Brazil that presented Ronaldo with a tap in, sympathised with Karius on German television: 'From a goalkeeper's point of view I don't recall seeing anything more brutal than that. Goalkeeping is never fair. There's nowhere to turn to ... Getting yourself out of this situation again, that takes a massive mental effort.' If not, Kahn worried about drastic consequences: 'An evening like this can ruin a career.'

There were touching scenes immediately after the final whistle as the German keeper slumped to the ground and embraced the pitch for minutes like a bundle of misery, kneeling, head and body bowed almost in supplication. He was alone, as his teammates clearly had their own disappointment to deal with, until Madrid players, including two-goal Gareth Bale, picked him up. Karius then approached the Liverpool support in tears and making apologetic gestures – and the fans answered him with encouraging applause. They had already struck up 'You'll Never Walk Alone' towards the end of the match to set themselves and the team back on their feet. Looking ahead, Klopp called on journalists not to constantly rub Karius's mistakes in his face in the future. Wishful thinking one suspects.

Karius had been under scrutiny ever since he arrived at Liverpool. Yet for such terrible mistakes, at the worst possible time, and when he had at last been showing some consistency – words were hard to find. Karius himself was inconsolable, apologising on Talksport to the team, the club and the fans he had 'let down': 'If I could go back in time I would.'

As much as Klopp stressed after the game that it wasn't about himself, it's fair to surmise that a sixth lost final in a row will have hit him hard. Not that he had anything to reproach himself for – after all, he had no control over the bitter injury to Salah and Karius's decisive mistakes. Speaking at the post-match press conference, Klopp concluded: 'We wanted everything and got minus something with the injury of Mo.' It will take all the manager's psychological finesse to raise the team's heads again after two European finals lost in three years – especially after such a dramatic turn of events, in which injury and a night to forget for the goalkeeper blocked their path to success. Still: Klopp had led Liverpool back to Europe's heights, defying all the criticism from sceptics who before the start of the season had questioned his grasp of tactics.

Also, perhaps, a show of defiance: defeat wasn't going to stop the party animal in Klopp. At a private party after the final, Klopp sang a specially written song at six o'clock in the morning with celebrity Liverpool fan Campino, the singer from the German band Die Toten Hosen, and other friends. 'We saw the European Cup, Madrid had all the fucking luck. We swear, we keep on being cool, we bring it back to Liverpool.'

* * *

In the Beatles' day Liverpool was a rock 'n' roll as well as a dock city; since his arrival Klopp was playing heavy metal. No team scored more league goals (71) during his first 365 days in charge and, in 2017–18, Liverpool netted an astonishing 135 times in all competitions. Is Klopp really as 'normal' as he describes himself? He has woken up a team and their supporters from a lethargic melancholy and Liverpool are ready to follow him to the ends of Europe – although the heights of messiah hysteria are on occasion perhaps a little overdone. Klopp has brought the fun factor back to Liverpool. One thing he doesn't like is when the fans sings his name. After all, it's the players, not him, who are running their hearts out for the badge. Whether he likes it or not, though, the star of the show at Liverpool right now is their charismatic manager.

Borussia Dortmund's motto is 'True Love' – the passion shared by the club and their former coach has never died, and these are two simple words that have lost none of their meaning for Klopp. Love can be shared without being diminished. Klopp proved that when he moved from Mainz to Dortmund. Two clubs that forever have a place in his heart. And, surely, Liverpool had already joined them.

17

FINAL GLORY

Summer 2018: Liverpool were licking their wounds again. Following 2007 (in the Champions League against AC Milan), 2016 (in the Europa League against Sevilla) and the most recent defeat to Real Madrid in 2018, this was the third European final they had lost in a row. Yet the season gone had also demonstrated that Liverpool were within touching distance of the European summit. The club drew the right conclusions in the transfer market and continued to strategically strengthen the team.

The Rolls-Royce transfer came in goal, Alisson Becker being brought in from AS Roma of *Serie A* – he was Brazil's number one, and one of the world's most promising players in his position. Quality like that came at a price in the dizzying European transfer market: £56.25 million (all transfer values from transfermarkt. co.uk), plus performance-related add-ons, amounted to a new world-record fee for a keeper, as had been the case for Virgil van Dijk for a central defender. In the past few years, a reappraisal has taken place. The days when big money was spent only on attacking players are over. It's not for nothing that the well-known football saying goes: 'Attack wins you games, defence wins you titles.'

From a purely sporting point of view, both transfers were to pay off. Introducing Alisson, Klopp paid tribute to his talents: 'In all goalkeeper departments the highest level.' Even before Klopp's arrival, when the keeper with German heritage was still playing in Brazil in 2015, the club are said to have been following his progress, but decided against making a move. At that point, any fee would have been a fraction of what they went on to pay, but the development of talented players is, of course, a guessing game. The big European clubs often track the progress of South American players at smaller clubs in Europe, waiting to see how they cope with a different culture.

Liverpool fans made a grand gesture at the first 2018–19 pre-season game, once again living up to their reputation for unconditional love for and loyalty to their club. Before their team beat sixth-tier Chester 7–0, they greeted Loris Karius with a standing ovation despite his unfortunate Champions League final. A few days after the game against Real Madrid, it became public knowledge that Karius had suffered a concussion during the final, clearly as a result of a penalty-box incident shortly after half-time, when his head had come into contact with Sergio Ramos's elbow. At that point, the score was still 0–0. According to a specialist in America, the blow led to 'visual spatial dysfunction'. It can't be proved that this was the sole cause of Karius's errors, but it certainly does seem to go some way to explaining them.

Be that as it may, the German's chances of regular starts in the coming season had been lowered to a minimum with the signing of Alisson. After all, Liverpool weren't spending that kind of money not to make Alisson their new number one. Considering the likelihood of a permanent place on the subs' bench, Karius accepted a loan move to Beşiktaş in Turkey.

There were changes in other positions as well as in goal. Reinforcing the squad both in attacking quality and breadth came Swiss winger Xherdan Shaqiri from Stoke for £13.23 million, along with two defensive midfielders: Guinean Naby Keita from

RB Leipzig for £54 million, and Brazilian Fabinho, with the Reds paying AS Monaco £40.5 million for his services. Striker Divock Origi returned from a loan spell at VfL Wolfsburg – to play a decisive role come the end of the season. Fellow forward Daniel Sturridge was also brought back to Anfield, following a spell on loan with West Bromwich Albion.

Of the regular starters alongside Karius, Germany international Emre Can also left the club. He declined to sign a contract extension and, seeking new challenges, joined Italy's record title-holders Juventus. The core of the team remained intact, despite what must certainly have been a number of suitors for Mohamed Salah & co. Jürgen Klopp made clear repeatedly just how much he was enjoying being able to keep hold of his best players – unlike during his time at Borussia Dortmund, when he had to accept the loss of Nuri Şahin (to Real Madrid), Shinji Kagawa (to Manchester United), Mario Götze and Robert Lewandowski (both to Bayern Munich).

Playing an important role in squad planning was Ian Graham, who as director of research within the scouting department takes care of data analysis. Alongside traditional methods – including the man in the stands observing players – data analysis provides another important tool for evaluating possible transfer targets. An article in the *New York Times* made plain the importance of Graham – who earned a doctorate in theoretical physics at Cambridge – to the decision-making process at the club. His approach takes into account the argument that scouting currently is less about unearthing hidden gems (in these high-information, networked days, an unlikely possibility) and more about 'matching' – that is, evaluating players and judging whether they would suit the playing philosophy of the club interested in them.

It is a part of the industry that has taken on even greater significance since the takeover of Liverpool by American sports company Fenway Sports Group, FSG itself giving equally high prominence to data collection and evaluation. Together with the know-how and the personal impressions of the coaching team around Jürgen Klopp – for raw data cannot completely replace the human factor – an extremely smoothly functioning combo has come into being, which so far has succeeded in minimising misjudgements in the transfer market. Further contributions come from players being tracked sometimes for years, and investments being made not just in terms of bringing in big names, but according to planning and positions.

* * *

Klopp's team started the new season with real fire in its belly. Despite the formidable attacking trident of Salah, Mané and Firmino, who in 2017–18 scored fifty-seven of Liverpool's eighty-four goals in the league (as well as thirty goals in the Champions League, the 'Three Musketeers' each bagging ten), the title had remained out of reach. With Alisson, Keita and Fabinho, an attempt was being made to balance the defensive half of the equation – and it worked. It was to be a historic season for the Reds, even if once again there was to be no coronation as Premier League champions. After thirty-eight games of football they had collected ninety-seven points – an unbelievable haul, the best in the club's history, which in almost any other season would easily have earned them the title. It just so happened that they were competing against the 'robots' at Manchester City under Pep Guardiola, who in the 2018–19 season amassed ninety-eight points. Thirty victories, seven draws and a solitary defeat (which, inevitably, came at Manchester City) – and not only that but also the best defence of all Premier League teams with a mere twenty-two goals conceded – wasn't enough finally to bring the title back home for the first time since 1990.

But to begin at the beginning: the team kicked off the season in party mood, putting four without response past West Ham at Anfield. Salah, Mané with a brace and the returning Sturridge served up an opening day treat with style. It was the start of a winning streak that would not be interrupted until matchday seven, by a 1–1 draw with Chelsea. Even that result felt almost like a victory for Liverpool, with substitute Sturridge nailing a stunner from distance in the eighty-ninth minute to level the scores. In the following top-of-the-table clash too, at home against Manchester City, the points were to be shared, this time with the game remaining scoreless. In a surprisingly lacklustre match, Liverpool were fortunate that City's Riyad Mahrez missed a late penalty. As it was, with eight games played, three teams were level on twenty points at the top: City, Chelsea and Liverpool.

Following four fixtures without a victory (in the league, Champions League and League Cup), matchday nine saw a return to winning ways at Huddersfield, managed by Klopp's best man, David Wagner. A laboured 1–0 win was decided yet again by Salah. From then on the cogs in the Red machine were running smoothly, powering them from victory to victory, with the only interruption being a draw in another classic clash: 1–1 at Arsenal. The Merseyside derby at Anfield offered a particular highlight: the only goal of a typically boisterous battle came not only in the sixth minute of injury time, but also in the maddest of manners: Van Dijk's shanked shot looping high before bouncing on the bar with keeper Jordan Pickford flapping – and Origi nodded in. Anfield exploded.

Nor was there any more holding back for Klopp. With the ball in the net he left his tactical area and stormed onto the pitch, celebrating the derby win with keeper Alisson. Directly after the match he apologised for his behaviour to Everton manager Marco Silva: showing a lack of respect had not been his intention, he had simply been caught up in the moment. Silva took Klopp's exuberance in victory in his stride, but Klopp admitted an FA improper conduct charge and had to pay a fine of £8,000.

A more collected Liverpool than in previous years were now capable of maximising their advantage against the 'small teams'. They also had the steel to believe in victory right to the final whistle, as against Everton, and they ended Boxing Day top of the league with half the season played. With sixteen wins from nineteen matches they were on fifty-one points, six ahead of closest challengers Tottenham Hotspur. They had conceded all of seven goals. To take nothing away from the contributions of the ever-improving Joël Matip, from Dejan Lovren or from Joe Gomez, the decisive stabilising factor in defence proved to be record transfer Virgil van Dijk, honoured by supporters with his own song to the melody of folk classic 'Dirty Old Town', which became a hit online as well as in the Liverpool pubs:

> *He's a centre-half,*
> *he's a number four,*
> *Watch him defend,*
> *And we watch him score,*
> *He can pass the ball,*
> *calm as you like.*
> *He's Virgil van Dijk,*
> *Virgil van Dijk.*

That the *difensorissimo* truly was practically unbeatable in the 2018–19 season is evidenced by a remarkable statistic from Opta Sports, according to which despite being almost ever-present on the pitch he wasn't dribbled past in a single competitive match – even though at six-foot-four, many might have been tempted to assume that the big man might not be the most mobile. Far from it.

Keeping how far the season had left to run firmly in mind, Klopp warned that 'no one should feel out of the title race'. A glance at the stats for the last ten years had given Liverpool fans pause for thought in any case: in this time period the league leaders at Christmas had always gone on to win the title – except in 2008 and 2013. The leaders then had been Liverpool. The prospect that bad things come in threes became a looming possibility at the Etihad.

The tide started to turn. Crossing the touchline with the self-assurance of league leaders who had just triumphed 5–1 at home against Arsenal, Pool suffered their sole defeat of the league season in Manchester. In the first match of the new year the guests missed out on the lead by millimetres as City defender John Stones scraped the ball off the line in the eighteenth minute. The action came directly after Mané hit the post. Sergio Agüero's strike for the Citizens in the fortieth minute was answered with a Roberto Firmino header in the sixty-fourth. Yet when Leroy Sané put Guardiola's team back in the lead in the seventy-second minute, Liverpool failed to find a way back. By beating Liverpool, City had reduced the gap at the top to four points; the Reds had missed their chance to put clear blue water between themselves and their rivals.

Following two wins, 1–0 away at Brighton & Hove Albion and at home to Crystal Palace (4–3, with an unusually wobbly defensive performance, though Firmino scored Liverpool's thousandth goal in the Premier League), Klopp's team gave way to their sole under par period in the league from matchday twenty-four on, with four draws in six games. A draw at Anfield with Leicester City (1–1) was followed by the same scoreline away to West Ham. An emphatic 3–0 win over Bournemouth was followed by another draw: 0–0 at Old Trafford. When this was followed on matchday twenty-nine by another goalless draw, of all places at local rivals Everton, Liverpool lost their position at the top of the league, one they had held for nearly three months. With England number one Pickford saving low to his right, Salah failed to convert the Reds' biggest chance when through one-on-one.

For Klopp it was cold comfort that he remained unbeaten in his eighth Merseyside derby, the 200th iteration of the Liverpool versus Everton clash, for the guard had changed. City won all fourteen of their remaining league fixtures and stayed on top until the end. It was of no use that after that Everton game, Liverpool took three points from each of their remaining nine fixtures, shouldering the pressure to win every single game as their title rivals refused to give way, and delivering a gripping toe-to-toe fight to the finish. In the end, the Man City 'machine' found the path to victory, taking control of matches through Guardiola's trademark possession football, seeking to the greatest extent possible to minimise the impact of chance, and performing with unparalleled consistency.

Klopp's system focuses more on attack than control, although in the final analysis the differences between the two sides in the 2018–19 league season were marginal. From one point of view, those 1.12 centimetres at the Etihad on 3 January, which would have put the whole of the ball behind the line before Stones's clearance, were the hair's breadth to the title. But what ifs are pointless.

* * *

There were mixed feelings at Anfield following the last league game of the season, a 2–0 win over Wolverhampton Wanderers, for Klopp, for the players and for the supporters. On the one hand, there was the disappointment of a missed date with destiny which, following months at the top of the table, was seemingly within touching distance; at the same time, Liverpool were still riding the high on the football miracle that had occurred just days before against Barcelona (and there's more to come on that). Klopp regretted that there was no 'Most Improved' award for his team: 'We should get an award for the biggest development jump I can remember.'

Indeed, certain players had come on in leaps and bounds under Klopp's management, two examples being full-backs Andrew Robertson and Trent Alexander-Arnold, who matured from talented prospects to world-class performers. Even players brought in as established 'difference makers', such as Van Dijk, were now displaying their full potential at Liverpool.

Full-backs Andrew Robertson (left) and Trent Alexander-Arnold (right) are assigned an important role in Liverpool's system. Liverpool's standard 4–3–3 formation does without a classic playmaker along the lines of Eden Hazard at Chelsea, prior to his move to Real Madrid in June 2019. Central midfielder Jordan Henderson is more of a number eight than a number ten, or as Klopp deployed him for a considerable period due to personnel issues, a number six. Attacks were generally launched down the wings, using their full-backs with attacking ambition.

The combative Scot Andrew Robertson and technically gifted Trent Alexander-Arnold counted among the best assist providers in the Premier League, thanks in no small part to their pace. Both are often to be found high up the pitch and in the 2018–19 Premier League season that tactic brought them twenty-three assists combined – but they didn't neglect their defensive duties, as evidenced by Liverpool being the meanest defence in the league. On the contrary: à la Klopp their defensive task involves intense, energy-sapping pressing – one reason the manager looks to younger players.

Next to swiftness of body in the duo's repertoire is swiftness of mind, as demonstrated by Alexander-Arnold's clever corner in the Champions League semi-final against Barcelona. According to assistant manager Peter Krawietz, quickly exploiting dead-ball situations is a regular part of training. Which is also why the incoming coaching team increased the number of ball boys at Anfield, reducing the time it took for the ball to return to play after interruptions.

In no small part thanks to the offensive output of the two full-backs, not one but two Liverpool attackers finished the 2018–19 season at the top of the Premier League scoring charts, alongside Arsenal's Pierre-Emerick Aubameyang. Mo Salah – proving his incredible first season with Liverpool, when he had won the Golden Boot with a fantastic thirty-two goals, was no fluke – and Sadio Mané each finished the season with twenty-two league goals of Liverpool's total of eighty-nine.

Tactical tweaks, greater calm and control on the pitch, no more unnecessary dropped points against 'little teams', impressive consistency – Liverpool may not have won the title, but the developmental step forward Liverpool had taken under Klopp was clear as day in 2018–19. In the previous season, relegated West Brom, Stoke City and Swansea had all taken points from them. That was all in the past.

Yet what exactly, combined with the quality recruitment, had made the tactical difference? Assistant manager Peter Krawietz gave some hints to German sports website spox.com: 'We improved the quality of our possession. Now, even under a high press from the opposition we manage progressive, creative build up play – and we can do that highly consistently. We have created variability to the extent that we can always implement different formations of build-up play. When we do that we can give our players simple signals and they are capable of reacting to them with great variability. For example, when build-up formations should change, when we should push one flank a little higher or a player should be more active between the lines. That gives us the potential to perform more dominantly and more consistently over the entire ninety minutes. We know now that even in the final minutes we can create new situations with a substitution or a change of system that increase the chances of a goal.'

This variability is demonstrated in attack, where Liverpool play without a traditional centre-forward between left-winger Mané and right-winger Salah. In Firmino they have something of a false nine, ready to drop into midfield to receive the ball in build-up play, rather than merely waiting statically in the box for chances to fall to him.

At the end of the league season, the team could have no regrets: they had played a season close to perfection. Yet in the form of Manchester City they had faced a competitor in the league that was 'even perfecter'. Nevertheless, Klopp had just enjoyed by far his best season with the Reds. He had developed the players, invested sensibly in the playing squad by addressing problem areas, and he had taken the team as the sum of its parts to a new level. The well-earned reward would come in another competition: one which Liverpool had dominated during the late seventies and early eighties, until the horrifying events in Brussels's Heysel Stadium at the 1985 European Cup final between Liverpool and Juventus led to the indefinite expulsion of English clubs from European competition, a ban that lasted five years, six for Liverpool.

* * *

It was all quiet in the cups, at least at the national level. Liverpool once again suffered inglorious exits, this time at the earliest possible opportunity. So the domestic cup story of 2018–19 isn't long in telling: in the FA Cup the Reds went out in the third round, the first round of the competition in which Premier League teams take part, beaten 2–1 by promoted – and impressive – Wolves. Coming just days after their 2–1 defeat away to Manchester City, it meant two losses on the trot. As is his practice, Klopp had rested some of his key performers, Alisson, Van Dijk and Mané included. By bringing on Dutch central-defender Ki-Jana Hoever early in the game to replace the injured Dejan Lovren, Klopp made the sixteen-year-old the record-holding youngest player for Liverpool in the FA Cup. Klopp had glowing words for the debutant after the game: 'It is only about if you are good enough and not how old you are.' And the self-confident Hoever certainly showed he could be good enough. Youngsters Rafael Camacho (eighteen) and Curtis Jones (seventeen) not only made their own bows in the senior team, they were in the starting eleven.

As they were competing in Europe, Liverpool also entered the League Cup in the third round, which was also where they left the competition. It was another 2–1 defeat, this time at Anfield to Chelsea, having led through Sturridge. Both teams had rested regular starters – indeed, Klopp started only three of the team that had beaten Southampton 3–0 in the league four days before. Certainly, the central argument for rotating in the cups, resting key players, is plausible. After all, teams playing in England don't enjoy a true winter break as, for example, German teams do, and play through the entire season. Yet there was a bitter aftertaste: along with an early exit comes the accusation that not enough respect is being shown, to the FA Cup in particular.

If this was night, then the Champions League was day. The previous year's finalists didn't exactly have the luck of the draw, though, with challenging opponents even in the group stage. Alongside Red Star Belgrade awaited Napoli and big-spending Paris Saint-Germain. Even so, Liverpool started their campaign in fitting style against PSG – with a taste of even greater European drama yet to come. A 2–0 lead through Sturridge and Milner was levelled by the French team shortly before the final whistle, only for Firmino to drive low into the far corner in injury time to win it.

The next Champions League group fixture was a role reversal for Liverpool in Napoli's venerable Stadio San Paolo. After one of the guests' most uninspired performances of the entire season, in which they failed to create a single genuine chance, Napoli claimed a 1–0 win with a goal in the ninetieth minute. Indeed, Liverpool seemed to have lost their teeth away from home in the group stage, almost as if they were out to confirm the old prejudice that English teams drop a level in performance as soon as they cross the Channel. A clear 4–0 win over Red Star at home was followed by an unexpected 2–0 reversal away in Belgrade, which gave Liverpool, although still in a favourable position, real cause for concern about qualifying for the next round. For they were now level on points with Napoli, with PSG one point behind and Red Star only two, all still in a position to qualify.

Red Star had surprised Liverpool with a blistering attacking display in front of a raucous crowd, giving regular cause for panic stations in the Liverpool penalty area, at least in the first half. Two goals down, once the second half got underway Klopp's team took the initiative, and managed to create chances against a now defence-minded Red Star, but as in Naples failed to get on the scoresheet. The Reds' attacking fury had stuttered away from Anfield.

At the press conference after the game, Klopp sought to laugh the defeat off. A Serbian journalist volunteered that his players had seemed lost on the pitch thanks to Red Star's tactics. Klopp responded: 'Is he angry? He sounds angry.' Asked by a British journalist if he could put his finger on what went wrong, the manager answered: 'I only have ten fingers.' And he went on to add: 'We made life a bit too easy tonight for Belgrade, that's the main problem. As I said, they deserved it with the passion they fought.' This was a quiet hint to his team as to where their problems lay: taking the match too lightly after winning so convincingly in the reverse fixture. 'In the end you have to score goals in a game and if you think about how often we were in the box and around, that's what you have to do in a game. But you have to make the last decision in the right way and we didn't. That's why we lost 2–0.'

The path through the group phase remained thorny, for the third away tie also proved to be a defeat. Liverpool got off to a bad start in Paris and found themselves pressed deep in their own half, although they did at least work their way back into the match somewhat in the second half. Milner halved a two-goal deficit from the penalty spot immediately before half-time. Yet with late substitutes Sturridge and Shaqiri unable to make a difference, the defeat was confirmed. Liverpool were now third in the group and facing a decider against Napoli – fortunately in front of their own fans this time. Only victory would seal first or second position in the group, and a place in the last sixteen.

Liverpool withstood the pressure and bagged the three points they needed from Napoli – and how! In an open game, the guests, who needed only a draw to proceed, refused to hide. Increasingly dominant, the Reds took the lead through Salah after the half-hour mark. Once again he had demonstrated his incredible acceleration, leaving his marker standing and Liverpool on course for victory. In the closing stages, with Napoli increasingly needing to come out to grab the draw they needed, the Reds squandered multiple chances to decide the game early: Salah, Mané and Van Dijk all had opportunities to put the game to bed, but either couldn't hit the target or couldn't get past keeper David Ospina.

This wastefulness in the dramatic closing stages was almost punished when the ball reached Napoli's Arkadiusz Milik on the edge of the six-yard box: he pulled the trigger, but Alisson pulled off an incredible reflex save to make himself Liverpool's hero. It was a save that had secured not just the win, but also Liverpool's progression to the knockout rounds. More drama was yet to come: straight afterwards, José Callejón did put the ball in the back of the Liverpool net – but the referee ruled it out for offside. Anfield breathed a collective sigh of relief.

Following the win, Klopp's thanks went most of all to his goalkeeper: 'It was not only one save. He had a lot of things to do tonight. How cool and calm he was with the ball helps us a lot in our build-up situations. When he comes out for crosses he is outstanding. And, yes, that save was just incredible,' he said at the post-match press conference.

On paper at least, the last sixteen was to be no less challenging. There, Bayern Munich awaited – in recent years a permanent fixture in the latter stages of the Champions League, and the opponent in some terrific duels during Klopp's time at Dortmund. Yet this

Bayern team were aging, their game-changers such as Arjen Robben and Franck Ribéry either injured or past the peak of their powers. A fact that should do nothing to diminish Liverpool's masterful performance in the away leg at the Allianz Arena: these were rare scenes of Bayern Munich appearing to be fainthearted in front of their own supporters in a key European match. Correspondingly great, clearly, was their respect for Klopp and his team.

This respect had already been shown in the first leg, admittedly by both sides. Liverpool, adjudged light favourites before the match by the experts, faced a Bayern who were defensively set up, giving barely anything away but failing to create anything themselves. The two teams neutralised each other and the 0–0 scoreline was the logical result. In the return leg Bayern could dominate only in the opening phases of the match, before Liverpool managed to shed their European away inhibitions. With one of his searching, game-changing passes, Van Dijk found Mané, who then bamboozled the onrushing Manuel Neuer before chipping in on twenty-six minutes. An own goal by Matip just before half-time as he attempted to clear from Bayern striker Robert Lewandowski brought Munich back into the game.

Anyone expecting all-out attack by Bayern Munich in the second half was about to be disappointed. Instead, it was Liverpool who dominated and reaped their well-earned reward following a corner from Milner: Van Dijk, who had missed the first leg through suspension, made full use of his frame, leaped highest to win the header, and restored Liverpool's lead on sixty-nine minutes. Bayern, who had failed to create any real chances in the second half, had had their wings clipped. Mané, once heavily linked with a move to Bayern from Southampton, put the match beyond doubt by completing his brace in the eighty-fourth minute: the opening toast to an English party night in Munich. The quarter-finals had been reached. It was a success that meant 'everything' to Klopp, enjoying the victory over an old rival in front of the Sky microphones.

Waiting for the Reds in the quarter-finals were two-time winners – but heavy underdogs – Porto. Especially since the two teams had met at this stage the previous season with Liverpool easing through the tie 5–0 and 0–0. And indeed the hurdle was taken at a gallop once again, even if Klopp – as is demanded of the conscientious coach – warned of Porto's strengths with light understatement: 'People with a proper idea about football did not want Porto.' His team was to give Porto the same respect they had Bayern Munich – but no more than that. After all, Klopp said, his team was 'on fire' – a claim they proved against Porto. A 2–0 win at Anfield was followed by a 4–1 win at Porto, a somewhat flattering scoreline given the numerous chances the Portuguese had, but proof of Pool's clinical efficiency, Liverpool scoring with their first four shots on target.

* * *

Superlatives should be used sparingly, but the semi-final against Barcelona was to prove one of the greatest events in Liverpool's long European Cup pedigree, if not *the* greatest next to the comeback against AC Milan in the 2005 final (from being 3–0 down at half-time to winning on penalties). Barcelona, complete with five-time Ballon d'Or winner Lionel Messi, were the bookies' favourites going into the first leg at the Camp Nou. Yet the guests came to play, attacked early and created numerous chances in an open encounter. Even going 1–0 down in the twenty-sixth minute, almost inevitably to former Liverpool player Luis Suárez, did nothing to dampen their spirits. (Before the return leg Suárez apologised to the Liverpool supporters for his extravagant celebrations against his ex-club, where he had plied his trade from 2011 to 2014.) Another blow, shortly before they conceded, was the injury that forced Naby Keita to be substituted.

As well as Suárez there was also a reunion with former Liverpool player Philippe Coutinho, who however remained below par in both games and was substituted early in both too. Suárez, who despite his apology was confronted with a hostile reception at Anfield, also failed to produce any magic in the second leg.

After the break Liverpool pressed undeterred for the equaliser. The otherwise always so dominant Barcelona found themselves forced into unaccustomed passivity. Yet neither Mané nor Salah could find a way past Barça keeper Marc-André ter Stegen. The clinical team here was Barcelona, superstar Messi in particular: first adding a second from close range in the seventy-fifth minute, then employing his 'magic foot' to fire in a sublime free-kick from thirty yards to seemingly settle it in the eighty-second. Was the Reds' own sublime season about to end with no reward? Even now Liverpool refused to give up and nearly pulled one back almost immediately, Salah slamming the ball against the post in the eighty-fourth minute. Deep into injury time, breaking from a Liverpool corner three-on-two, Dembélé had a golden opportunity to make it 4–0 after receiving the ball from Messi in the box, yet scuffed a weak shot straight to Alisson – much to Messi's irritation. Perhaps he was already anticipating the possibilities of a comeback and Anfield's irresistible magic on European nights.

Coming on the back of a 3–0 defeat, Klopp's demeanour seemed more appropriate to a different match, telling reporters: 'I enjoyed the match', apart, obviously, from the result. In true sporting manner he spoke with awe of Lionel Messi, particularly the free-kick for Barcelona's third: 'What a crazy shot!' It was a fact that Liverpool had by no means been second best against the Barcelona passing machine, with the stats – fifteen shots to twelve, five corners to three, and 52 per cent to 48 per cent possession – lightly in the Reds' favour. But when it came to being clinical, the statistics were entirely in Barcelona's favour. And their chances at Anfield? 'We will play again,' declared Klopp laconically.

And *how* they played again. Before the second leg, the Catalans had to deal with much talk about their collapse against Roma in last year's edition of the Champions League, when a 4–1 win at home was followed by an abject 3–0 defeat in Rome, which sent them out on away goals at the quarter-final stage. Perhaps a bit too much talk. For Barcelona were about to experience déjà vu. The rub of the green that had been so sorely lacking in Camp Nou was now firmly in Liverpool's favour. Of their feared attacking trident of Mané, Salah and Firmino, only Mané was fit enough to start. Salah and Firmino were replaced by Origi and Shaqiri – and it fell to one of those replacements, Origi, to open the scoring in the seventh minute. A perfect start for Klopp's team: not only was it a psychological boost in their comeback hunt, it fed the hopes of the fans, who carried their team on a tidal wave of support for the entire ninety minutes.

Still buzzing, left-back Andrew Robertson described the magic moments on the athletes' internet platform, theplayerstribune. com: 'We knew that the supporters believed in us because we could hear them. My God, we could hear them. And, probably most important of all, we knew that we believed in ourselves and in each other. That's why when Divock scored in the seventh minute, I didn't just believe. I knew. I knew what was coming – what Anfield was going to create. I hope that doesn't sound disrespectful in any way, because I couldn't have more respect for Barcelona, but on that night it wasn't about them. It was about us. We were fired up by the fans and our hunger was on another level.'

After surviving the opening phase of the game without conceding any more, the Catalans pulled themselves together and started taking the initiative, as Liverpool had managed to do at times at the Camp Nou. Before the break in particular, Barça managed to build pressure and work some decent positions, but they were lacking that final piece of quality that would have led to a goal and quelled the growing Anfield euphoria. Pulling just one goal back would have left Liverpool needing five. Still – even that wouldn't have been out of the question on a night like this ...

At half-time Klopp brought on Wijnaldum for the injured Robertson – and the Dutchman didn't waste a second. Disappointment at not starting was transformed into livewire energy: in the space of 122 seconds, starring in the fifty-fourth minute, he guided in Alexander-Arnold's deflected low cross and powered home a header from Shaqiri's cross. The score was now 3–0 – and the tie started afresh! Anfield was transformed into bedlam, betwixt and between passionate support and sickening angst at who might score the next, decisive, goal. Neither team was prepared to do open battle now, stabilising their defences and lying in wait for that potential decisive opportunity. It came in the seventy-ninth minute, with something of slapstick about it. Trent Alexander-Arnold, the only born Liverpudlian in the team and once a ballboy for the Reds, seemed to be winding up to take a corner before walking away from the ball as if he wanted to let a teammate take it. Then he dashed back and pinged the ball to Origi, lurking in the box, who coolly steered the ball into the corner of the net to make it 4–0.

Not everyone understood straight away what had happened, or if the goal stood. That included Jürgen Klopp, who caught as little of the corner as the Barcelona players. ('I had no idea who took the corner and who scored because it was too quick for me,' confessed Klopp at the post-match press conference. He hailed Origi and Alexander-Arnold's quick thinking: 'just incredibly smart'.) He had to have events explained to him by the rest of the dugout. The goal, of course, stood. The bewildered visitors had fallen into a collective slumber and let the situation pass them by. A sleight-of-hand move that might have worked against a schoolboy team – but against the mighty FC Barcelona? It's not something you're ever likely to see at this level. But then, there are more things in football than are dreamed of in philosophy.

Liverpool saw the lead out to the final whistle and found themselves for the second year running in the final of Europe's premier club competition. Klopp had now reached three European finals with Liverpool – Europa League, 2016, and Champions League, 2018 and 2019 – within four years.

After the final whistle had blown, the team, including the injured Salah, suitably wearing a T-shirt bearing the slogan 'Never give up', lined up as one in front of the Kop and celebrated in full measure with the fans, still in a state of disbelief at what had just been achieved. Warhorse James Milner shed tears of emotion, which in turn set off the empathetic Klopp. Returnee Suárez, stunned, commented that his team had 'looked like schoolboys' defending the fourth goal.

Plaudits soon piled up, even the royal family offering congratulations via Prince William on Twitter: 'Well done Liverpool – an incredible result, what a comeback! W'. The *Guardian* wove its analysis into a declaration of love for football in general: 'It was nothing short of extraordinary – one of the all-time Champions League comebacks and a reminder, amid all the euphoria, about the greatness of this sport, with its capacity to surprise and conjure up barely conceivable storylines.' Spanish sports paper *AS* wasn't quite so poetic: 'Anfield crushed a trembling Barça like a cockroach.'

Klopp glowed after the game, talking about his 'mentality giants': 'I said to the boys before the game it was impossible. But because it's you, I say we have a chance … After the season we played, the games we had, the injuries we had now in this moment, if you go out there and ask who bet a penny on us, I don't think you find a lot of people. So, and then going out there and putting a performance like this on the pitch is unbelievable … I am really proud to be the manager of this team. I will remember it forever.'

Alisson returned the praise and saw in the manager the decisive factor in the unthinkable turnaround, with the ability to transmit his belief in the impossible to the players. Captain Jordan Henderson: 'Within the team as well we believed. And that's the great thing about this team. The manager always believes, you can see that, and the talk he gives before we come to the stadium, that helps – that helps the players believe.' Even directly after the end of the first leg in Barcelona he had built them up again in the dressing room, underlining how good their performance had been, so that the belief that they might just have a chance was restored. Indeed, Liverpool really had performed far better than the scoreline suggested.

Andrew Robertson gives an impression in *The Players' Tribune* of how Klopp worked his magic after that first-leg defeat: 'The manager came into the dressing room, bouncing and wearing his trademark massive smile. "Boys, boys, boys!" he says. "We are not the best team in the world. Now you know that. Maybe they are! Who cares? Who cares! We can still beat the best team in the world. Let's go again."' In hindsight, Robertson finds, that was the moment that changed everything.

No less dramatic was the second leg of the semi-final that was to decide Liverpool's opponents, Tottenham Hotspur or Ajax. With Spurs 2–0 down in Amsterdam at half-time they needed their own comeback saga – which they sealed in the form of an injury-time strike to make it 3–2 and take them to the final. The purely English final was symbolic of an at least temporary weakening of Spanish dominance, after a Spanish team had won the competition in each of the past five years, four of those wins being by Real Madrid. That the final of the Europa League was also an all-English affair, Arsenal facing Chelsea, completed the European success story. No trace of Brexit in football at least …

* * *

The special challenge for Klopp leading up to the final in the Wanda Metropolitano, Atlético Madrid's renovated stadium, consisted not just of getting the two previous lost finals out of his players' heads, but also making best use of the three-week break between the last Premier League game of the season and the final. This was new territory even for as experienced a manager as Klopp. How would they avoid losing their rhythm? How would they maintain their intensity without burning out before the final? One part of the plan was a six-day training camp in Marbella in Spain – exactly what they had done so successfully before the tie with Bayern Munich, making good use of the break from competition their early exits from the League and FA cups had afforded them.

Klopp wanted to leave nothing to chance as they prepared for the final. Although he was highly familiar with Spurs from their many clashes in the Premier League, he had them simulated in a friendly. As Renato Paiva, the coach of Benfica's second team, revealed to Portuguese sports newspaper *A Bola*, Klopp had realised that the playing style of Benfica B resembled that of Tottenham. To prevent Liverpool getting rusty, a friendly was organised to take place a week before the final. The Lisbon players were to match as closely as possible the play and positioning of Tottenham's offensive trio Harry Kane, Dele Alli and Christian Eriksen, as well as the team's attacking and defensive plays and the expected routines for dead ball situations.

Then, finally, the long three-week wait for the fans for '*el duelo*' was over. Excepting the injured Keita, the Reds had their strongest first eleven available, Firmino having recovered in time from a muscle injury. And the sequence of events was to be quite different to the previous year. The course of the match ran in their favour right at the start: twenty seconds had gone when the Reds were awarded a penalty. Tottenham's Moussa Sissoko was struck on the outstretched arm – with which he was attempting to direct a defensive colleague – by Mané's cross. The referee blew his whistle. The penalty was put straight down the middle by Salah – who with his early injury in the previous season's final had rivalled Loris Karius in tragedy and left the pitch in tears. It was 1–0 to Liverpool in the second minute. Benfica B coach Paiva revealed in a newspaper interview that Liverpool's play in the lead up to the penalty reminded him of a move from the friendly.

Contrary to what one might expect, the early goal did no favours for the neutral spectator. Liverpool were prepared to wait for their next opportunity and ventured only the occasional counter, while Tottenham, although to the casual eye lightly in the ascendant, never found a way to generate clear-cut chances. Coming back from nearly two months out injured, goal-guarantee Kane failed to have an impact. Liverpool searched for the optimal strategy following the unexpected start to the game: defend the 1–0 lead and not risk too much, or attempt to find a second goal and kill the game off. The Reds decided on the more defensive option, with little to be seen of their usual aggression.

It developed into an untypical game for Liverpool. But this time the result was all that mattered. Not that there was much chance of topping the drama and emotion of the semi-final. The long three-week break before the match, which applied to both teams, may well have combined with the natural tension of a final, and the Spanish climate, to dampen any footballing spectacle. Klopp made his changes around the hour mark, bringing on semi-final hero Origi for Firmino and then Milner for Wijnaldum. And it was to Milner that the first big chance of the second half fell – but his shot from just inside the box fizzed past the right-hand post.

Even if they weren't scoring the goals, it was the two record transfers, Alisson Becker and Virgil van Dijk, who proved to be true matchwinners. They were the rock on which the Spurs attack foundered – especially towards the end of the game as Tottenham were forced to come out in search of an equaliser. Van Dijk stood steady and cleared what needed to be cleared. The same went for his underrated partner Matip, whose play was often less conspicuous but immensely effective, earning him Dejan Lovren's place in the starting eleven. Alisson proved to be the deciding factor, dealing with a number of good Spurs opportunities, including an excellent Eriksen free-kick, as the clock ticked down.

Once again, a goalkeeper made a big contribution to the final result. This time, in Liverpool's favour. For, just as against Barcelona, it was to fall to Origi to score the killer goal. With the ball bouncing around the Spurs box following a Liverpool corner, it dropped to Matip who tapped it to Origi on the left-side of the box. The Belgian slid it past Lloris into the far corner of the net. It was 2–0 to Liverpool with three minutes of normal time to go, and Spurs' resistance was broken. The Reds saw the game out. The goalscorer had proved himself the model of efficiency: in the entire Champions League season he had three shots on goal – and all three went in!

* * *

Klopp's Heroes – the players in the final

The team that brought the European Cup back to Liverpool after fourteen years:

Alisson Becker – Alexander-Arnold, Matip, Van Dijk, Robertson – Henderson, Fabinho, Wijnaldum (Milner, 62) – Salah, Roberto Firmino (Origi, 58), Mané (Gomez, 90)

Scorers: Salah (2) and Origi (87)

* * *

This was Liverpool's sixth title in the competition; only AC Milan (seven) and Real Madrid (thirteen) can boast more European Cup and Champions League triumphs. For Klopp it meant – after six lost finals, three of them with Liverpool, and after two runners-up medals in the Champions League – finally a gold medal, finally a chance to lift a pot (even if, modest to a fault, he was quick to give his players precedence during the award ceremony). It was Klopp's first win in a final since the rollicking 5–2 cup win with Borussia

Dortmund over Bayern Munich in 2012. Following Jupp Heynckes (1998 with Real Madrid), Klopp is now the second German manager to win the Champions League with a foreign club, definitively establishing himself as one of the managerial greats.

Speaking to Sky, Klopp conceded that they hadn't played well – neither team had. Nevertheless, the final was emblematic of the Klopp plan – team-oriented, with group success being at the forefront rather than individual glory. It was the result of a development process that Klopp had been pursuing with his coaching team since 2015. The squad had learned from the previous finals, when Liverpool had won hearts but not cups with their attacking play. Like in the 2016 final – when Liverpool started strongly but had nothing left in the tank in the second half against an increasingly dominant Sevilla. A final is there to be won. The Reds took on the task soberly and rationally this time, and were rewarded. A lesson learned, a mark of intelligent reflection, recognising when pragmatism and not prettiness is called for. If not in a final, then when?

When the whistle has been blown and the heavy burden of significance has been lifted from shoulders, it's a time for big emotions. It is now that the spectator sees moving scenes on the pitch, the players jumping around drunk with joy or on their knees in grief. Jordan Henderson, who as a boy watching the 2003 final between AC Milan and Juventus had already determined 'Dad, I'm going to play there one day', sobbed in the arms of his manager, without whom this triumph would have been 'impossible', as he told television journalists. He praised above all the togetherness in the dressing room that Klopp had managed to generate. 'We all love him.' The players carried 'King Klopp' across the pitch to the end accommodating 15,000 Liverpool supporters and gave him the bumps. Henderson revealed that he had wanted to lift the trophy together with Klopp, but the manager had refused, telling him it was the captain's job.

Just as they did after they had beaten Barcelona to qualify for the final, the team and the coaching staff lined up arm in arm, this time in front of an impressive Red block in the Wanda Metropolitano, with the European Cup in front of them. They all sang together: 'You'll Never Walk Alone'. Moving images which, however many times they see them, the supporters will surely never tire of feasting their eyes on.

* * *

Klopp had matured. After the final whistle he showed dignity not in defeat, but in victory. There was no ecstatic celebration, no spaced out gurning grimace of triumph, no wild run across the pitch. While the rest of the Liverpool bench stormed the pitch in celebration, Klopp preferred to shake hands with Tottenham's Argentinian manager Mauricio Pochettino, because: 'I know how Tottenham feels in the moment better than anyone else in the world.' Klopp had previously been backward in coming forward after the tachycardia tie against Barcelona at Anfield, though after matches against Málaga (with Borussia Dortmund) and against Borussia Dortmund (with Liverpool) he had crowned a successful goal hunt with a memorably passionate celebration. Jürgen Klopp is not someone who can be put in a box of stereotypes. Perhaps the party animal in him needed some time to assimilate – based on the importance of the title – the greatest success of his management career. The next day, though, at the grandiose reception in Liverpool, it was time to release the party animal again …

In the press conference after the game Klopp underlined that the title wasn't so important for himself, but that he was overjoyed for the 'boys': 'It feels really good, but I am much calmer than I thought I would be when it finally happened. It was not important really to touch the cup or whatever. I love the pictures when the boys held it aloft. I saw a few faces in the stands. That is what gave me everything I need. But tomorrow, going to Liverpool and having something to celebrate is big and I am really looking forward to that.' This was 'big' – an observation that Klopp was to repeat many times that evening.

When the alteration of his public perception as being the 'manager who loses finals' was touched upon, Klopp responded: 'We spoke two days ago about my unlucky career, somehow, and when I hear it, I think, yeah, people could see it like this, but I don't feel it, to be honest, because I always see the way to a final as well. Because of course that's important for me as well. I think my life is much better than I ever expected it. So winning something is good, cool, but it's for all the other people. I'm not so much in it, I'm interested really in development. But I get it, we have to win things, so it's for us really important that people don't ask now all the time about not winning or winning things. We won something and we will carry on, we want to win things one hundred per cent.'

Something that bothers Klopp is that the quality of a team's coaching is often judged according to a few contingent factors in a football match, which then decide first or second place. Or as some people choose to look at it, first is everything, second is nothing. This is anathema to Klopp, for it's a viewpoint that fails to take into account the long line of opponents left behind by 'second' on the way to the final.

Klopp was enjoying the victory not just for his players, but for himself and his family: 'I feel mostly relief, relief for my family. The last six times we flew on holiday with only a silver medal it didn't feel too cool. It's different this year, it's for them.' In the moment of his greatest triumph Klopp was thinking of the people around him, taking note of his responsibilities. The inner satisfaction he felt in this moment was derived from the happiness of others, his family, the supporters, the players and the club staff.

Fitting then, considering how Klopp motivates his players. He strengthens the sense of community, produces a feeling of togetherness, shares responsibility among all the players. In the 'ego business' of professional football he asks that players play not for themselves, but for everyone who is involved with the club, the staff as well as the supporters, who give their all day in, day out to make Liverpool Football Club successful. 'Everyone who is connected with Liverpool, you want to make them proud,' confirmed Van Dijk.

* * *

The manager showed off some of his talents during the well-lubricated post-match celebrations. Like after the 2018 Champions League final, he sang a song, composed by the coaching team, with Die Toten Hosen frontman and LFC fan Campino – this time not in defiance, but in pure joy. Die Toten Hosen shared the witty song on Instagram with all the fans: 'We're sending greetings from Madrid, tonight we made it number six. We brought it back to Liverpool, 'cause we promised we will do.'

Karaoke Klopp could hardly believe it himself that the wish expressed in the song a year ago, when he and Campino had announced that the cup would be coming back to Liverpool, had become a reality at the first possible opportunity: 'But after the final last year, when we came home to Liverpool, it was not cool. One of my friends is a singer and my assistant coach, we sang a song: "We saw the European Cup, Madrid had all the luck, we swear we'll keep on being cool, we'll bring it back to Liverpool." Nobody thought in that moment it would happen. In that moment it was only to lift our mood a little bit and now it happened actually, so we have to think about what we will sing now because obviously it means something.' As it turned out, it didn't take long to think up some suitable lyrics!

It was not to be the only demonstration that evening of Klopp's vocal stylings. He also loosened his vocal cords for Jan Åge Fjørtoft, the former Premier League and Bundesliga target man, now a pundit on Norwegian TV. Mashing up Liverpool's sixth triumph in Europe's premier club competition and Salt-N-Pepa's 1991 classic 'Let's Talk About Sex', Klopp sang 'Let's talk about six, baby!'

'This is maybe the best night of my life, at least professionally,' Klopp told English TV journalists. The finals curse had been lifted. Klopp can do more than 'just' develop, he can win titles – for the fourth time now, following two league titles and the cup with Dortmund in Germany.

* * *

The international press had a lot to say about Liverpool's success – less about the unspectacular final, much more about the club's development under Klopp. Spanish sports paper *Marca* went as far as practically deifying Klopp as a kind of 'football god'. This is just a selection of the emotional responses from the press:

England

Liverpool Echo: 'Liverpool are Kings of Europe once again after a night of pure ecstasy in Madrid. Jürgen Klopp is the class act who in four short years has transformed Liverpool from also-rans into the most feared side in Europe. This is a special team with an incredible, inspirational leader. Ol' Big Ears is coming home to Merseyside for the sixth time. This party has started and it won't be finishing any time soon.'

Daily Mail: 'This was not a night to marvel at the football but to revel in the history. It was only twelve months ago after all, when they were leaving the pitch at the Olympic Stadium in Kiev, desolate having lost to Madrid in the final, haunted by nightmarish images of two macabre bloopers from their goalkeeper, Loris Karius, and a stunning overhead kick from Gareth Bale. They have lived through this season determined to purge themselves of that disappointment. So what have you actually won, Jürgen Klopp? No longer can the accusation that the German is a nearly man be levelled at him. Never again. He is one of the great ones now.'

Daily Telegraph: 'The sixth star sewn onto the Liverpool shirt, a club that keeps winning the biggest prize of all through different eras and generations. A place for Jürgen Klopp amongst the greats at Anfield, where they have a European history unsurpassed in the English game of stupendous performances and great finals – of which, strangely, this, the occasion of their sixth European Cup, was neither. It is hard to reconcile the immense achievement of Klopp's Liverpool, the transformation of a mediocre Premier League team into the champions of Europe in less than four years, with this: a final forgettable in every aspect save the outcome.'

The Times: 'An unlovely spectacle but who from Liverpool cared? Control replaced chaos, sparse notes the heavy metal, and in a manner opposite to how they reached Madrid, red rule enveloped Europe again.'

Spain

El Mundo Deportivo: 'Liverpool touch the Madrid night sky. Crowned Kings of Europe for the sixth time. Klopp grabs the handle of the cup at his third attempt. The early penalty hit Tottenham hard and determined the course of the game. Origi was the Champions League hero again. Their patience with Jürgen Klopp has paid off for Liverpool.'

Marca: 'Liverpool raises the sixth title to the sky! Apotheosis of Rock 'n' Klopp. Van Dijk is a giant. Klopp has entered the Olympus of the great coaches. A great atmosphere in the stadium, but little football. Spurs deserved more, but Van Dijk and Alisson prevented worse.'

AS: 'Eternal Liverpool. Sixth title for the Reds. The curse of Klopp comes to an end. The time of high expectations and low results is over. The patience has paid off. *Danke*, Mister Klopp. You'll never walk alone ... Oh Jürgen, it would be nice if we could experience you sometime in Spain as a coach.'

Italy

Gazzetta dello Sport: 'Liverboom! After losing two Champions League titles Klopp is now celebrating a deserved triumph. With pragmatism and intelligence, he conquered the Champions League at the third time of asking. The wound of having lost the final last year is healed. Salah, who was sunk by Sergio Ramos last year, celebrated his revenge at the end of an extremely tactical and "Italian" match.'

Corriere della Sera: 'Red paradise: twenty-five seconds were enough for Jürgen Klopp's troops to subdue their opponent and conquer their sixth Champions League title. This victory is first and foremost Jürgen Klopp's triumph. Klopp conquers a place in football history alongside Bob Paisley, Joe Fagan, and Rafa Benítez.'

Corriere dello Sport: 'King Klopp: He had long dreamed of this moment. His victory is fully deserved. This time, he also had the luck on his side that was missing in the six lost finals. The deadly disappointment of the lost victory from last year is forgotten. Liverpool are celebrating their best season of the last twenty years. After a continental masterpiece, Klopp wants to extend his contract with the Reds. The negotiations have already started.'

Tuttosport: 'Salah and Origi conquer Football Olympus. The match was not nice to look at. A game that was heavily influenced by the Reds' goal in the first few minutes. Pochettino's men kept fighting, but Van Dijk and his colleagues closed down every gap. Keeper Alisson was also decisive.'

Germany

Kicker: 'King Klopp. The German coach has finally won the Champions League with Liverpool. But this should just be the first step.'

faz.net (*Frankfurter Allgemeine Zeitung*): 'Mission accomplished. On Saturday evening the toils and tribulations of the past three-and-a-half years in Liverpool were crowned with success.'

Süddeutsche Zeitung: 'At the end of a hero's journey. Klopp rewards himself with the title at his third attempt.'

* * *

Emotional too was the triumphal reception for the team in Liverpool on Sunday 2 June 2019, with an incredible 750,000 people packing the streets to give the winners the welcome they deserved as they toured the city for hours in an open-top red bus, shrouded in red fog. A red cordon, starting at the airport, ran for miles all the way to the city centre. The whole city, except for hardened Everton fans, was on its feet, a city of music rocked by heroes in red jerseys. 'I cannot really describe it, because I cried a little bit as well, because it's so overwhelming what the people are doing,' Klopp said as he gave his impressions of the scene to club website liverpoolfc.com. 'When you have a direct eye contact and you see how much it means to them that's touching, to be honest. It's brilliant.' Klopp isn't ashamed to shed a tear, and why should he be?

Victory in the final was one element of a three-part promise, two of which were now fulfilled, with one remaining open. Promise, Part I: At his introductory press conference in October 2015, Klopp had promised a title within four years. Promise kept, just in time. Promise, Part II: In 2018, together with Campino after the Champions League final defeat, he had announced that he would bring the European Cup back to Liverpool. Kept in style. Promise, Part III: 'This is only the start,' Klopp said after the victory over Tottenham. 'It's still a wonderful age group, they all have the best times in their careers ahead of them.' Klopp isn't finished yet.

Some commentators too were already daring to dream about a new era for Liverpool, one in which the Reds would once again dominate the European stage. Daring dreams given the density of talent available to Europe's elite clubs, and their perennially aggressive transfer policies. On the other hand, Liverpool's key players were all on long-term contracts, and being an average 26½ years old (2018–19 season), the squad was at the perfect footballing age. Those were conditions that did allow LFC to dream of a new golden era – with 'Development Meister' Klopp ideally there to deliver more magic moments for the club and its supporters for a long time to come.

Prior to the Champions League final, Liverpool's American chairman Tom Werner had already made his unbounded admiration for the manager clear to the *Liverpool Echo*, telling them that 'he can stay as long as he likes'. Can anyone be surprised? Klopp has delivered not just sporting but also financial growth for the owners. According to transfermarkt.co.uk, the squad is worth more than £887 million as of July 2020 – more than three times as much as when Klopp took the reins in October 2015 (£262 million). During this period, in absolute terms, no other football team has appreciated as much in value.

Despite investing around £230 million in the squad during the 2018/19 business year, the club announced in February 2020 that the Reds had banked a pre-tax profit of around £42 million. This was made possible by achieving a turnover of over £500 million for the first time. For the 2015–16 season, during which Klopp was appointed, turnover had been around £300 million – making a more than 50 per cent increase within four years. Somewhat the worse for wear in the autumn of 2015, less than five years later English football's Old Masters had been restored to pristine condition financially as well as on the pitch.

In summer 2019, Klopp's contract was set to run until 2022. He had been in charge for seven years at Mainz and Dortmund respectively; 2022 would also mark seven years at Liverpool. Did the club have to worry about keeping Klopp past that date? Fresh advances arrived from the south of Germany: Bayern Munich's honorary president Franz Beckenbauer, a friend of Klopp's going back years, made known via *Bild* newspaper that he 'longed' for him to become their manager.

In December 2019, business was taken care of: Klopp extended his contract in the North West for a further two years, until 2024.

'We decided to continue what's worked so far, not too bad,' he announced with typical understatement on a short video clip on the club's channel, LFCTV. 'We love it here. First and foremost, it's a wonderful club, we really feel at home.' For him, this was 'a statement of intent, one which is built on my knowledge of what we as a partnership have achieved so far and what is still there for us to achieve,' he added in a statement on the club website.

And indeed, there was plenty still to do. As they say, after the game is before the game, and even at the post-match press conference after the final in Madrid, Klopp had already had an eye on the upcoming 2019–20 season. Klopp revealed then that his management colleague Pep Guardiola had just called to congratulate him. And they had agreed that 'We will kick each other's butts again next season.' The hunger for victory hadn't been sated: it was now more intense than ever. Mission number one remained: win the nineteenth league title. And there was also the allure of winning the FA Cup, which Liverpool had 'only' won a comparatively modest seven times – and which under Klopp's management had been treated rather as the poor relation. Or the Club World Cup, a trophy conspicuously absent from the Reds' cabinet.

* * *

Even before the magnificent efforts of the 2018–19 season, Thomas Helmer regarded the positive assessment he made at the start of Jürgen Klopp and Liverpool Football Club's relationship as more than confirmed: 'The Premier League is balanced, anyone can beat anyone else. I've been impressed by how Klopp has imposed himself on this tough league – huge compliment to Klopp. That Liverpool are competing right at the top again is largely down to him. And in terms of his personality too, he's a perfect fit for

Liverpool. People love his charisma and his emotionality, which are the real deal. This passion on the touchline is a novelty for the Premier League. When I think of former Arsenal manager Arsène Wenger: most games he spent sat stoically on the bench. Klopp offers you a completely different spectacle and lets people share in his emotions. That's great for the fans. And I find that very refreshing too, when he gets so wonderfully wound up.'

Klopp has continued his development in England, Helmer believes, taken the next step and won people over with his open manner. The Euro 96 winner is convinced of that, and also believes his estimation of the type of player who would have difficulty with Klopp has been confirmed: 'Today as yesterday Klopp has no time for egocentric stars, you can see that at Liverpool now too. First he let Mario Balotelli go, and he dropped Mamadou Sakho as well.' For Klopp, the team comes first.

Early retirement?

In the medium term Frank Dopheide sees Jürgen Klopp managing Germany. Yet would this job (when World Cup winner Joachim Löw finally decides to pass on the baton) really be suitable for a man who belongs on the training pitch, ideally daily? Being able to work with 'his boys' only at irregular intervals, for only a few days at a time? Being able to coach only every few weeks, for only a couple of matches? At this stage, it's hard to see Klopp getting much out of that any time soon.

But what does the man himself say about how he sees his future? When asked during his Dortmund days about a possible life plan, Klopp's answer may well have come as something of a surprise to outside observers: 'At home sometimes we talk about what's going to be happening in ten years' time. It would really be cool to stand there then and say: "Thanks, it was great, no end of fun, that's enough." And to have thirty years' time. I haven't seen anything of the world. I haven't been on holiday much.'[8] Klopp was able to make that good during the months after the end of the BVB chapter of his life.

A management career ending as soon as 2021, as he had in mind ten years before, was no longer up for discussion in 2020 – given that he had signed a contract extension at Liverpool through 2024. But retiring from football at fifty-seven, when his contract expires? It's something you wouldn't put past Klopp, given how uncompromisingly he's always followed his own path. He had already spoken in quite similar terms previously: 'To be able to enjoy that feeling of calm ... where I wouldn't care one way or another if a football team won at the weekend or not ... This would be cool, if we could pull it off somehow: with the kids and the grandkids in a big house somewhere just lounging in the sun and being happy. Now that would be really being able to relax.'[9]

Saying this, Klopp looks down, absorbed in his thoughts, lets his words sink in for a moment, before adding: 'And ideally living abroad, not working.' At the moment, though, he has made his mind up to work abroad – and at his third managerial position, too, is rising magnificently to the challenge of making his players the best footballers they can be. And anyone who sees Klopp in full flow on the Anfield touchline will know that this is a man living his dream – and in no hurry to retire from football.

18

A SEROTONIN SEASON: WINNING THE PREMIER LEAGUE

So great was the trust in the squad's capabilities that Liverpool did without any big-name signings for the upcoming 2019–20 season. Dutch youngster Sepp van den Berg (just seventeen at the time) was brought in as a future prospect for central defence; sixteen-year-old Harvey Elliott, a winger who had already played in the Premier League for Fulham, was another long-term prospect; and Spaniard Adrián succeeded Simon Mignolet as back-up keeper, the Belgian preferring to return to his homeland and get game time with Club Brugge. Where indeed could the squad have been improved? After enjoying great success, teams often need to bring in fresh, hungry players to avoid complacency setting in. But 'Klopp's boys' had had nowhere near their fill: united by the grand goal of winning the league, their motivation levels were as high as ever. Key squad members couldn't be tempted away; for Klopp, contract extensions for core players such as Salah, Mané, Henderson and Alexander-Arnold were just as valuable as any new transfer.

Still, in the January transfer window Liverpool did add to their squad, bringing in Takumi Minamino. The Japanese winger from Red Bull Salzburg was considered potential back-up for the heavily relied upon Roberto Firmino. And there was a welcome financial side-effect for the club: Minamino's transfer was expected to boost support in his homeland, opening up a new market. For a modern football business that understands itself as a global player, it's an aspect of the game that can't be underestimated.

The 2019–20 season was going to be one to remember – for the love of the game for starters, as Liverpool's mastery of the Premier League bordered on perfection, assuming with no lesser aplomb the mantle of Manchester City's previous dominance. But then – much more seriously, tragically and completely unexpectedly, encompassing the entire world with effects reaching far, far beyond football and its often exaggerated importance – COVID-19 brought football to a standstill. First, though, the sporting story.

As league runners-up, Liverpool faced double winners Manchester City in the Community Shield. The loss on penalties, with Georginio Wijnaldum failing to convert, was soon put behind them. Ten days later, Liverpool returned to Istanbul to face another English team, Europa League winners Chelsea, in the UEFA Super Cup final – the first all-English final since the competition officially began in 1973. The destination of another trophy was to be decided after a penalty shootout, with newcomer Adrián taking the place of injured number one Alisson and making himself the matchwinner. With the scores tied at 2–2 after extra-time (Mané bagging a brace), Adrián saved Chelsea's final penalty, with all of Liverpool's takers converting. Their reward was Liverpool's fourth success in the competition and their second European trophy of 2019.

In the league, the Reds couldn't stop winning; in contrast, Manchester City were showing unfamiliar signs of weakness and, along with Leicester, were losing the struggle to prevent the gap between them and the top from growing. The raw numbers, a smorgasbord of record breakers and fantasy-football figures, speak for themselves:

- The 3–2 win against West Ham at Anfield on matchday twenty-seven was their twenty-first home win in a row, a run extending back into the previous season – a new league best. The previous record had also been set by Liverpool – in 1972, almost half a century prior.

- Eighteen wins in succession, home and away, equalled Man City's record streak from 2017–18.

- The Reds won twenty-six of their first twenty-seven Premier League games, the only imperfection being a 1–1 draw at Old Trafford in October. Including the winning run at the end of the previous season, they had bagged an unbelievable 106 from 108 possible points in thirty-six matches.

- Their lead over 'challengers' Manchester City, who had already lost an unexpected six times by matchday twenty-seven, now totalled twenty-two points. Liverpool could have forfeited seven games and still topped the league.

Even Klopp, never usually one to get too caught up in statistics, had to concede, 'It is so special. The numbers are incredible.'

The one-on-one duels at the top of the table left a lasting impression on their competitors. The 4–0 defeat of Leicester at the King Power Stadium on Boxing Day was a demonstration of strength, expressing their iron will to maintain focus until their mission was accomplished. Klopp had drilled this attitude into his players: take it one step at a time, never slacken, never let the growing public euphoria become a distraction. Before their game against Liverpool, Leicester had gone eight months undefeated in front of their own supporters. Klopp was fuming at half-time: Liverpool had failed to turn their crushing superiority into more than a one-goal lead (Firmino). In the second half they were more clinical, with Milner scoring a penalty, Firmino completing a brace and Alexander-Arnold adding the finishing flourish to a well-earned victory.

The year 2020 was ushered in with high praise from Chris Wilder, the manager of newly promoted but high-flying Sheffield United. He and his team had just lost 2–0 at Anfield, in itself hardly a surprising result. But how that result was achieved, thanks not only to the outstanding individual quality that the Liverpool players possessed, but also more fundamental footballing attributes, drew admiration. These were stars who weren't shy of getting mud on their boots, who kept doing their work even with the clock ticking down on a comfortable lead. 'So, they won every first ball, every second ball, dropped on every second ball, ran forward and ran back and they did that miles better than us,' Wilder said. 'They played in second and third gear but still had the humility and desire to do that as world champions, European champions and obviously, they're well on the way to being Premier League champions.' United couldn't lay a glove on them; in short they were, as Wilder put it, 'outstanding'. Klopp must have been tickled pink by the comments: they highlighted that the hard work his players put into training every day was being transferred to the pitch and paying off.

* * *

Liverpool is worth a trip: whether it's for the music-centric atmosphere of the home-city of the Beatles, which is reflected in the supporters' creative song culture, or its trendy, colourful cultural scene, or the historic docks (a UNESCO World Heritage Site), varied architecture and attractions such as ... Anfield. Street art can be found in the city, for example on the side of a building on the corner of Jordan Street and Jamaica Street. An imposing mural by the artist Akse covers several square metres. His giant Jürgen Klopp, in that familiar, affectionate pose showing gratitude for the fans' support, right hand over heart, a fond gaze directed towards what must be the stands, has graced the brickwork since 2018. The eye is drawn down towards the club's mantra, whose first line derives from the legendary Bill Shankly: 'We are Liverpool. This means more.' Two sentences that are omnipresent in the stadium, at the training ground, in the city.

Klopp gave expression to this identity in his own inimitable way, in a moving club video that gave goosebumps not only to Liverpool fans. Accompanied by reactions to memorable moments from the Reds' sporting history, disaster as well as triumph, ecstasies of passion and silent despair of players and supporters alike, Klopp's voice comes from 'offstage'. He speaks without rhetorical flourishes, calmly conveying emotion: 'For others it's sport, for us it's a way of life. They have a stadium, we have a home. They have songs, we have an anthem. They have a manager, we have a guardian [Bill Shankly, who passed away in 1981]. They have supporters, we are a family.' At the end of the video, Klopp himself appears and simply states: 'We are Liverpool. This means more.' Some may find it emotionally overblown; for others, it sums up the aura and uniqueness of this club. A club that after the stadium tragedies of Heysel in 1985 and Hillsborough in 1989 can never be a 'normal' one.

German former sports journalist Lissi, now retired, is going to the match against West Ham United on 24 February. The night will be spent at the Royal Hotel, Crosby, on Merseyside, the meeting place for many Liverpool fans who come from out of town, especially when there's an evening kick-off. The hotel barman is friendly with Liverpool's kitman, and has a few stories. 'They don't go past these four walls, though.'

Neil is at the hotel, too, but not to spend the night, no, he lives nearby. He's there to meet up with friends before they head to the stadium. Neil hasn't missed a home game in thirty years, as he proudly declares, but now he's got a problem, a luxury problem, admittedly. 'If Liverpool keep winning like this, they'll clinch the title in three weeks at Everton – just when I'm on holiday in South America!' Of all teams, their city rivals. That's right, Liverpool isn't all Anfield and red. Blue and Goodison Park too – just five minutes from the LFC stadium at that. The Toffees, though, have been enduring some fallow years. Klopp's Reds outshine everything.

Neil's secret hope, one he scarcely dare say out loud: he must root for the opposition. 'Perhaps they'll drop a few points before then, so I won't miss the celebrations ...'

That the title celebrations might be postponed indefinitely, that it would be uncertain whether they would even take place because football would be brought to a halt by the coronavirus ... Neil wouldn't have thought it possible. The pandemic spread across the planet; football wasn't so important anymore. Did Neil ever board the plane for South America? And if he did, was he able to get back home before his flight was cancelled? These are uncertain times.

An English friend of Lissi's has been living in Germany for thirty years, and that friend's sister lives in tranquil Formby just up the coast from Liverpool, half an hour by car. This is also where the Klopps have made their home, like many Liverpool players, past and present. Here, away from the big city, the beach is a standing invitation to switch off. Emma, the Klopps' pet dog (named after the nickname of BVB's legendary striker Lothar Emmerich) brought with them from Dortmund, can be taken along the coast for long walks. The friend relates how her sister gushes about Kloppo whenever she talks about him: 'When youth teams spot him and ask for a photo he takes care of everyone, he always stands there patiently.' There you go, away from the pitch, he's a laid-back kind of guy. And one who shares the famous English sense of humour. Not a bad qualification for feeling at home here!

Klopp often pops in to his cosy traditional local, the Freshfield. Rustic, the way you imagine an English pub, and the hub of the community, complete with fish and chips and Sunday roasts, real ale on tap, of course, and pub quizzes. Even the dog is welcome. 'The Boss', as he is affectionately known, often mingles with the regulars. 'He really is the "normal one" there. If he'd known you'd come from Germany specially for the game, he'd have come and sat with you to have a bit of a chat,' the sister is certain. He's well liked here for his uncomplicated manner. Lately, these spontaneous encounters are becoming a rarity, much to Klopp's regret. His visits were attracting too many people, it was getting too much. A downside to fame.

Even before Klopp's time, Lissi was a follower of English football in general and Liverpool FC in particular. 'It's football in its purest form – the narrow confines of the smaller stadiums, the closeness to the pitch, the atmosphere at the games, it's unique,' she says passionately. 'No one is jeered, even when an opposition player is down on the pitch. In Germany, there'd be a concert of whistles at once, because everyone would assume they were putting it on. When an opposition player does well, they'll even applaud respectfully, and even the players complain less. Nothing else matters except football.' Liverpool and England: worth a visit.

The Reds didn't play spectacularly against West Ham, but they won 3–2. Sadio Mané scored the winner in the eighty-first minute. Another late winner, another comeback win. The league is another step closer. In Liverpool, Lissi checks out the Beatles statues and predicts: 'One day there'll be one of Jürgen Klopp here as well.'

* * *

The 3–1 win over Man City at Anfield on matchday twelve, back in November, had been an early indication of which way the title was heading. The victory had been well-earned, although a little luck had been involved: immediately before Fabinho's early goal, Alexander-Arnold had unintentionally but clearly touched the ball with his arm in his own penalty area – the referee waved away what could have been a City penalty. Pep Guardiola was absolutely furious. That was of no consequence to Salah and Mané, who scored to set the Reds on their way to victory.

It spoke of an astonishing level of fitness, of a carefully calibrated intensification of training and effort, that Liverpool turned around a remarkable number of matches in the final minutes, often sealing the three points in injury time. The team demonstrated the toughness of a boxer in taking blows on the chin and coming straight back – with the belief and will to win right to the final whistle to decide a match in their favour. The term 'Kloppage time' was soon doing the rounds.

One example was the league clash at Villa Park at the start of November. Liverpool were anything other than convincing. Yet when Robertson levelled the scores at 1–1 in the eighty-seventh minute, he didn't waste a second celebrating, but signalled that being satisfied with a draw wasn't good enough. And indeed, Mané still had time to make it 2–1. That goal meant that the Reds had already bagged ten points from a losing position that season. For midfielder Adam Lallana, the late turnaround was an expression of inner conviction, as he declared in the wake of the match: 'It's almost like a sixth sense. We knew at half-time that, if we got one goal, it's going to count. We got it late but we still had time. It doesn't surprise me that we got a second goal.' The more times they staged a successful fightback, the stronger their conviction they would do it – and the more fear was instilled in their opponents. It's scarcely worth mentioning that this comeback capability was something Klopp worked towards in training, focusing specifically on pressing.

Not that Klopp ever leaves anything to chance. On his initiative, since 2018 the team behind the team has even included a throw-in coach. The Dane Thomas Grønnemark works on the players' technique at regular intervals, as well as advising several other clubs. Nutritionist Mona Nemmer joined Liverpool's specialist squad back in 2016; like fitness coach Andreas Kornmayer, she was headhunted from Bayern Munich and works concurrently for the German FA.

Veteran *Bundesliga* pro Erik Meijer, who spent the 1999–2000 season at Anfield, is a fan of his ex-club's power football: 'The pressing full-back combo of Alexander-Arnold and Robertson together with their offensive power is triple plus! The backline stays very high and defends to the front, never back. The three-man midfield counterpresses very aggressively and the attackers pull off deadly solo plays. The numerous victories in the final minutes are the result of pressure, pressure, and more pressure until the opposition is broken,' is the Dutchman's compact summary of their style of play. Meijer is impressed that Klopp had come through a league season without much in the way of rotation:

'The back four is nearly always the same and in attack Salah, Mané and Firmino play over 90 per cent of games. It's only in midfield that you see more changes.' And the title? 'They'll do it this year, finally,' Meijer was certain in February.

Meijer sees 'The Boss' as the main architect of this success: 'Liverpool's development is naturally in very large part down to him, but also to his purchases. He was able to invest big money in players who perfect his system. What's also decisive is the drive that he brings to the team, every single day. The players follow his example. He's kind, he's direct, but also hard as nails if you're not putting the effort in or not doing what you should be.' Former striker Meijer would have loved to play for Klopp: 'Characters pick themselves up after a setback, again and again. Just like Klopp managed to do so impressively after losing those finals. And with success, with trophies, the trust is even stronger. *Follow the winners ...*'

* * *

At the same time as Liverpool's dominance in the league was piling the pressure on their challengers in February, a charming story was made public. For a school project, ten-year-old Daragh Curley had written a letter to Liverpool FC, yet it was anything other than ordinary fan mail: 'Liverpool are winning too many games. Being a United fan that is very sad. The next time Liverpool play please make them lose. You should just let the other team score. I hope I have convinced you to not win the league or any other match again.' The boy had spoken!

Jürgen Klopp took the time to answer the youngster personally, with his own letter. 'It was nice, it was cheeky,' Klopp had said of the letter at the next press conference after the news had leaked, although he regretted that a private matter had become public. In his answer, he praised Daragh's passion for football and stressed that Manchester United should consider themselves lucky to have such a devoted fan. Yet he was in no position to fulfil Daragh's wish, not voluntarily at least. 'As much as you want Liverpool to lose, it is my job to do everything that I can to help Liverpool to win as there are millions of people around the world who want that to happen so I really do not want to let them down. Luckily for you, we have lost games in the past and we will lose games in the future because that is football.' He gave Daragh hope that even Liverpool wouldn't be invincible forever.

It was a strange twist of fate that Liverpool then did go on to lose several games in a short period of time, namely in the Champions League, the Premier League and the FA Cup. The defending European champions had drawn Atlético Madrid in the round of sixteen. Under Argentinian manager Diego Simeone, they are a team with a fearsome reputation in European competition for their almost unparalleled defensive commitment and solidity. There was no understatement in Klopp's warnings about their opponents ('If there's one team where you have to be at your absolute best ...' he repeated 'have to' for emphasis, 'it's Atlético.' Not to mention that 'People say I'm emotional on the sideline. I am only on level four, Diego is level twelve! Really I am the kindergarten cop against him!'). Atlético demonstrated their prowess in their 1–0 defeat of Liverpool in front of their buoyant home supporters in Madrid, a deflating return to the host city of last season's final. 'It was clear the crowd wanted to help tonight, in a different way to how our crowd help.'

Relegation-threatened Watford then put an end to the winning run in the league on matchday twenty-eight with a limp Liverpool deservedly losing 3–0 at Vicarage Road. It was an uninspired performance; only human after all, after months on a high. Some commentators suggested that the defeat had been on the cards, Liverpool having recently put together a string of weaker performances. Yet was it not their great strength to win even these kinds of games, ones they didn't 'deserve' to win? And Klopp refused to accept that the unexpected defeat had been coming. With it, the Reds missed out on setting the record for Premier League victories on the trot, and they'd also failed to match the 2003–04 Arsenal Invincibles, who had gone the whole season unbeaten. That was a record that only Preston North End had achieved previously – 115 years before! 'Arsenal's best result of the season,' tweeted Gary Lineker mischievously (the Gunners were spending the season muddling along in mid-table).

Klopp wouldn't be Klopp if he hadn't wrung a positive out of the ending of a super series of forty-four league games, across two seasons, without defeat: 'Now we can play free football again and don't have to try to get a record.' The constant, irritating inquiries as to what records Liverpool might still break would be put to bed.

* * *

The cup competitions provoked much debate, the root of which was the ever-more unsparing international football calendar, the goal of which was clearly to have football being played at all times. As Champions League winners, Liverpool took part in the FIFA Club World Cup in December 2019. Quite the honour, were it not for the fact that the club had to undergo squad mitosis. Within two days, Liverpool were supposed to play in Birmingham against Aston Villa in the quarter-final of the EFL Cup, as well as contest the semi-final of the Club World Cup in Qatar against Mexican side Monterrey. 'Sensationally good organising,' Klopp summed up the fixture list with biting sarcasm. The solution to the puzzle: Liverpool split their squad in two, taking the first team to Doha and having the under-23s play at Villa Park. The EFL Cup, and therefore another shot at a trophy, would have to be practically given away. At least the planned Premier League clash away to West Ham could be rescheduled to the end of January 2020.

Klopp and the first team followed the action in Birmingham from their hotel in Doha, Qatar's capital. The youngsters gave their all but as expected came off worse in a 5–0 scoreline. The first team was more successful against Monterrey, Firmino with his goal to make it 2–1 – once again in 'Kloppage time' – securing their passage to the final. And it was Firmino who would be the matchwinner in the final against Copa Libertadores winners Flamengo. Scoring the only goal of the game against his Brazilian compatriots, this time in extra-time, he ensured that Liverpool would be crowned club world champions for the first time. A fantastic success!

Liverpool FC could now call themselves the best team in the world and mark it officially for a year with a golden world champions badge on their jersey. The one bit of bad news was that for the time being they wouldn't be able to wear this outfit in the league, with an exception for only one match being granted. Changing the appearance of a kit while the season is underway isn't provided for in the Premier League rules – the exception being for charity – so the Reds would have to wait for next season and their new kit.

In light of the successful end to the tournament, Klopp could take a conciliatory view of things. And while he hadn't known beforehand what it would feel like to win the title, he could now say, 'It's outstanding. Absolutely sensational … I'm really happy.'

Klopp can't do finals? After winning three in 2019 alone – the Champions League, the UEFA Super Cup and the Club World Cup – that trope really had been put to bed. And Pool had 'popped out to pick up' the club world championship during the middle of the season before picking up where they left off in the league: winning. For they simply did not allow the energy-sapping tournament travel or the traditionally tightly packed English Christmas schedule to put them off their rhythm.

Before that, Klopp's film-star charisma had also been on display on the stage of La Scala, the world-famous opera house in Milan, when he was voted world manager of the year in September 2019 at the Best FIFA Football Awards gala. He had reached the top, both with his team and in his management career. 'I don't 100 per cent understand individual prizes but I get it. I'm here for a lot of people,' he said modestly. 'It's great, nobody would have expected that I stood here twenty years ago,' Klopp continued, looking back, and thanked his family and everyone who had contributed to Liverpool FC's success. He turned to Mauricio Pochettino, manager of defeated Champions League finalists Tottenham Hotspur: 'Mauricio, we won that game, that's why I'm here and not you, so that's how football is but we all know what an incredible job you did, what an incredible job Pep did, what so many coaches out there did.' Pep and Poch landed in second and third place respectively.

* * *

Meanwhile, the extent to which Borussia Dortmund were still pining for their previous manager – even four-and-a-half years after his departure – was made clear in October 2019. Would-be title challengers BVB were playing below their potential in the

Bundesliga, Klopp had been voted world manager of the year the month before, and Dortmund's CEO Hans-Joachim Watzke presented his book *Echte Liebe – ein Leben mit dem BVB* ('True Love: A Life with BVB'), written in collaboration with journalist Michael Horeni, at Signal Iduna Park's media centre. Here, Watzke pondered whether it may have been a mistake not to try to persuade Klopp to change his mind after he decided to quit: 'Maybe it would have been better if we'd replaced all the players and not the manager; because you can never get a manager like that again, that was obvious, but you can always get good players. But it's always clearer in hindsight.' Nevertheless, the BVB boss believed: 'Jürgen wouldn't have done it anymore, you could sense it.' Due to their close friendship, Klopp's departure following the cup final in 2015, his last match in charge of Borussia Dortmund, was particularly hard for Watzke to take: 'I was in tears, no exaggeration. The kind of relationship I had with Jürgen at BVB over the course of seven years, that hadn't been a thing before. And probably won't be again, either.' He particularly missed Klopp's 'whinnying laugh' on the training ground: 'I was always reassured: everything is as it should be.'

Watzke also revealed his attempt to bring him back in May 2018. BVB had just parted ways with Peter Stöger and were looking for a new manager. So Watzke chanced a phone call to his old friend, never rating very highly his chances of success. But he wanted to have at least tried. Klopp's response was unambiguous: 'Are you crazy? What are you thinking?'

Even though the book presentation had long been in the works, it can't have been pleasant for the current and much-criticised BVB coach Lucien Favre, making as it did the (unfulfillable) expectations surrounding him all the clearer. There was a steady ebb and flow of accusations from fans and media alike that the Swiss manager was too cerebral, simply not passionate enough for BVB. It was hardly a fair criticism: everyone knew what kind of manager he was when he was appointed. And you can't clone Jürgen Klopp.

* * *

There was another scheduling clash to come, this time in the FA Cup, though the clash was not with another competition but between time off and a replay. Liverpool faced third-tier Shrewsbury Town at New Meadow in the fourth round. Once again, Klopp rested almost his entire first team, and as a result came away with a 2–2 scoreline and exactly what the manager had been trying to avoid given the fixture congestion: a replay. This was scheduled for the start of February, just when English football was to enjoy its first ever winter break – and Klopp had no intention of denying his players the necessary rest. So Liverpool sent out their under-23 team under Neil Critchley once again. Neither the first team nor Klopp himself was present at the game. It was a decision that aroused much controversy – after all, there was no time constraint preventing them from appearing this time.

Jürgen Klopp came in for some harsh criticism for his choice – especially from Andy Holt, owner of League One Accrington Stanley, who complained that the FA Cup was being disrespected, and accused Klopp of being a 'disgrace' and of 'pure selfishness of the highest degree'. Klopp was showing a lack of solidarity with lower-league clubs, according to Holt, clubs for whom the FA Cup was not only of footballing but also great financial importance. Shrewsbury Town manager Sam Ricketts feared a major loss of income from a game against Liverpool's teenagers, since in the FA Cup the guests were entitled to a cut of the ticket sales – and now a significant price reduction could be expected for the match at Anfield. Klopp attempted to discuss the matter with Ricketts after the first match and win him over to his position. It seems doubtful that he enjoyed much luck.

Ex-Liverpool defender Jamie Carragher could well understand that Klopp wanted to protect his players, but not why he wouldn't take charge of the under-23s: 'Senior players having a winter break is right, you can't implement one and then have a replay in the break,' he tweeted. 'But Klopp should take the team, his young players will be delighted.'

Klopp didn't see himself as a revolutionary: this was no labour dispute, he only felt 'a responsibility for the players'. If people considered him lazy for not being at the game, there was nothing he could do about it. For Klopp it was the principle, about standing up for his conviction that awareness needed to be raised about the problematic packed football calendar and consequent strain on the players. Given how often and adamantly he had publicly spoken out about it, he would have considered it 'folding' to rob his pros of part of their winter break now. Klopp hoped that his boycott would focus attention on the problem and give the schedulers pause for thought. So was Klopp's behaviour admirable consistency, or was it disrespectful towards football's most hallowed competition? Would it not indeed have been a highlight for the youth players to have Klopp in charge? But on the other hand, would that not have been disrespectful to U23 coach Critchley, who instead of taking charge on the big Anfield stage would have found himself demoted?

Klopp wasn't to be prevented from at least getting in touch on the phone, calling before the game and also at half-time. Critchley later revealed that 'The Boss' had given him some words of advice and encouragement and that the team should play 'like Liverpool'. Moral support also came from vice-captain James Milner, who wasn't posting holiday pics on Instagram, but trained with the youth players after consulting with Critchley, watched the game from the stands behind the subs bench, and supported them with advice in the dressing room at half-time.

Oh yes, and besides all the ballyhoo there was a game to play as well. The under-23s Klopp called 'kids' did a cracking job of it on the pitch and surprised Shrewsbury Town to win 1–0, admittedly thanks to an own goal, but also thanks to a brave performance, buoyed by fantastic support from the Liverpool crowd. It was a performance that was overshadowed by all the noise surrounding the game. The 'kids', with an average age of 19 years and 102 days, were the youngest team Liverpool had ever fielded for a competitive fixture. Curtis Jones, nineteen, was the youngest captain in the club's history. For eighteen-year-old full-back Neco Williams it was 'Just unbelievable. It was a night that we will remember for a long time.'

* * *

Next stop in the FA Cup was Stamford Bridge, where Chelsea were waiting for the Reds in the fifth round. Klopp turned on the rotation machine again, and only around half the starting eleven were regulars. The two youngsters Curtis Jones and Neco Williams got another opportunity in the first eleven, this time with the seniors. Klopp had kept his word: he had dangled the prospect of one or two of the youth players getting a start in the next round if they managed to beat Shrewsbury.

The 2–0 defeat to the Blues, more with a whimper than a bang, posed questions as to whether a shot at another trophy hadn't been carelessly conceded. With ten games to go before the end of the season, the Reds had a twenty-two-point lead, having played one game more than second-place Manchester City – even if City managed to win their game in hand, they would still be nineteen points behind. Wouldn't it have made sense to play the big guns? Klopp was mild in his assessment of his protégés; in comparison with the defeat at Watford they were 'not bad'. The coaching staff had made changes in personnel because 'we knew it would be intense'. The amount of goals they had been conceding, eight in the last four fixtures, was certainly something he was well aware of: 'Usually you don't get a lot of chances against us.'

After Watford, this was now the second defeat on the trot – unfamiliar feelings of vulnerability crept in after months in a daze of victory. Had the letter from the ten-year-old Manchester United fan done what was intended, and given other teams a boost? Not quite. After three away defeats in the last four competitive fixtures, a 2–1 win in the league against relegation candidates Bournemouth was a step back in the right direction – a sluggish one perhaps, having to come from behind again and putting in a rather ordinary performance, but rewarded with three points. Now the Reds needed only two wins to seal the title, regardless of what any other team did. The Premier League trophy was close enough to touch. The red part of Liverpool was counting down how many points were still needed game by game and looking forward to an almighty party, thirty years in the making. That's what should have been, anyway. Yet that match against Bournemouth was long to be Liverpool's last game of the 2019–20 Premier League season.

What was to be the Reds' last match for the foreseeable future was the Champions League return leg at Anfield against Atlético Madrid, a match that afterwards was to be the subject of intense debate as to how much it might have contributed to the spread of the coronavirus. The stadium was sold out, away fans (around 3,000 of them) were allowed to attend, some of whom may have brought the virus with them to England or taken it back with them to Spain. Indeed, that deaths from the pandemic spiked in Merseyside in early April strongly suggested a link.

The tie on 11 March 2020 was the last professional football match in England before lockdown was imposed. By mid-March the pandemic had the world and therefore football too so firmly in its grasp that on urgent medical advice all games had to be called off indefinitely. In Europe, attempts were at first made to put on matches behind closed doors, to avoid exponentially increasing the transmission of the virus through mass events (and also to secure TV revenues) – but the experiment soon had to be abandoned, for people were gathering to watch football in pubs or meeting in front of stadiums. A counterproductive effect. In short order the leagues shut football down completely.

* * *

Liverpool entered the enforced break on the back of another defeat, and a needless one. Klopp's team threw not just the sink but the entire kitchen at Atlético, but their inability to convert their chances was costing them. The hosts had predictably dominated the game, but in extra-time, as their batteries ran down, the Spaniards hit them on the counter. For a time it had looked as if it was going to be all right on the night for Liverpool, as Roberto Firmino gave them the two-goal lead they needed at the start of extra-time, with Wijnaldum having levelled the tie when he made it 1–0 just before half-time. The Anfield mythos seemed to be in effect once again, turning another deficit into triumphant comeback victory.

But then things changed. Keeper Adrián, standing in for the injured Alisson, made a decisive error. Under no pressure, he played the ball straight to João Félix's feet, who quick-wittedly played in Llorente. The sub placed it in the bottom corner to open Atlético's account. With the score now 2–1, Liverpool were heading out on away goals. The Reds pushed on, leading to spaces opening up at the back that Atlético well-knew how to take advantage of: Llorente added another and Morata put them in the lead on the night. Anfield had been cut to the quick: 4–2 on aggregate, and the defending champions were out. It was the first time under Klopp that Liverpool had lost a European knockout tie over two legs. Since he had taken charge of Liverpool in autumn 2015 they had reached the final of every European competition they had competed in. Without exception.

'I loved our first 95 minutes,' Klopp declared at the post-match press conference, regretting however that his team had failed to get the second goal in normal time. At the same time, he was ticked off by the destructive tactics of the opposition: 'When you see a team like Atlético packed with world-class players in their positions and they play the way they play, it is the most difficult thing to do … But the way they play… I just don't get it. I don't get it,' he added in irritation. 'I am really an under-average loser, to be honest. At least tonight, if I would say all the things I have in my mind I would look like the worst loser in the world, so I best stop here.'

Yet for all that, before the tie Klopp had actually praised Atletico's disciplined defensive style, even defended it against its critics in its homeland: 'Successful football is what is attractive and for me it's attractive. It's very intense, with speed. It's aggressive with a clear plan and a clear philosophy. I know we are in Spain, in the country of tiki taka, and maybe people say it because of that.

But I am from Germany and I admire things like that.' Following elimination, admiration mutated into frustration. Yet for all of Atlético's resilience, Liverpool's exit from the competition was ultimately due to profligacy in front of goal – thirty-four shots, eleven on target – as well as an individual goalkeeping error.

* * *

And this was the end of football, of sport in general, for the foreseeable future. In Britain, in Europe. Not just football, but public life itself came to a stop. The coronavirus and potential measures to stop it were the topics that dominated everything. The European Championship planned for 2020, to be hosted by twelve different cities in twelve different countries, was postponed until the following year. This gave the national leagues the chance to extend their seasons into the summer to allow them to be completed. That brought up the question of how to deal with player contracts that would be expiring on 30 June, the usual end-of-season date. A complete abandonment of the season was also in question.

But if you did that, how would you actually go about it? Stop the clock on the league tables as played, and award titles and European qualification based on that, as well as promotion and relegation? Or call the competitions off, declare the results null and void, and reset everything to summer 2019? Question after question. No one knew what to do. From now on the schedulers of the football calendar were medical professionals, especially virologists, and politicians. France's *Ligue 1* and the Dutch *Eredivisie* were abandoned. In France the clear frontrunners PSG were awarded the title, and the two clubs propping up the league, Amiens and Toulouse, were relegated, while in the Netherlands the entire season was declared void, with no champion and no relegation. Some clubs were ready to pursue legal recourse against the decision.

For Liverpool, a void season would have been particularly bitter. A quite phenomenal season down to the twenty-ninth matchday, with at most six more points needed to secure the league for the first time in thirty years, and it would all have been for nothing. And even if the remaining games were still played, the title party wouldn't be the same in the eerie atmosphere of an empty stadium. Celebrating with the supporters, an open-top bus parade with the trophy as for the Champions League triumph the year before, hundreds of thousands of fans packing the city: all that was unthinkable until some unknown future date due to the terrible danger of the virus spreading.

At the end of March 2020 the Reds released an emotional video message in which, after introductory words by Jürgen Klopp, many of the club's players and staff, in their respective mother tongues, thanked health workers and everyone else contributing so selflessly to the effort against the coronavirus. The video closed with a plea to do your bit: 'Stay home. Save lives.' Klopp has always been one to speak his mind, and that wasn't going to change during the coronavirus crisis, speaking out in June about Britain's delayed public health reaction, such as the reluctance to prescribe the wearing of masks for example, in comparison to other countries. The UK at that moment in time was recording a very high number of infections in comparison with the rest of Europe.

What would be the impact of the crisis – and this time the overused word was completely justified – not just on health, but also economically? The wages of the players, manager and all the rest of the club staff were still being paid, but what about the revenues from sponsorships if companies ran into financial difficulties? What was going to happen about the TV money when matches weren't being played? LFC decided, as did four other Premier League clubs, to furlough many of their non-playing staff. The furlough scheme was backdated to March 2020 and provided for the government paying 80 per cent of wages for three months, up to a maximum £2,500. 'That's not what the scheme was designed for,' Didi Hamann tweeted. 'Contrary to the morals and values of the club I got to know.' The emergency assistance programme was intended to support small businesses whose very existence was in danger, not prosperous, investor-backed football behemoths with easy access to additional capital. It was a truly spectacular own goal, one that cost the club no small amount of goodwill among its traditionally working-class fans. As CEO Peter Moore had said six months previously, 'What would Shankly have done?'

The Reds faced a backlash so intense that they sheepishly reversed their plans a few days later. Peter Moore apologised in an open letter to the fans on the club's homepage, at the same time offering an apologia for their original plans: 'We believe we came to the wrong conclusion last week to announce that we intended to apply to the Coronavirus Retention Scheme and furlough staff due to the suspension of the Premier League football calendar, and are truly sorry for that. Our intentions were, and still are, to ensure the entire workforce is given as much protection as possible from redundancy and/or loss of earnings during this unprecedented period.' LFC was faced with 'unprecedented operating losses', according to Moore, for: 'despite the fact we were in a healthy position prior to this crisis, our revenues have been shut off yet our outgoings remain'. The club was now going to find 'alternative ways to operate'.

Training during the break represented another new challenge. Training at Melwood was not possible at first due to the lockdown; an alternative had to be found. The planned move to the new training complex in Kirkby, just north-east of Liverpool, had to be delayed, with the final building work having to be put on hold. Like for so many other workers whose only option was now the home office, video conferencing became the norm for Liverpool players as for others in team sports, with online team training supplemented by individual fitness work. Modern communications technology at least made it possible for the players to still enjoy individually tailored training plans.

* * *

The FA and the Premier League were both seeking to get football started again. The enforced break was originally set to run until 3 April, but the public health situation was such that it had to be repeatedly extended. The model for a restart was the *Bundesliga*, which kicked off again in mid-May, the first of the big European leagues to do so. The new concept provided not only for behind-closed-doors games, but also quarantine regulations for the players as well as regular coronavirus testing, mask wearing for the staff and a limit of 300 people inside the stadium. The seventeenth of June was the red-letter day: the hiatus was over and the Premier League could continue. After weeks of worry, Liverpool could now attempt to accomplish Mission: Title.

Liverpool's first game after three-and-a-half months out of action was a scoreless draw with Everton at Goodison Park, the first of 236 derbies without spectators. It was a dull match, absent the usual charisma and dynamism for which Liverpool had come to be known. Concerns that the team might have grown rusty during the long pause were swept aside during the following encounter, against Crystal Palace on 24 June. The commanding 4–0 win was Liverpool's twenty-eighth in thirty-one league matches and, it turned out to be the case one day later, the final step of their journey to the title. For Manchester City lost 1–2 at Stamford Bridge, sealing the title for Liverpool 'on the sofa' – thirty years of hurt finally at an end! Another chapter in the Reds' history, one replete with sporting drama and human tragedy, had been written in the most momentous of circumstances.

The players and manager had gathered on the terrace of a Liverpool hotel to follow Chelsea v. Man City, and partied their hearts out afterwards, if only among themselves, of course, due to the virus. Amid all the jubilation, Klopp did a little dance for 'his boys'. The day after he revealed that he tried to come up with a speech for his players, but was so overwhelmed that even thinking about it made him start to well up. He compared the moment to his similarly emotional departure from Mainz in 2008.

Despite Klopp's call for Liverpool fans to celebrate safely, hundreds also went to Anfield – in defiance of the continuing social-distancing rules and restrictions on gatherings – to celebrate the end of Liverpool's thirty-year title drought cheek by jowl. Thousands gathered the next evening at Pier Head on the waterfront, blatantly ignoring coronavirus safety and generating numerous 'incidents'. In a joint statement, the behaviour was condemned by the club, the city authorities and the police as unacceptable.

* * *

Although it had been on the cards for weeks and months (despite being threatened for a time by the pandemic), Klopp was still overcome by the intensity of his feelings once the league title was confirmed. In a TV interview with Sky Sports he struggled with his emotions, wiping tears from his eyes more than once, very likely in part due to the tributes coming from Reds legends Sir Kenny Dalglish and Graeme Souness. 'This is a big moment, I have no real words. I am completely overwhelmed. I never thought I would feel like this! It's just big,' Klopp explained, before his voice went and, overcome, he had to break off the interview with the words: 'Sorry, gentlemen.' The next day he went into more depth during a virtual press conference: 'I know it means the world to the fans. It means the world to me. It's just exceptional. Maybe since last year I was waiting … It's massive, absolutely massive.' For all the euphoria, Klopp didn't forget to highlight the contribution made by the supporters, players, coaching staff, backroom staff and legends such as Dalglish and Steven Gerrard (whose successes made it easy for him to motivate the team), and he praised his team above all for their exceptional consistency over the past two-and-a-half years.

The champions enjoyed a special treat at the next game following the confirmation of the title, when the opposition gave the new title holders the traditional guard of honour. The team was Manchester City, the now former champions and their great rivals of recent seasons. 'We are going to do it because they deserve it,' said Pep Guardiola in recognition and respect.

Towards the end of July, Liverpool hosted another great rival, Chelsea, at Anfield for a late kick-off. There were no fans present, but the match was being specially broadcast on free-to-air Pick TV, as one of twenty-five matches from the restarted Premier League season. Liverpool led 3–0 and then 4–1, repelling a Chelsea fightback to seal a 5–3 win in the final minutes with fireworks bursting in the sky above. Vibrant red in the darkness. Twenty minutes after the final whistle, the time had come. On a podium specially constructed on the Kop, Sir Kenny Dalglish handed the Premier League trophy to captain Jordan Henderson. The league was theirs.

Speaking to the BBC before the destination of the title was finally confirmed, Klopp had promised Liverpool supporters a celebration fit for the achievement – one day. 'If we become champions, whatever celebrations are possible we will do as a team internally and with all our supporters in the moment we are allowed to do so again,' he said. 'I can promise that if it happens, there will be a parade as well. Whenever. Who cares!'

Even without the spontaneity of the moment, the joy of the Liverpool fans would still be great once the crisis had been overcome: a heady mixture of love of life, relief at an end to lockdown, social distancing and quarantines, as well as the pure pleasure of knowing that the Reds are finally, finally back on their perch. For Klopp and his team the motivation remains to double down on the success and if possible celebrate a 'normal' title in 2021.

* * *

The press on Liverpool's first title in thirty years:

England

Daily Mail: 'From the start, he and Liverpool felt made for each other. He got the club, he got the city, he got its people … He didn't spend months discovering English football, he didn't study the peculiar psychology, glean information from books. He knew it, he knew us.'

Daily Telegraph: 'For Liverpool to have beaten this Manchester City team by such a margin is one of the all-time great achievements.'

Guardian: 'From late summer into spring Klopp's team seemed to be operating to a different set of physical laws to everyone else.'

Spain

Sport: 'Liverpool are champions again after thirty years! The curse is laid to rest. This Liverpool is one of the best teams in the history of the Premier League. Jürgen Klopp has that winner gene, even after setbacks, he proved that already at Dortmund and Mainz.'

Mundo Deportivo: 'The long wait is over. Kenny Dalglish's legendary 1990 Liverpool have a worthy successor. When are they erecting the bronze statue of Klopp at the Anfield gates?'

Italy

Corriere dello Sport: 'Historic title for Liverpool. Rarely has one seen a football team so perfectly reflect its manager. There are managers who do everything to buy top players. Klopp makes them.'

Gazzetta dello Sport: 'Liverpool are back on the throne after thirty years. Klopp has proved himself the real alternative to Guardiola and has risen to be Liverpool's fifth Beatle. He has created a masterpiece.'

APPENDIX

KLOPP IN QUOTES

KLOPP ON KLOPP

On his initiation as manager in 2001: 'There's nothing in life I've been better prepared for than that. I have more trust in my capabilities as a manager than I had in myself as a player.'

On his career as a player: 'Unfortunately, during my active days as a player I wasn't able to do on the pitch what was happening in my head. I had the talent for the sixth-tier *Landesliga* and the brains for the *Bundesliga* – and what came out was second-tier *Bundesliga*.'

On his active transition to his dream job: 'I regarded my time as a professional as a transitional period before becoming a manager.'

On his squad's style of play: 'None of my teams have ever played lawn chess.'

On his career ambitions: 'I want to be the best manager I can be.'

On the strain of a match, speaking to Schalke's then manager Fred Rutten: 'If it smells like sweat, then that's me. The match was so exciting.'

On the joys of high-class football: 'I've spent enough time on bad football – and I mean my own.'

On today's generation of players: 'Relating with the lads isn't hard. I like football players in general. It's better when they're young and listen than if they're older and want to tell me how things work – that's obvious. But whether I get on with someone or not depends on whether he wants to learn something, not how old he is.'

On the large number of missed major chances in the Supercup match loss to Schalke in 2011: 'I wasn't interested in this debate last year either. Last season we wasted more big chances than Leverkusen even managed to produce.'

On the debate about the absence of leadership on the field: 'Nuri [Şahin] was far from being a big character when he arrived at Dortmund. There's no point in pushing anyone into an office. I prefer no one talking than anyone spewing bullshit.'

On the goal in a game against an underdog in the DFB Cup: 'Anyone who thinks a bad pass in Sandhausen should be treated differently to one against Bayern is simply crazy.'

On his team's attacking strategy: 'No one needs to worry that we'll build a second wall in front of the *Südtribune* [South Stand].'

OTHERS ON KLOPP

Andreas Rettig, CEO of the German Football League (DFL) from 2013 to 2015, now chairman at St Pauli: 'I remember well an encounter in a café in Mainz where we met for breakfast. At the time I was sporting director at Cologne and wanted to get to know Jürgen Klopp, basically scouting him as a manager. I have to say that I've rarely sat so long at breakfast and still hardly ate a thing. I sat there, astonished, and thought: "Man, you sure can listen to him talk!" He's one of those guys who want to bounce out of bed every day and conquer the world and show everyone what they're capable of. Klopp is smart and knows how to have the right people around him in the right moment. What I like about him in particular is that he is also capable of laughing about himself and doesn't take himself too seriously. I was also pleased by his unbelievable rhetorical skills and technical knowledge. At that breakfast table Klopp demonstrated perfectly how pressing works using egg cups. That impressed me.'

Klopp's fellow manager Friedhelm Funkel, long-time *Bundesliga* **pro at Bayer 05 Uerdingen and Kaiserslautern, most recently manager at 1860 Munich:** 'I think back ten years, to Klopp's start at Mainz. I remember when I was still manager at Cologne that Jürgen had his team play very, very aggressively against the ball. With a squad I'd venture wasn't so strong individually as Borussia Dortmund is today. That he started in the second division and tried to mould that style with increasing precision – very successfully. And now at Borussia Dortmund, with the individual class, the strength of the individual players, he's naturally even more successful. They're much stronger at getting the ball and quicker in front of the opponent's goal than might have been the case ten years ago. I remember very clearly how our players had great reverence, or at least respect, in our matches in Mainz. We knew what was headed our way, how Kloppo had set up his team back then, and it was always very, very difficult to play against them. And it's naturally improved remarkably over the years.'

Mirko Slomka, former manager of Schalke 04, Hannover 96 and Hamburg SV: 'The system [that a manager has chosen for his team] has to fit the team and to some extent the club's philosophy as well. I believe one can develop something within a club. And that what Kloppo does fits extraordinarily.'

Michael Oenning, former manager at Nürnberg and Hamburg: 'One also has to put the team front and centre and think what you can do with them. Of course it's great if there's a unifying concept. We don't even have to go to Spain [Barcelona] for that. I really enjoy orienting myself around Dortmund.'

Christian Nerlinger, former *Bundesliga* pro and former sporting director at Bayern: 'If you see him on the touchlines: that's not emotional. To some extent that has psychopathic excesses.'

Hans-Günter Bruns, long-time *Bundesliga* pro with Borussia Mönchengladbach and currently manager: 'I get furious about the purely defensive teams these days. For me, precisely the way Dortmund play is football! Today there are only a few managers like Jürgen Klopp, who have their teams play offensively. Dortmund are oriented forwards and are still solid at the back. They demonstrate wonderfully how this 'third way' can work.'

Klopp's managerial role model Wolfgang Frank: 'First and foremost, Jürgen has a good character. He's been formed by his parents and school. Then his intellect was able to develop on this basis ... He understood things very quickly and wanted to develop tactically because he wasn't a giant when it came to football skills ... He was always a good guy. Honest, open, able to take criticism, serving the team. He always liked joining the discussion. He even sometimes flipped out on the pitch because he had so many good ideas that he wasn't able to realise with his football skills. Sometimes that frustrated him so much that I had to take him to one side … Jürgen doesn't forget people he's benefited from. He's a very respectful person.'

JÜRGEN KLOPP:
THE FACTS

Name:
Jürgen Norbert Klopp

Born:
16 June 1967 in Stuttgart, Germany

Family :
Married to children's book author Ulla Klopp
From 2010 to 2012, son Marc played for Borussia Dortmund's U23 team
before injury forced an early end to his career at the age of twenty-three

Siblings:
Two elder sisters

Height:
6'4" (193cm)

Nickname:
Kloppo

Star sign:
Gemini

Education:
Diploma in sports science from Goethe University Frankfurt (his thesis
was on walking, although Klopp himself prefers jogging)

Played for:
1972–83 SV Glatten (youth)
1983–87 TuS Ergenzingen (youth, then seniors)
1987 1. FC Pforzheim
1987–88 Eintracht Frankfurt (Amateurs)
1988–89 Viktoria Sindlingen 1989–90 Rot-Weiss Frankfurt
1990–2001 Mainz 05

Playing stats:
- 325 second division games for Mainz,
making him the club's record appearance holder
- With 52 goals second behind Sven Demandt (55) in the Mainz
goalscoring rankings for the second division; Klopp scored four
times in a 5–0 win at Erfurt in 1991
- Klopp was deployed in various positions over the course of his career:
as a striker, in midfield, as well as in defence

Managerial positions:
2001–08 Mainz 05
2008–15 Borussia Dortmund
2015– Liverpool

Managerial successes:
With Mainz 05
- Promotion to the Bundesliga 2004

With Borussia Dortmund
- Bundesliga champions 2011 and 2012
- DFB Cup winner 2012
- Supercup winners 2008 (unofficial), 2013 and 2014
- Champions League finalist 2013
- Bundesliga runners-up 2013 and 2014
- DFB Cup finalists 2014 and 2015

With Liverpool:
- Premier League 2020
- Champions League 2019
- FIFA Club World Cup 2019
- UEFA Super Cup 2019
- Champions League finalist 2018
- Europa League finalist 2016
- Premier League runners-up 2019

Personal honours:
German Football Manager of the Year 2011, 2012 and 2019
FIFA Manager of the Year 2019
Second in voting for FIFA Manager of the Year 2013
Deutscher Fernsehpreis (German Television Award) 2006 and 2010 in the
Best Sports Programme category, both for World Cup commentary (2006
together with Johannes B. Kerner and Urs Meier on ZDF, 2010 with
Günther Rauch on RTL)

AN INTERVIEW WITH FRANK DOPHEIDE

HOW KLOPP ADDED VALUE FOR BORUSSIA DORTMUND, SEPTEMBER 2011

Frank Dopheide is an expert on marketing and brand formation. However, his career path initially had a completely different starting point: he was trained to be a lifeguard and studied at the German Sport University Cologne with an emphasis on journalism. Then he got his start in the field of advertising in 1990 writing copy, quickly climbing the corporate ladder, becoming the head of the well-known German ad agency GREY in 2004.

As managing director, Dopheide has headed the company Deutsche Markenarbeit GmbH since the beginning of 2011. Dopheide and his agency teams have been repeatedly distinguished with awards. In 2014 Dopheide was named managing director of customer development and brand management at the Handelsblatt publishing group, but continues his work at his agency.

* * *

Mr Dopheide, what characterises the 'Klopp Brand'? Where does its power come from?
Klopp derives his power from being down-to-earth. He speaks the language of the people and also makes appearances in a tracksuit. His external appearance is not a means to an end. He's actually the

way he presents himself. He always remains similar and has changed little over the years, from the perspective of appearances, language or habits. He's true to himself and that's also what makes his brand so valuable. The fact that Klopp keeps his own sense of style is something that gives him great power. Just look at the way he parts his hair in the middle, which he persistently retains – regardless of whether it's in style or not. Klopp stays steady!

He's very convincing rhetorically, and what he says fits with what he embodies. This leads to credibility that is very decisive for brand formation. He has a big mouth, speaks metaphorically and understandably so that you don't have to be a football pro to follow him. He doesn't beat around the bush, which is also good for the BVB brand, because Klopp's down-to-earth, honest appearance overlaps with the mentality of the Ruhr region. In addition, I believe Klopp is very attractive to women and has great power over young people. You just have to look at the young and powerful squad he's formed.

With Klopp's passionate explosions on the touchline, he can lose his grasp on his down-to-earth nature ...
Sure, he's very impulsive when he's on the touchline. One often has the feeling that he's not always 100 per cent content, after the event, with what he did on the touchline. But somehow he just has to let it out.

In addition, he appears to be very consistent and very straightforward in his approach.
Precisely. The exciting thing is: Jürgen Klopp is so steadfast in what he does that he will grow stronger. It's an exponential development factor. At the beginning it takes a while, similar to endowment

insurance: month after month one makes deposits in the brand account, in this case through his actions. Over time, an accelerating power develops and all at once, a brand is very valuable. And because Klopp has been making these 'deposits' for so long, he really sticks out in the fraternity of managers.

You just mentioned that Klopp fits well with the mentality of the Ruhr region. Is my impression also true, that he is a particularly good fit with Dortmund?

That's right – and on the basis of the Limbic® Map from Gruppe Nymphenburg Consult AG [a brand consultancy based in Munich] I can show you what I like to call value spaces. With it, every individual value a figure or company stands for can be tied to a particular overarching concept. I've done this for Klopp as well as for Dortmund. If we start by considering what the Borussia Dortmund brand stands for, I think of concepts such as friendship, home or loyalty. The Dortmund brand is based in being deeply rooted in the region. So the overarching concept of 'Balance' is very important in the field of values [as can be seen in the illustrations overleaf]. Here, one can also see why Dortmund sporting director and legendary player Michael Zorc is such an important figure at the club: because he conveys this connection with Dortmund, this feeling of home.

* * *

Gruppe Nymphenburg explain the Limbic® Map as follows: 'The Limbic® Map shows an overview of the entire gamut of human emotions at a glance. All human motives, values and desires can be displayed and correlated on the Limbic® Map. How was the Limbic® Map created? The positioning of the values in the Limbic® Map was initially determined based on expert assessments provided by psychologists and

The values of Borussia Dortmund represented as a Limbic® Map

ADVENTURE THRILL

STIMULANT

BALAN[CE]

extravagance

impulsiven[ess]

adventuresomeness

creativity

individualism

spontaneit[y]

art

variety

fun

curiousness

humour

easiness

fantasy

tolerance

pleasure

candour

dreaming

poetry

flexibility

friendship

loy[alty]

family

sensuality

cordiality

safety

trust

sociability

home

nature

security

nostalgia

FANTASY PLEASURE

rebellion

ourage   victory

fight   power

DOMINANCE

autonomy   elite

assertion

freedom   fame   status

effort

pride

efficiency

honour

diligence   ambition

functionality   tenacity

logic

order   precision

discipline

justice

morality   duty

obedience

hygiene

cleanliness   asceticism

reliability   thriftiness

health   quality

tradition

DISCIPLINE CONTROL

The values of Jürgen Klopp
represented as a Limbic® Map

rebellion

ourage   victory

            fight   power

autonomy   elite

                              assertion

    freedom   fame   status

              pride   effort

        honour   efficiency

              diligence   ambition

    functionality   tenacity

              logic

        order   precision

    justice   discipline

        morality   duty

obedience

        hygiene   asceticism

cleanliness

    reliability   thriftiness

health   quality

tradition

DOMINANCE

DISCIPLINE CONTROL

Two versions of the Limbic® Map represent the values of Borussia Dortmund
and Jürgen Klopp respectively. The Limbic® Map was developed by Gruppe
Nymphenburg Consult AG of Munich. The values in the two diagrams
were identified by Deutsche Markenarbeit GmbH of Düsseldorf.
© Dr. Hans Georg Häusel/Gruppe Nymphenburg Consult AG.

was subsequently empirically validated using distance analysis. The Limbic® Map is a unique navigational tool to demonstrate motive and value structures of brands and products.'

Bernd Werner, Partner and member of the board at Gruppe Nymphenburg, explained the meaning of the terms in the Limbic® Map: 'The three instructions of "balance, stimulant and dominance" are overarching concepts. Discipline/control, adventure/thrill and fantasy/pleasure represent "mixed forms" of the three: the mixture of stimulation and dominance is adventure/thrill, the mixture of dominance and balance is discipline/control and the mixture of stimulant and balance is fantasy/pleasure. The individual placement of every person, company or a given brand is carried out subsequently. For every one of these, values are located upon which individuals or companies are oriented.'

Dopheide offers some comparative examples from the world of business: 'The beverage manufacturer Red Bull clearly stands for impulsiveness, adventuresomeness, and spontaneity, so is categorised under "adventure/thrill". Deutsche Bank, in contrast, stands for dominance, elite, status, pride. The same thing can be done with a Bundesliga *club, naturally. And when we are to advise their decision-makers and say whether a given player or manager fits well with them, then we do it in just this way.'*

A more detailed explanation of the Limbic® Map can be found on Nymphenburg's website at http://www.nymphenburg.de/292.html.

* * *

What would happen if Borussia tried to acquire values other than the ones already ascribed?

That would only work if they were near the previous values. For example: in the 1990s Borussia wanted to ape Bayern Munich, which I situate in the area of 'Dominance' – so precisely the opposite area of the value map. This reorientation didn't work because it couldn't be supported by the brand and it's not where the brand is rooted. That's not how branding works.

And Jürgen Klopp's values …

… are in a very similar area to those of Dortmund. Klopp covers all of what Dortmund stands for. As was already the case in Mainz, where he influenced these values and was active as a player and manager for what feels like an eternity. Family is important to him. Klopp stands for friendship: he's a mate, is approachable. He had demonstrated the 'home' value through his long tenure at Mainz. And the security that is important here is the skill of a master craftsman: he's being doing his job for quite a while and has proven that he's capable. This is already the basis for being able to say: it's a fit with Dortmund and Klopp. In contrast, managerial types like Louis van Gaal wouldn't work well at all at Dortmund because they stand for other values – 'dominance' in this case. This is not a judgement about which area is better. They're simply different. Yet in order to achieve harmony, the values represented by individuals and companies, in other words, manager and club in this case, should overlap as much as possible.

The value area you've outlined for Jürgen Klopp is clearly broader than that of Dortmund. How do you view this from a brand perspective?

The fact that Klopp adds values that Dortmund didn't previously possess is extremely valuable for the club. In other words, values such as comfort, humour, candour or flexibility are worth a great deal. If you ask people about what they associate with Jürgen Klopp, they all say: 'His broad grin and cheeky answers.' And then they often add the way he jumps around on the edge of the pitch. These three points are it. That is why it's interesting that one of the *Bundesliga*'s new target groups is located in that quadrant: women. And in this way, Dortmund also profits from the additional values that Klopp brings to the table.

And precisely how can Borussia Dortmund profit from it?
The older a society becomes, the more important aspects like security, safety and family become. In addition, women stand for values like comfort, humour and candour, often paired with sensuality and fantasy. Jürgen Klopp can capture this target group for Dortmund. And that's what makes him five times as valuable, because regardless of the fact that he's first and foremost a good manager, he adds new values. He becomes an additional identification figure for the fans, a magnet for young players, a steroid injection for journalists, and an anchor of trust for sponsors. So independent of his actual professional work, he is five times as valuable for the Dortmund brand.

But doesn't Klopp also stand for values such as courage, due to his impulsiveness, emotionality and positive extravagance – in the sense of non-conformity? If you notice how much he puts youth before experience in his team, then courage must be one of his characteristics?
Careful. Here there has to be a distinction between the values Klopp stands for – so what is important for him in life – and those he projects in his appearance. One is important for the 'what' and the other the 'how'. It's right that he's very emotional. However, I define extravagance differently: extravagance contains a glamour factor – and Klopp doesn't have that. He's unique in his character because he's independent. He may seem extravagant, but that doesn't have to be important for him. The fact that Klopp puts his

money on young players is a courageous decision but it is also a question of the way in which he does it, so the 'how'.

But you do admit he had courage? After all, he played the youngest central defensive duo in the Bundesliga *after being installed at Dortmund.*

He was at Mainz for a very long time, but now he's clearly been loyal to Dortmund for a long time as well. You'd expect larger breaks in his biography with courageous decisions, which would cause people to say: 'Look at the unusual things he always did.' For me, he doesn't seem to be someone who needs to take risks. When we locate 'courage' in the value space, it is with people who consider everyday life too boring, and who consciously expose themselves to danger. That's not the impression Klopp gives me. I believe he knows exactly what he's doing, so confident he is in himself. And returning to values: he comes from the area of 'security' and adds 'easiness'. Of course that involves a little courage, but that can't be a core element. The same is true for impulsiveness, another 'how'. That's what his character is like, but it's not essential for him.

There were other clubs besides Dortmund interested in Klopp in 2008. Let's speculate a little: where else would he have been a good fit?

I spontaneously have to think of Werder Bremen because it's positioned similarly to Dortmund from a branding perspective. Werder stands for friendship, family, loyalty, solidarity and safety. By the way, that's why manager Thomas Schaaf was allowed to stay in office during the disappointing 2010–11 season [Werder ended the season thirteenth in the table and were in danger of relegation for a while]. When values such as those mentioned are important, then you can tolerate these situations. Klopp wouldn't have fit well with Bayern because their values are situated completely differently: with dominance, power, pride, in keeping with their *Mia san mia* motto – we are who we are.

And with other Bundesliga *clubs?*
Bayer Leverkusen wouldn't have fit either because I place that club with functionality, logic, discipline, duty and asceticism. Today, of course, Schalke 04 would be unimaginable because of their status as Dortmund's arch-rivals, but before his stint at Dortmund it might have worked. But Schalke is scarcely defined as a brand for me. I can discover a lot of nostalgia, home and friendship, but also extravagance, individuality, divas – so a certain glamour. It's difficult to situate and at any rate it wouldn't have been as clearly positive for Klopp as Dortmund.

You say that Klopp is an 'anchor of trust for sponsors'. Which advertising partners could be a good fit for him?
The advertising partners who would profit the most would be those who need his easiness the most and those who come from a very security-oriented, even familial background – probably even banks, surprisingly. In general I think of fields in which there hasn't been much 'emotionality' yet, that have seemed stiff and dry up to this point. Insurance companies could profit from Klopp as an advertising partner, just as estate agents and building societies or energy providers would. Perhaps also media, where one would say: 'Look at that, good old Klopp is reading this, or watching that.' And with his broad grin, he'd always be a good match for toothpaste ... Klopp has a connecting element because he stands for friendship, family and loyalty. So the fundamental question is: where do you feel like you belong?

Sticking with the 'connecting element': taken literally, his adver-
tisement for glue would also work wonderfully ... but in all seriousness:
what's your assessment of the Klopp brand and how well it fits with
Borussia Dortmund?

It fits 100 per cent – with Klopp himself as well as in connection with
Borussia Dortmund. And that's exactly what makes the brand so
convincing: the external appearance corresponds to the inner values.

AN INTERVIEW WITH CRISTIÁN GÁLVEZ

ON KLOPP'S PERSONALITY AND PUBLIC IMAGE, SEPTEMBER 2011

The fact that Jürgen Klopp is a man of public interest is part of his profession. Life coach Cristián Gálvez knows how this effect is produced. His motto is 'character makes a difference' and this versatile coach makes a difference as a life coach, as an author of self-help books and as a speaker with a wealth of experience, having given more than 6,000 presentations: his clients include a 'who's who' of the business world. Gálvez studied business as well as social and business psychology in Germany and the US. He is particularly interested in the influence of emotions on people. Business communication is also one of his core areas. He was among the top-ten business speakers at the prestigious Conga Awards in 2007, 2008 and 2010.

The following is a conversation with Gálvez about leadership training, world views, the process of development and of perfection, as well as factors from the field of the psychology of character that are relevant to success – success that can be observed in the career of Jürgen Klopp.

* * *

Mr Gálvez, what characterises Jürgen Klopp as a personality?

In the highly results-oriented world of business Klopp enjoys a very high level of regard – and this is completely deserved. Through my work as speaker and coach I look into the corridors of power in German and international companies on a daily basis. Again and again I discover that Germany is missing the truly great leaders in comparison to the international scene: the leadership role models. Our German businesses are frequently *managed* excellently, but actually *led* all too infrequently. Perhaps that is exactly the reason why a figure like Jürgen Klopp generates such enthusiasm – even among top German managers. For Klopp embodies the characteristics of excellent and contemporary leadership.

How would you differentiate between 'managing' and 'leading'?

This distinction has existed since the end of the 1980s. At the time, Professor John Kotter from Harvard Business School differentiated between management and leadership. On the one hand were the managers who administered, maintained and imitated. These are people who ask: 'How are things going? How can it continue?' It's worth noting that the term 'management' comes from the Italian *maneggiare* and originally meant 'leading a horse in the circus ring'. In that regard, this understanding is very close to the world of football with its sports arenas and highly paid two-legged thoroughbreds. These people always have their eye on the prize. Their perspective is short-term.

On the other hand, Kotter speaks of 'leadership'. This concerns the future, motivation, vision, orientation and, above all, sustainable change. These personalities are not copies, but rather originals who think long-term. They build up trust, are enthused and enthusing, have clear visions and always question the status quo.

And then we come to Klopp ...

Exactly, very quickly – because Jürgen Klopp is a very authentic leader. Authenticity means that thought, feelings and actions are always in harmony. What he thinks is clearly shown through his actions. In addition, Klopp understands quite well how to bring both sides together: as much as he makes appearances as a figure of leadership, his manager side is also strongly displayed. He always emphasises that techniques are the tools of football. And even if that means his players need to handle the ball cleanly 850 times in training, then it's pure management.

Can leadership be learned? Or is it more instinctive, making it purely a question of type?

Naturally, leadership coaches like saying that successful leadership can be learned. At any rate, Klopp grew up with leadership roles: he was elected 'class spokesman' in school, team captain at his youth club – so always the role of someone who pushed things forward. Klopp soaked up leadership skills at an early age: he is social, communicative and integrative. Other people who weren't taught these skills have to learn them with great effort. There are top business managers who are great at converting analytic processes, but then enter into a leadership position and fail completely. Companies always need both: leadership and management. And with Klopp I can recognise a very, very strong leadership component. At the same time, he understands how to translate this practically: 'How do we apply it so that we're successful?'

You just said that leaders call the status quo into question. How is this demonstrated by Klopp?

He doesn't just follow developments within his field, but also intentionally thinks outside of the box. A typical leader from the realm of business was Steve Jobs, who was CEO of Apple until August 2011. Jobs wasn't oriented on what the competition was doing, but rather looked into how beauty and aesthetics could be brought to life – even with computers. Long ago, Jobs dropped out of college and became engrossed with calligraphy. Klopp is also someone who in his public statements has repeatedly made it clear that he does think outside of the box and, in doing so, questions the status quo.

Can you give me an example?
We humans are very adaptive creatures. We really like to look around at what others in our area are doing successfully and try to copy it. Klopp goes beyond that and fixes his gaze on something more distant. In an interview with the weekly newspaper *Die Zeit* [6 August 2009], Klopp said: 'I just watched a film about a drummer who said that he repeated a single sequence up to 1,600 times until he had truly internalised it. Then he no longer thinks about it, but just plays it.' This shows you that he is consciously looking at other worlds. Leadership personalities perceive life's opportunities differently.

And within sport …
… Life Kinetik is a great example of mental as well as physical training. Klopp appears to be quite enthusiastic about it. This is a very decisive quality of leadership personalities: not just watching what prevails in one's own field, but also looking elsewhere. He seems open and that is why his character has a broad basis – that's a leadership quality.

In your opinion, leadership personalities have clear visions. Former German Chancellor Helmut Schmidt once recommended that

'Whoever has visions should go to the doctor.' How can 'visions' be filled with life and where can you recognise them with Klopp?

Tangible goals can be defined from visions. Visions define goals – naturally with all the vagaries that the path there contains. A vision makes a person palpable and trustworthy. For we are always particularly fond of personalities when we know where we stand. In this way, American President Barack Obama propagated 'change' in his campaign. This allows us to derive concrete goals, for example for health care or tax policies. Even when we watch television or go to the cinema, we always want to know what the characters want: James Bond wants to save the world, ET wants to go home, Graham Norton wants to entertain and Jeremy Paxman wants to explain the world – every one of these figures first becomes familiar to us through their visions. They constantly act with harmony between their goals and visions. That creates trust!

And what does Klopp want? His vision is making the world a little better. That is not only noticeable in his wording, but above all visible through his actions. It's that determined will that makes his visions tangible. He wants to make his team better as manager. As a TV expert he wants to explain the events on the pitch to the viewers. I can only emphasise: he just wants to make it better. Such a strong will comes from the heart, isn't put on. Others might say: 'I want to earn lot of money, become famous, become number one, want this or that.' But Klopp says, 'Even if it sounds melodramatic, for me that means making where I am a little better,' which he said in the *Zeit* interview. And this approach isn't limited to the realm of sport, but is more fundamental. Not only on the football pitch, but rather everywhere, wherever he happens to be, the world should be made a little better. That's his basic attitude.

Do you think there's a trigger for this self-understanding?

I assume he comes from a very stable home background and was lucky enough to always be able to do the things that came from the heart. He also wants others to be part of that. It would be presumptuous to guess where it comes from exactly.

Returning to Klopp the leader, how can his leadership style be described?

There are two basic leadership styles: one is authoritarian, as typically represented by Louis van Gaal. Then there's the participatory, inclusive style – and this is where Jürgen Klinsmann is very strong, if I think back to his time as manager of the national team. The secret recipe of the duo of Jürgen Klinsmann and Joachim Löw consisted in Klinsmann embodying leadership and Löw the manager who analysed, implemented and rolled up his sleeves. An ideal partnership. Klopp, on the other hand, embodies something that could be characterised as 'enlightened patriarchy'.

'Enlightened patriarchy'?

With that I mean that here as well, Klopp is able to access a valuable mixture from both approaches: when it comes to basic values, he's very authoritarian. He gives a clear sense of direction. But then Klopp becomes very participatory when it comes to processes and details. So on the one hand he is seeing himself as a leader, but on the other hand, giving players their individual freedoms. This leads to him standing for concrete values: trust, reliability, responsibility. They are strongly represented in his statements.

Many people try to gain trust but not all succeed. How does Klopp manage to build up trust?

His rituals play an important role in building up trust in him as a leader. Klopp cultivates rituals that attempt to bring people within a group together – for instance, the raffle at the training camp to see which players share a room. He makes a real happening out of it and, in doing so, creates a shared identity. Klopp's very good at that. I would even include the ritualised celebration of trophies. We experience how he participates in the celebration – as an equal: the man doesn't distance himself, he's in the middle of it. For group cohesion it's import to celebrate successes like that together.

What does it mean to create a 'shared identity' in football? Forming the classic 'we' feeling that people are so fond of attributing to the days of Germany's 1954 first World Cup glory?

Creating a shared identity is no anachronism. Klopp very much creates identity. This means: where he goes, he's also there – fully and completely. However, it's not just about him, but the identity of the whole: he wants to form a team that consistently and mutually pursues the given target. Klopp spent long years in Mainz, but when he went to Dortmund in 2008, he had immediately arrived and told himself: 'Now I'm going to make the world a little better here.'

What role does worldview play when pursuing a goal? To what extent does it influence behaviour?

Our worldview fundamentally steers our behaviour. Worldviews arise from learned experiences. Either on the basis of one's own experiences or on the basis of the patterns we are taught. The influences can be parents, authorities, friends and social surroundings: what we think about ourselves and the world guides our behaviour. Our personalities are fundamentally influenced through our world of thought. So when I believe performance is important, then I'll demand performance. If I believe that fun is important, then I'll demand fun.

In your opinion, which worldviews are dominant with Klopp?

I believe that Klopp has internalised a very performance-oriented worldview. Apparently his father was very influential in this regard. According to Klopp himself, his father was a real sports enthusiast who attached very high athletic expectations to him. Through that, he developed further and learned at a very early age that personal growth, success and satisfaction can only arise when people move outside of their comfort zones. Thanks to sheltered and trusting surroundings, Klopp was also strengthened mentally at an early age. He learned certain things about himself and life during his childhood, which he can naturally pass on wonderfully as a manager now. This worldview about performance was given to Klopp in the cradle.

And how can these worldviews be transferred? Because if the players don't accept them for themselves, they will only follow their manager to a certain degree.

From Klopp's statements you can hear that he has a positive worldview about himself and the world. And this is transferred, for people always follow along when they listen or watch. Why are we touched when top athletes celebrate their successes? Why do we let ourselves be caught up in their tears of joy? Because they're real. Why don't we cry along with a reality show? Because it's feels as though it's just acting, and isn't reality embodied with heart and soul. People have a fine sense for that and recognise the difference. To sum it up: Klopp believes what he says. We sense that. And that's precisely what makes us empathise. It creates emotions.

To what extent are your statements dependent on which club Jürgen Klopp works for? Would his character unfold in the same way with a different employer than with Mainz 05 and Borussia Dortmund?

I believe Klopp found an ideal club in Dortmund. Let me once again make a connection to business: there's a fundamental difference between the business of rebuilding and the business of perfection. The well-known professor of business and business consultant Hermann Simon differentiates between these two business models and comes to the conclusion that in the two cases differing kinds of personalities are at the top. They also demand different kinds of leadership systems and styles.

Which kinds, precisely?

The leadership personalities that have built up a company generally have different qualities than those who later join a settled system. This can be observed particularly well with small and medium-sized businesses. With these, characteristics such as determination, vitality, endurance or inspiration are especially important. I believe that Borussia Dortmund was also a business of rebuilding when Klopp took office in 2008 – especially after the significant economic problems in the years before.

And with businesses of perfection?

They include Bayern Munich within German football. Their ambitious goals are articulated publicly and aggressively. Market leadership should be defended, global presence achieved. Correspondingly, Bayern always has to play in the Champions League. Dortmund was first and foremost concerned with forming a team as good and inexpensive as possible. With a rebuilding business like that, Klopp's energetic, visionary manner can engender trust and success. Which doesn't mean that Klopp couldn't be successful at Bayern. But the difference lies with the time and patience before success has been achieved: he would presumably be granted less time with a business of perfection than with a company of rebuilding.

And how did he help with the 'business of rebuilding'?

By demanding and cultivating. I like always to look closely at language patterns that can be observed. Klopp has the idiosyncrasy of always challenging journalists in some way in interviews. For example, by answering completely differently than expected, and being smug all the while. It never sounds like a power struggle, more like a demanding do-gooder with positive intentions. Along the lines of: 'I'm a manager, I have to challenge people. I always have to pull them out of their comfort zone so that something special can happen.' He prods the best out of everyone. Of course that raises the activation level of listeners – people enjoy listening because something is happening. Leadership always has something to do with change. And with Klopp, the interlocutor always has the feeling that something's changing – in contrast to the case with politicians on numerous talk shows. Because there, it's usually not really about change.

Do people actually let themselves be pulled out of their comfort zone by Klopp?

Yes. There are new insights from the field of neuropsychology regarding what people actually want. There are reportedly three basic needs: security, self-worth and attachment. Klopp is unbelievably good at strengthening people in all three areas. That's what makes up his motivating power. By the way, people can only create the security, self-worth and attachment they embody themselves. Leaders must lead themselves first.

It's not only Klopp's players that frequently express enthusiasm about him, but the wider public also views him very positively. Why is this?

We love people with congruency, those who have inner coherence.

This is joined by the positive characteristics like the constant smile, that casual blond mane. We view him as an appealing figure. The man's having fun, and one quickly feels like an equal with him. He doesn't give his interlocutors the feeling they need to look up to him. He isn't 'high status'. Klopp gives his fellows undivided attention – a valuable commodity. He's very respectful to other people. That also helps establish an identity. And of course what's also very important: Klopp is very competent on a technical level, demonstrates expertise.

Could this be summarised by saying that for Klopp, football isn't just his very personal passion, but rather he views it as a social task?
Absolutely, he emphasises again and again that football is joined by a social component. Worldviews are not just a part of football: what do I believe about football as manager or player? If football is exclusively a means to make money for me, I will behave differently than if I believe football has an important societal task, and that through it I want to provide people with moments of joy. And that's what Klopp wants, as was expressed during the celebration of the *Bundesliga* title. He was moved that so many people were happy about the success, from the bottom of their hearts. And in return, it also made him happy – an interplay.

AUTHOR BIOGRAPHIES

THE EDITOR

Elmar Neveling is a freelance football and business journalist whose work has appeared in the official *Bundesliga* magazine, the *Ruhr Nachrichten* newspaper and German football website RUND. He is the co-author of the book *Football Tactics: The Anatomy of the Modern Game* (2015).

CONTRIBUTORS

Matthias Greulich is a freelance journalist and editor. From 2001 to 2003 he was deputy editor of the FC St Pauli magazine *1/4NACH5*. From 2005 to 2007 he was managing editor of the football magazine *RUND*. Since 2007, he has been running the magazine's online version (www.rund-magazin.de).

Roger Repplinger studied at Tübingen and has a doctorate in sociology. He lives in Hamburg. He has won many awards for his work as a writer, and lectures at Macromedia University of Media and Communication Hamburg as well as the Institute of Sports Science at the University of Tübingen. His book *Das Höchste: Was Menschen am Everest suchen, finden und verlieren* (*The Pinnacle: What We Seek, Find and Lose on Mount Everest*) was published in German in 2011.

Saban Uzun is a defensive midfielder, central defender and sports media research student at the University of Tübingen. He has played for TuS Ergenzingen to Under-17 *Oberliga* level, has been a press officer for the women's *Bundesliga* team at VfL Wolfsburg and is a UEFA 'B' Licence holder. He supports VfB Stuttgart and Trabzonspor and worked as a coach for the German Football Association. Since 2014 he has been in charge of the women's second division team VfL Sindelfingen.

NOTES

1 'Rubbing the cat' is a saying from the Middle Ages. At that time a purse was also called a 'money cat'. The purses were on long round belts made from leather and were bound around the belly. If merchants wanted to spend money, they stroked their purse, so 'rubbed the cat' – probably to make sure that there was still enough money inside. 'Rub the cat' was also a request to make a quick decision and open the money-belt. Today it's a synonym for doing things faster.

2 Mainz had actually scored twice in the first game of the season against Hannover 96, which ended 2–2. However, the scorer of the first Mainz goal, Thomas Ziemer, hadn't been properly registered by the club, and Hannover were awarded a 2–0 win.

3 Bruchweg was the home stadium until July 2011. Mainz 05 now play in the newly built Coface Arena. The new office of Mainz 05 and Christian Heidel is located in Isaac-Fulda-Allee 5 in Mainz, not far away from the Coface Arena.

4 The following Jürgen Klopp quotes (and all others in this book for which no source is given) are from the International Coaching Conference in Bochum in 2011 (25–27 July). On the final day of the event, Klopp was interviewed by Sky TV presenter Max Jung, before taking part in a podium discussion with fellow managers Friedhelm Funkel, Michael Oenning, Mirko Slomka and Matthias Sammer (also moderated by Jung). The theme of the conference was: 'Fast transitions to attack and defence – technical and tactical aspects.'

5 The data was published on the Borussia Dortmund homepage on 6 August 2011.

6 'Jürgen Klopp rallies neutrals to support "special" Borussia Dortmund', *Guardian*, 21 May 2013.

7 In Germany, anyone who coaches in the top three divisions is required to have either the UEFA Pro Licence or the *Fussball-Lehrer* qualification, the latter an equivalent German qualification. In most European leagues, it is only in the top division where such qualifications are mandatory.

8 Quote from Klopp from an interview with the Swiss newspaper *NZZ*, Sunday 24 April 2011

9 Appearance by Klopp on 'Audi Star Talk' on the Sport1 TV station, broadcast 22 March 2011